1989

# The American Writer
# and the University

# The American Writer and the University

EDITED BY

*Ben Siegel*

**DELAWARE**

Newark: University of Delaware Press
London and Toronto: Associated University Presses

Associated University Presses
440 Forsgate Drive
Cranbury, NJ 08512

Associated University Presses
25 Sicilian Avenue
London WC1A 2QH, England

Associated University Presses
P.O. Box 488, Port Credit
Mississauga, Ontario
Canada L5G 4M2


The paper used in this publication meets the requirements
of the American National Standard for Permanence of Paper
for Printed Library Materials Z39.48-1984.

**Library of Congress Cataloging-in-Publication Data**

The American writer and the university.

Includes index.
1. American fiction—20th century—History and
criticism.  2. American literature—20th century—
History and criticism.  3. Universities and colleges
in literature.  4. College teachers in literature.
5. Education, Higher, in literature.  6. Authors as
teachers.  7. English philology—Study and teaching
(Higher)—United States—History—20 century.
8. Creative writing—Study and teaching (Higher)—
United States—History—20th century.  I. Siegel, Ben,
1925–       .
PS374.U52A44  1989  810'.9'355       87-40499
ISBN 0-87413-336-X (alk. paper)

# Contents

Preface   7
Introduction: Poets, Novelists, and Professors—A Bittersweet Mix
    BEN SIEGEL   9

### *Novelists and the University: Critical Views*

Desire, Hypocrisy, and Ambition in Academe: Joyce Carol Oates's
*Hungry Ghosts*
    STANLEY TRACHTENBERG   39
Academia and the Wasteland: Bernard Malamud's *A New Life* and His
Views of the University
    JAMES M. MELLARD   54
The Gnomes of Academe: Philip Roth and the University
    ERIC SOLOMON   68
John Barth, the University, and the Absurd: A Study of *The End of the
Road* and *Giles Goat-Boy*
    ELAINE SAFER   88
Joseph Heller and the Academy
    JAMES NAGEL   101
Saul Bellow and the University as Villain
    BEN SIEGEL   114
Making the Best of Two Worlds: Raymond Federman, Beckett, and the
University
    MELVIN J. FRIEDMAN   136

### *The Poet on Campus*

A Personal View: Poetry, Pedagogy, and Per-versities
    THEODORE WEISS   149

### *The Playwright on Campus*

A Personal View: The Academy and the "You Know?" Generation
    JAMES RAGAN   161

5

*The Novelist on Campus*

A Personal View: The "Real Life" Fallacy
    DAVID MADDEN                                        179


Notes on Contributors                                   190
Index                                                   193

# Preface

No other institution rivals the American university in harboring so many who criticize and even revile it while refusing to leave it. No other nurtures so much internal factionalism and strife. And certainly in no other area of the university are the internecine hostilities as frequent and vocal as those between its professional teachers or professors of literature and its invited poets or novelists. The latter are, of course, the "creative writers" appointed to teach literature or composition or—God help us all—"creative writing." Here resentments and bruised sensitivities on both sides appear most bitter and open. What are the causes of this anger? The essays gathered in this volume speak to this point. To my knowledge, this is the first book to do so in an extended or fully developed fashion. Both "factions" are represented here: critics and scholars as well as novelists and poets. All the contributors are teachers, and several fit validly into both categories. Three deal not only with their own experiences in the classroom but they also relate these personal experiences to the general cultural and academic scenes. The others discuss seven major American novelists who have made the university an important setting or reference point (or target) in their fiction. Hence this volume's purpose is not to suggest a debate between the university's professional teachers and its invited or appointed writers; instead, it offers differing responses of creative writers to their respective institutions or to the idea of the university and to academe's varying effects on the sensitive individual. The cumulative result of these ten essays then should be to provide the reader interested in the contemporary American university with new insights. He or she should derive a much sounder understanding of the place and attitudes of those creative writers who inhabit academe and of the trials and tribulations, satisfactions and joys these special people experience there.

In editing this volume I wanted to present the American writer's role in the university in as balanced and detailed a fashion as possible. Therefore, I invited contributions from those members of the academic community whose experience and achievements would give them, I felt, much to say on the subject. I am satisfied I have chosen wisely. I hope the reader will agree that these essays offer a broad and richly textured portrait of academic life (warts and all) and the varied ways writers confront and react to it.

Most of these essays were presented first as papers for Modern Language

Association programs (sponsored by the Popular Culture Association) on "The American Writer and the University." The contributors are teachers with distinguished publication records. Each agreed to develop his or her MLA paper into a full-length essay for this collection. Although two of the papers (on Heller and Bellow) have been published previously, both have been revised for inclusion here.

Many individuals merit thanks for helping to make this book possible. In addition to the contributors—all of whom have displayed great patience and forbearance—I wish to thank Professor Ray B. Browne, the executive secretary of the Popular Culture Association, for his unfailing cooperation in allowing me to use that group's MLA panels to gather and test out these papers. I wish to thank, too, those Cal Poly Pomona administrators at department, school, and university levels who have made available to me the needed time and travel money. I am indebted also to Carol Follett and Sherry Allen, English department secretaries extraordinaire, whose magic fingers, unflagging energies, and unfailing good humor produced a computer-clean manuscript. And when second copies of individual articles were needed, my daughter Sharon repeatedly came to Dad's rescue. My wife Ruth and son Kenneth also helped—generally by not taking my frenzied efforts very seriously and by laughing at all the wrong times.

# Introduction
# Poets, Novelists, and Professors—
# A Bittersweet Mix

## Ben Siegel

MANY academics argue that the creative artist is simply an anomalous figure on campus. They appear to feel this way even when the writer holds a Ph.D, but they do so in particular when he is a writer-in-residence (long or short term) without the customary academic degrees. He (or she) generally is appointed to add a cultural veneer to the literature department and perhaps to attract students. What the writer inevitably attracts is his academic colleagues' envy and hostility. He is for them one of those literary itinerants or "freelance cavaliers," notes an only slightly joking George Garrett, who "come and go, brightly, according to their current rating on the board of the literary stockmarket." There may be "no harm there," adds Garrett, except for "the gut-gnawing and teeth-grinding of simple deadly Envy." Then again the Local Man may find the Distinguished Visitor adds to more than his emotional burden, as his superiors naturally assume "one writer will best know how to handle another." In addition to giving his time, the faculty member must also consider the political ramifications. "If X comes to visit and snubs you or cuts you dead, it is noted. One's local standing drops. Or the opposite. If Y comes to town and boozes like a trooper and chases cheerleaders and (ever and always) ends up, at best, with a lean myopic lady graduate student or a frigid faculty wife, is a hit or a bomb out, somehow *you* are responsible."[1]

In addition to these extra difficulties, the regular faculty members are reacting also to what they interpret as this scribbling interloper's genial contempt and his conviction that he alone possesses a creative or imaginative mind. On occasion, more general prejudices may surface. The campus writer's difficulty "is compounded," warns Leslie Fiedler, when "he is not merely an intellectual among anti-intellectuals, but also, say, a Jew among Gentiles, an Easterner among Westerners, a radical among conservatives, a European refugee among the native-born, or simply an urban type among defensive provincials." These plights, variously altered, are among those that campus writers like Joyce Carol Oates and Bernard Malamud, Philip Roth and John Barth have depicted in novels and short stories. In such narratives, the "final horror" of academic life is not represented by defeated intellecturals who flee the campus or die defeated on it. It is exemplified by those deflated creative souls who have adapted to the university's demands and remained in the classroom. Usually they have done so "to teach literature, and, presumably, to write novels on the side."[2]

Garrett and Fiedler could have been describing the disoriented, disheveled faculty types that people Joyce Carol Oates's seven short stories in *Hungry Hearts*. Her academics, complains Stanley Trachtenberg, are "uniformly portrayed as egocentric villains...[who] are comically frustrated by their inability to impose a subjective vision upon the solidity of experience." Their frantic attempts "to do so result in joyless lives, shaped by the funneling of desire into an increasingly narrow vision. Malicious, petty, self-serving, pompous, frightened, they frequently conceal the shallowness of their thoughts behind inflated claims of importance for obscure literary figures with whom their scholarly reputations are linked." Few of Oates's frenetic scholars appear "aware of the disparity between the manic intensity of their efforts and the worth of the advantages they seek." Even fewer reveal "concern for the humanistic nature of their vocation; instead, they disguise mean self-interest by pious professions of concern for some ennobling ideal. Typically ineffectual, they find that their inability to control or even influence events only intensifies the anger that is their most authentic emotion." As for their vaunted "academic integrity," says Trachtenberg, "Oates makes clear...[that it] constitutes only a pose of rectitude that masks a hypocritical venting of personal spite."

Many of the tragic consequences they experience derive from "the sterility of the university environment," the "deadness" of its life, says Trachtenberg, "and the emotional rigidity it fosters." Too often Oates's teachers and their spouses and students "are defeated by a life-denying aridity whether they reject the claims of humanity or attempt to respond to these claims." For in Oates's rigid Ivory Tower the individual's "fragile grip on reality... dissolves completely" under personal or professional pressures. Yet despite the emptiness of her university setting and its denizens, Oates views her fiction as a positive assertion of human potential. Indeed, she criticizes, says Trachtenberg, "the attenuated process of consciousness" in Henry James and Virginia Woolf. She believes their writings reduce "the range of human experience as it is actually lived and people it instead solely with 'spirits without personal bodies [who] inhabit time and space in a ghostly manner.'"
She finds more valid the novels "of Fielding, Austen, or Thackeray, for whom identity is defined in terms of social judgment." This literary schism moves her to ask: "Why must art be painful?... And if it is deliberately

conceived of as a negative human activity, how can its products be anything less than death-affirming, despairing, an unnatural distortion of one of the most joyful of all human adventures, the mysterious flowering of the imagination into conscious forms?" She is suggesting, explains Trachtenberg, that "Such...forms are systematically reduced to nihilistic utterances by the academic refusal to accept mystery over reason. Academic ritual substitutes a desacralizing separation of incantation from sacrifice and so proves incapable of a healing violence."

Oates's anger at the refusal of many academics "to accept mystery over reason" is shared by many creative writers. (Saul Bellow is also bitterly outspoken on this point.) Her concern for the "visionary possibility," observes Trachtenberg, may be why Oates ignores in her academic fiction many of the truly "complex educational or economic problems that currently beset the campus." Nor does she suggest "how these problems affect or are affected by what was once innocently thought of as the life of the mind." She presents no "characters struggling to develop their personalities in the recognizable fullness of human conflict; they offer no contrasting typological figures." Among the missing are the "kindly if absent-minded professor and the stern pedant who sharpens his students' minds by demanding an uncompromising intellectual rigor.... [Instead] instability is an occupational hazard for Oates's academics, who refuse to acknowledge the murderous consequences of rationalizing their desires. The conflict between their inner compulsions and an unyielding reality often drives them beyond sanity....For academics who inflate their petty concerns into broad moral issues, Oates reserves a special comic punishment—that of ridicule."

Trachtenberg concludes that Oates's teachers, writers, and critics "shape their fantasies into obsessive concerns that continue to haunt them even as they themselves victimize others." A teacher, writer, and critic herself, Joyce Carol Oates appears "haunted by these same controlling roles and by the hypocrisies and desires they project. To the degree that her characters' morbid passivity and violent frustrations are enacted in her fiction," states Trachtenberg, "she can exorcise these ghostly figures. At the same time she takes revenge upon them for their attacks on man's knowledge of a shared, universal condition. No matter how ingenious or arrogant, the individual ego—Oates is convinced—can never erase the memory of that knowledge from our collective consciousness. In her fiction it seems to be in the academic nature never to stop trying."

Faculty people appear equally obsessed and driven in Bernard Malamud's *A New Life*, despite the pastoral setting in which they find themselves. Indeed, the beauty of their surroundings quickly proves secondary to the moral choices they make or refuse to make. This Malamud novel has received varied readings, but each reading, notes James Mellard, should be perceived in terms of "the book's most dominant generic form—

that of the academic novel." Still it could be argued, concedes Mellard, "that neither Malamud nor any other novelist sets out *merely* to write an academic novel. The novelist has to consider many elements, including his need to provide a detailed context for characters, themes, and plots." Among other things, he has to "bring his special qualities to it." Malamud does so in *A New Life* by working "into the academic genre those elements of pastoral long identified with his fiction." Hence if he expresses here "his views of the university and its possibilities...those views prove to belong within more pervasive concerns associated with pastoral archetypes."

Not surprisingly, the academic or college novel, says Mellard, reveals the author's "reactions to the college institution itself, its faculty, and the cycle of events linked to an academic calendar." In most of his novels Malamud draws his narrative "elements through the alembic of pastoral archetypal conventions." But in *A New Life* he treats "the pastoral conventions somewhat more ironically." His college community, for example, "is situated in a stunningly natural beautiful setting," but it may be seen as "a garden or a wasteland, or even both at once, depending upon the individual perspective." His protagonist, Seymour Levin, soon finds that landscape and weather, like his new acquaintances, are quick-changing and complex. Everything living "must be read within other contexts. They are not simple pastoral icons or signs. They take on deeper meaning and value within a human purview at each instant. So the newcomer should resist making too much of surface beauty and variableness." What Levin also will learn, says Mellard, is that a true education's real purpose "is to teach one that something conducive to humane pursuits results from any setting's natural beauty. For in itself a physical setting is merely a given, an accident of circumstance—not the end of one's existence. This idea is particularly evident in Malamud's handling of the college itself." Therefore, "what the place is will rest largely on individual perception, and that perception of one's values."

In the terms provided by this novel, original sin proves to be "the separation of the human spirit from the material world, of humane values from our human acts. The Fall, as Malamud represents it in academia, occurs when the liberal arts are separated from the crafts, imaginative vision from practical application." Hence his hero's "perception of Cascadia as an academic wasteland is reinforced by his gradual penetration to the real identities of his employers and friends.... His inevitable disillusionment forces him into conflict with his colleagues, for their primary aim is not to redeem the arts, but to be good team players, cooperating, often enthusiastically, in carrying out the school's illiberal, antihumanistic curriculum." Levin had come to Cascadia "as a thirty-year-old ex-drunkard and naive liberal idealist, who believed that things always are what they appear to be." He quickly discovers "that few things at Cascadia are what they seem, least of all his own innocence. Hence his new life brings with it as much of the detective story as of traditional Western or frontier or proletarian plots." Mellard notes that "Levin becomes more shamus than Oedipus, a scruffy, over-age Hardy boy solving mysteries of identity and morality in which he himself is somehow deeply implicated." But the deepest secret he has to penetrate is that "of identity." For if Levin is to fashion a new life, he must determine "the most valid role models after whom to pattern himself. Roles and succession emerge as major elements of the novel."

Levin rejects the lives of his colleagues as possible guides for his own. But "as his own experiences unfold at Cascadia," says Mellard, "Levin learns that at every important turn [a now-dead predecessor] Leo Duffy has... 'already been there.'" Seeing his life follow the pattern shaped by Leo Duffy, Levin realizes "that in some mysterious way he *is* Leo." What this means is "that his new life is not new at all." In essence, therefore, says Mellard, "Levin has chosen little. He has been chosen by the archetypal role he must play in this mythic rite of the sacrifice of the scapegoat." Yet Leo Duffy "is not the force that frames the fearful symmetry of the two lives. Pauline Gilley is—or at least represents—that force, which is the force of life itself. Typically, Malamud locates the primal force of material and spiritual life in a woman, the *right* woman." Embodying the force lying behind Levin's new life, Pauline provides him with "a means of attaining his primary goals: 'Order, value, accomplishment, love.'"

What *A New Life* provides, says Mellard, is "a view of sexual initiation, but it also traces the initiation of an extraordinarily innocent academic into the sad realities of college life." In a "true pastoral fashion," it presents Seymour Levin as a total "naïf, albeit an urban one, when he arrives at Cascadia. He has a totally idealistic notion of academe." After a brief but turbulent stay at Cascadia College, Levin sees some of his proposed humanistic reforms adopted. "In his personal life, Levin makes a commitment to Pauline Gilley that similarly displays his values in action. He will assume responsibility for her and her children, even if it means loving Pauline merely 'on principle.'" To have Pauline he also has to promise her husband Gerald to give up teaching. In addition, he learns belatedly that Pauline had "chosen" him for the job at Cascadia because he resembled a Jewish boy who had once befriended her.

Malamud thereby seems to be acknowledging "his hero's role in a still broader archetypal ambiance," concludes Mellard. "Bringing new life to a wasteland—academic or otherwise — is heavy going, but somebody has to do it. If many are called, few are chosen. Seymour Levin is one of the chosen."

Like Oates and Malamud, Philip Roth also makes clear in his fiction just how emotionally and socially unstable American academics can be. Not until his ninth novel does Roth present a professor, says Eric Solomon, who may be "making his intellectual and emotional peace with the university." Inspired by Kafka and other literary masters, David Kepesh—Roth's "Professor of Desire"—is trying hard to integrate those "worlds that usually split Roth's protagonists into schizoid halves. These 'worlds' include life and literature, society and the academy, reality and books, sexual rage and intellectual order, Jewish *angst* and American assimilation, and passion and control." For Kepesh, as for Roth's other "academic" heroes, his best hope for finally comprehending his life's meaning lies in talking in the classroom "about great works of fiction." Indeed, Roth's professors desire to discuss not only great books but also "the intimate facts" of their personal lives. What this means, explains Solomon, is that Philip Roth has been from the start "an academic to his marrow" whose pages "inevitably echo the literature professor's analyses of great novels" and his own fears and actions.

Yet to many critics Roth's fictions represent the very "opposite of academic order." These critics see his writings "as wild, childish, obsessive, whining...and, of course, hysterically sex-obsessed." But for Solomon what has proved most significant is that whenever Roth has presented life and the university in conflict, he has revealed himself to be "an intensely academic novelist." He also has long been a man of the university. His academic degrees and teaching experience "all emphasize that Roth's academic career, in its essential outline, is indistinguishable from that of thousands of others." Despite his having "diverged, rejected the Ph.D. for life and writing, 'Professor Roth' has remained close to the university." He has continued to teach until the present. Yet he has "resisted the obvious. He will not write the traditional academic novel," and in his fiction "he has insisted...that the dual worlds of academy and society remain distinct."

What Roth tries to do, says Solomon, is "write—like his master Flaubert—of extreme behavior in ordinary situations, trying to control life so the work can be impassioned." Having used this tension effectively in his early fiction, Roth "finally resolves the strain in his crucial academic novel, *The Professor of Desire*." Earlier, for example, in his novella *The Breast*, Roth had provided "a comic model for... [his] ultimate combining of his two worlds of literature and life, of the grotesqueness of art and the disorder of sexuality." But only in *The Professor of Desire*, states Solomon, does Roth's hero move from a rakish existence to one of self-acceptance as a teacher of literature. In short, it is at that point that "Kepesh achieves the ability to...'connect' by teaching and living the professor's life." Only at that point does David Kepesh do "what Philip Roth the novelist does." Like his chosen literary masters (Tolstoy and Mann, Chekhov and Kafka), Roth depicts "the invented, certainly, but also authentic, life of the author. Having reached this point, Roth then can truly start his Zuckerman books—orderly, shorter narratives joining the worlds of literature and life."

Roth sums up the recurrent theme of his academic narratives when he declares that he tries to discover "the means to be true to these seemingly inimical realms of experience that I am strongly attached to by temperament and training—the aggressive, the crude, and the obscene, at one extreme, and something a good deal more subtle, and, in every sense, refined at the other." Responding to such thoughts and to Roth's depictions of his academic heroes, Solomon observes that "Professors of literature every- where may well breathe sighs of relief that Professor Roth of the University of Pennsylvania has not committed himself to depicting fully the life of the writer in the university. Given his satirical knowledge, his academic novel undoubtedly would have made those of Mary McCarthy, Randall Jarrell, John Barth, and David Lodge seem sentimental and forgiving."

On the other hand, Roth may leave unanswered some questions raised by the sheer outlandishness of some events in his fiction. "But for Roth the dangers of extremity can be as real and distorting in university teaching as in sexual activity. His two worlds prove equally threatening." At the same time, Roth can offer, says Solomon, "marvelously comic dialogues in the form of arguments about whether a story is 'universal' or a character is 'sympathetic.' He also details the controversies over realism versus prose poetry and symbolism." In addition, Roth is given to "having fun with his own work and his critics." This is especially true, Solmon makes clear, in *My Life as a Man*, where Roth offers thinly veiled criticism of his own *Portnoy's Complaint* and underscores the predictability of many of the critical comments directed at his characters and plots.

This leads Solomon to observe that this Roth novel then "*is* academic in its pervasive literary criticism and its onion-like peeling of its own reflexive technique." It is in *My Life as a Man* that Roth's hero, Peter Tarnopol, cites Flaubert's advice to writers: "Be regular and orderly in your life like a bourgeois, so that you may be violent and original in your work." Philip Roth himself, notes Solomon, achieves this aim. This "quiet privatist" and university professor "writes violent and original novels about erratics... who fail to achieve such a balance." Yet Flaubert, says Solomon, is the literary master "who most clarifies Roth's double vision." Still he offers Roth a "mixed message." For Flaubert and the other modern masters who intrigue Roth and his academic heroes "all write to excess and mostly about themselves." So if Roth's "major novels take the forms of autobiographies, that is the master's lesson Philip Roth encodes in his fiction and criticism." Hence Solomon concludes that Roth, having finally achieved "the balancing act" between his real and fictional lives, "now appears to be free of the academy, free to live the examined life in that world of reality where the writer fantasizes for himself, not for his students in a university."

John Barth also has made consistent use of academe in his fiction. But if critics have examined many aspects of his novels, states Elaine Safer, they have not probed carefully what Barth terms "the spectacle of these enormous universities." Like all of the contributors to this volume (and their subjects), Barth has spent his adult years teaching. Endlessly fascinated and repelled by the university, he has woven unabashedly into his satirical novels many of his own experiences as teacher and writer. In this he differs little from those literary contemporaries (Mary McCarthy, Randall Jarrell, Philip Roth, and Saul Bellow, among others) who also reveal a strong interest in "the frailties of university teachers and students." In two of his novels, *The End of the Road* and *Giles Goat-Boy*, most of the action occurs on campus. In fact, in all his novels Barth not only includes his major characters' academic backgrounds, but he also draws upon his own academic experiences for specific incidents and details.

Not surprisingly then, Barth's essential audience, says Safer, is made up primarily of academics who enjoy his scathing satires of contemporary "educational practices and the theoretical suppositions that lie behind them." Often the academic reader recognizes in Barth some essential "truths about the profession, the university community, and himself." In those instances, "Humor collides with a more painful tone, and the reader, because of his similar experiences, becomes strangely affected by the tales." He may notice also that in *The End of the Road* and *Giles Goat-Boy* Barth develops his "comic vision" by means of "ironical allusions" to traditional educational values and works. Emerson's "The American Scholar" (1837), for example, serves Barth as a primary "paradigm for the American educational ideal." Without alluding to it directly, Barth makes it clear, Safer points out, that he views Emerson's essay as "a respository for many of the notions that encompass the American ideal of teacher and scholar." Certainly he develops "ironic counterparts" to it in his two academic novels. To a lesser degree, Barth does the same with *Magnalia Christi Americana*, Cotton Mather's histoical paean to Harvard College and its Puritan ministerial faculty.

For example, in his *The End of the Road*, Barth "burlesques the Emersonian educational ideal of 'Man Thinking' and reasoning." He does so by employing "as protagonists two university professors who represent the extremes of super-rationality and unreason." History professor Joe Morgan "is a rigid thinker." English instructor Jake Horner proves "the epitome of unreason." Barth's emphasis on Jake's "purposeless movement" is a parody of Emerson's "concern for meaningful action," states Safer, "that is, [for] the education of the scholar by action." The very "mindlessness" of Jake's actions offers "an ironical contrast to this concept." Barth underscores the comic "discrepancy between the educational ideal and its loss" by using traditionally affirmative words such as "reason," "light," "eyes," "eternity," "ultimacy," and "the cosmic view." Hence for Jake the light of reason "is a bright glare in a world denuded of reason and order and meaning." He can find in the world about him "no reason to do anything."

Jake's mentor in nonreasoning behavior is his doctor. "Each aspect of the Doctor's educational therapy for Jake," Safer notes, "gains its comic quality by being an ironical contrast to the life of reason as stipulated by traditional thinkers like Emerson and Cotton Mather." The Doctor encourges Jake to "engage in Mythotherapy, a method that emphasizes that a man must choose his myths and ideologies anew in each situation." Like an actor trying out different roles, if he finds one mask is ineffective, he should try another. He "should not be concerned about general truths. He should just act the role most appropriate in each setting."

Jake Horner then is the "university instructor as non thinker," and as such he represents "an ironical reversal of the educational ideal of scholar-teacher. The contrast is the butt of many humorous episodes in *The End of the Road.*" That John Barth should focus "his comedy on the disparity between the scholarly ideal and its gross manifestation in the teachers of the academy," says Safer, "shows his hostility toward educator 'types' who have been his colleagues for years. In fact, Barth seems to find professors of English—his own field—particularly comic." In contrast with Jake, history professor Joe Morgan "relies solely on his mental powers, even though they may be in conflict with his emotions...The absurdity of depending on reason alone is underlined by the contrast between Joe's high seriousness and the crude language that characterizes his philosophic observations." The pseudo-rational behavior of Joe Morgan and his wife, Rennie, and the nonrational actions of Jake Horner cause "postulates—such as 'Man Thinking' and being self-reliant—[to] seem preposterous in relation to the university professors in *The End of the Road.* The connection between the scholarly life and the productive life for the individal and society, so paramount for Emerson, is acted out as farce in this novel of the absurd."

Barth offers another thematic variation on the gap between the ideal and the real in *Giles Goat-Boy*. After creating "nostalgia for an educational ideal...[he] then frustrates the reader's expectation by developing a contrast to the standard model of excellence." He does this, in part, by repeatedly pointing up the lack in Tammany College's students of "the educational and moral standards of early scholars." In effect, Barth is criticizing a university community whose actions offer a direct contradiction to the three major Emersonian tenets for the scholar: "to be an observer of nature, a reader and creator of books, and a thinker who has duties in the world." Instead of striving for such goals, Tammany College professors "pursue abstract theories and talk nonsense."

To emphasize his contempt for "the corruption of training in the contemporary university," says Safer, Barth uses "scatological imagery." He also relies once more on earlier classical works as his intellectual touchstones. Specifically, he "casts a comical light on the role of saints' lives as a model for instruction." But instead of Foxe's *Book of Martyrs* or Cotton Mather's *Magnalia*, Barth offers the reader a bitingly ironical *Giles Goat-Boy*. In this "academic travesty, the heroes are 'saints' of the absurd, far fallen from the exemplary lives described by Foxe and Mather." To his hero, Giles, Tammany College is the "place that will help him to progress toward the truth, in the Emersonian sense." Instead, Giles is increasingly frustrated by the "futile confrontation between...[his] serious desire to gain knowledge....and the frivolous attitude of the student body." But Tammany students have little cause for concern, as no lengthy preparation is expected of them either for admission or graduation. Traditional matriculation requirements and religious instruction have been abandoned.

In this novel of black humor, Barth satirizes "all aspects of university life," says Safer, "from the perspective of Giles the goat-boy, who has left the farm to attend the great institution of higher learning." Giles tries "to affirm order and meaning as he studies to be a Grand Tutor at Tammany College." But Barth literally inverts "traditional standards of educational excellence." He sees "disorder, rather than unity and meaning," as the culmination of Giles's experiences at the academy. In doing so, Barth not only underscores "the futility of the pedagogic process in the academy," but he also appears "to doubt whether even the best instruction can actually help man to use reason to understand an illogical world." He is reaching beyond his fictional characters, observes Safer, "to educate the reader." He wishes the reader "to question his own basic assumptions." In effect, Barth is deriding the reader for "relying on societal myths (and the educational researchers for contributing information that helps to form these myths)." He mocks such researchers. He ridicules their obsession with the kind of "narrowly specialized material....that...is associated with the work of recluses, valetudinarians, and 'squint-minded antiquarians' in the university." Barth is here at one with Emerson in suggesting that such individuals "are unfit for public labor in the academy."

In doing so, Barth is offering himself as a target, warns Safer, for Professor John Barth is himself "preoccupied with his own type of esoterica." The basic and most familiar irony, of course, is that despite (or, perhaps, due to) his criticism of academe, Barth "gains his primary readership from university faculties and students."

Joseph Heller, too, finds much to ridicule in academe. And like that of Oates, Roth, and Barth, his life and work have remained entwined with the university. Indeed, his university training literally proved for Heller, states James Nagel, "a vehicle for both socioeconomic advancement and self-discovery." In fact, despite his highly successful literary career, Heller has returned repeatedly to Yale, the University of Pennsylvania, and the City College of New York, among others, to teach writing. Even the stories he published in *Esquire* and the *Atlantic Monthly* as a New York University undergraduate dealt with college or academic "opportunities." These early creative efforts, says Nagel, "hint at . . . a [later] preoccupation with universities and education, with educational background as a means of defining character, and with related themes of assimilation and social justice, of snobbery and exclusion, of access and denial." These concepts prove an important but "persistently overlooked subtext in Heller's most notable works, *Catch-22, Something Happened*, and *Good as Gold.*"

Clearly then, Heller, "far from being an antagonist of the academy...is very much a product of it." In addition, his letters indicate that he was extremely pleased "that *Catch-22* quickly made its way into American literature courses at major universities." Yet if critics have examined *Catch-22* "from nearly every conceivable angle," says Nagel, not one "has thus far observed that virtually every major character in the novel is identified in terms of institutional affiliation and that socio-academic status is a central element in the method of establishing character." Many of the most satirical references to the university and the types of characters it helps form are to be found only in Heller's notes and early drafts of the novel. For a variety of reasons, Heller cut them from his final manuscript. Still it remains "clear... that education in *Catch-22* is not so much a vehicle for social mobility for the disadvantaged as an emblem of prestige and privilege for the rich." Hence in Heller's war narrative "moral virtue is inversely proportionate to the amount and prestige of collegiate training." The more educated the character, the less sensitive he "is likely to be to the prerogatives and feelings and very existence of others." The more prestigious his institution, the more likely that he will grow "obsessed with defending an insensitive capitalistic system and with issues of exclusion and class distinction." Given the ethical structure of *Catch-22*, "the better educated a character is, the less he is likely to understand" others' needs and feelings.

Heller's next novel, *Something Happened*, says Nagel, "is much less significant in its development of the academic theme." Its hero, Bob Slocum, is of uncertain educational background, but "always in the swirl of...[his] neurotic introspection there is an awareness of education, of institutional status, of culture and intellectual cultivation." In fact, his "habits of mind often lead...[Slocum] to think of things in terms of their impact on campus." For from his "perspective, identity is often an extension of, or at least related to, education." Summing up this work, Nagel states that "Although *Something Happened* is in no sense an 'academic novel,' it is also true that this remarkably personal study, perhaps the most agonizingly introspective novel in American literature, presents 'identity' consistently in educational terms."

For Nagel, Heller's most detailed treatment of the university comes in *Good as Gold* (1979). This novel not only offers an English professor as protagonist, but it "also has him working a good deal of the time on an essay entitled 'Education and Truth or Truth in Education.'" Bruce Gold sends his children to highly rated schools and is keenly aware of his friends' educational backgrounds. Yet he declares education to be "the third greatest cause of human misery in the world." He reveals little interest in literature and hates teaching. What he wants is a job in government. "In fact," observes Nagel, "some aspects of...[Gold's] position strain credulity." He is a full professor but does "no scholarly work and writes only familiar essays." Most strangely, "despite his rank, he is untenured and appears not to understand tenure." He also opposes academic freedom, "rarely attends class, never prepares, and only groans at the thought of the term papers about to come due." Gold's major academic asset is his ability to write outlandish course descriptions that attract students to classes. "'Professor Gold,'" says Nagel, "is more a satirical construct than a believable human being, as are most of the [novel's] other characters." Heller employs him to satirize most of this country's prestigious institutions. Heller also satirizes "real" people—in particular Henry Kissinger—by using "their own public statements to reveal their intellectual and moral limitations."

As in *Catch-22*, Heller here views any education linked to wealth and prestige as being, says Nagel, "not only empty but also a source of villainous insensitivity to social issues." In addition, *Good as Gold* "combines the two major lines of development" of this university theme in Heller's fiction. "The first is the satirical deflation of institutions of prestige on the grounds of their social insensitivity and lack of substance beneath the ivy walls.... The second line of thematic thrust has an even more explicitly social edge: it is becoming increasingly difficult to move upward in American society, increasingly difficult to get the requisite education." Nagel sees much of Gold's bitterness about education as deriving from his conviction "that the traditional opportunities have broken down, that the lower classes, especially the ethnic minorities, have almost no chance." But the true culprit here is less education itself and more—as in *Catch-22*— "an insensitive and inhumanly bureaucratic system of government."

Ultimately then, concludes Nagel, Heller's portrayal of universities and of education in his fiction should be seen to be "an instrument of social satire directly analogous to his treatment of the military in *Catch-22*." But the university theme strikes "a deeper satirical vein in that it runs throughout the Heller canon, linking and enriching the novels and stories along the way." This theme grows steadily darker, as Heller's fiction offers a progressively more intense and "satirical antipathy toward the role of education in American society." For him higher education is no longer the possible "mechanism for the eradication of injustice that it was...in his early short stories." It has become instead, in his eyes, "one of this nation's institutions that perpetuate social stratification and moral insensitivity."

To this point the novelists discussed have conveyed their essentially negative views of the university in their fiction. Saul Bellow is more direct. He deals with academe only tangentially in his novels (that is, in *Herzog* and *The Dean's December*), but he levels in his essays a deeper anger and more personal resentment toward it than do they. Indeed, few American novelists talk about the university as much as does Bellow. Certainly no other subject stirs in him equal rancor and bitterness. Still he does not underestimate the university's importance. His attitude suggests a familiar paradox. Like many American novelists and poets, Bellow remains rooted in academe while making it a frequent target. He refers to himself as a "professor," but he attributes much of what is wrong with this nation's culture, especially its literary culture, to the university and its professors. He sees these professors as the prime cause of America's "literary situation." This Bellovian phrase covers not only recent writers and writings but also the several decades of postwar media intellectuals shaping the country's thought and expression. Just prior to the Second World War, Bellow declares, America's "highbrow public" was small, but after the war, thanks to the G.I. Bill, it exploded with a "new class of intellectuals or near-intellectuals."

These new university graduates formed a serious "minority readership," Bellow states, but one different in taste and size from "that handful of connoisseurs that had read *Transition* in the twenties and discussed 'significant form.'" Yet if deficient in taste, this audience proved insatiable in its cultural hunger, viewing literature as both "swallowable" and "enormously profitable." Its members contributed to the "university boom" and to the expansion of journalism and publishing. Hence the postwar years, he recalls, found the universities newly prosperous and at the center of an enlarged but artificial "literary culture." Now, with all of culture's great "national capitals" (like Paris) gone, artists and writers have turned for "asylum" to the universities and transformed them into "the sanctuary, at times the hospital, of literature and painting, music and theatre."

Yet if writers find shelter on campus, observes Bellow, they are not truly comfortable there. A major source of their discomfort is their awareness of the popular conviction that "the intellectual life is somehow not virile." This widely held view moves the artist to downplay his true concern with thought. Perhaps this may be why, Bellow suggests, American literature does not "have more novels of ideas." In addition, novelists and poets are not clear on what their cultural obligations are. A few writers may believe their efforts belong to society, but most simply do not care. Bellow does care. His fiction and essays reveal his deep concern for the nation's intellectual life, on campus and off. He emphasizes repeatedly how damaging to humanistic thought is the university's increasing commitment to technology and to the sciences, physical and behavioral. Ideas there are flattened, packaged, devalued. So are standards and life styles. This negative effect on the nation's "independent literary culture," says Bellow, can be traced in part back to the fifties and sixties when the universities bought up most literary publications. Soon unaffiliated writers had "no extra-institutional and independent environment," while sorry academics or quasi-academics have been able to disseminate their personal (if borrowed) cultural ideas through the captive quarterlies, which now function as "attitude sources." Most of these university-subsidized quarterlies are typified by shoddy thinking and writing, and they share with popular magazines like *Playboy*, *Esquire*, and *Evergreen Review* a bohemian disdain for serious art. The literature professors who run these publications are primarily responsible for the university's pernicious influence on literary thought and culture.

Bellow divides professors into two general types: antiquarians and modern lit profs. The first group are essentially "stony old pedants" who amuse Bellow. A small minority are "quite useful," and the others are rather harmless textual fuddyduddies. Overall, the antiquarians are no longer significant. Their power was broken in the 1930s, when the universities turned to modern literature and contemporary writers. So Bellow's anger is directed at the modern lit profs. These people number in the thousands and turn out "millions of graduates in literature." They, like the antiquarians, wish to keep any literature limited and manageable. They proclaim the novel's imminent demise and that of literature in general. They move Bellow to wonder whether novels can be studied or even read if writers do not continue to write them. For such negative talk renders the novelist uneasy and undermines his confidence in exercising his imagination.

The role playing and dire prophecies of such people are bad, but even worse is their ineptitude. Bellow is astonished "at the ignorance of learned people." He thinks many literature and writing teachers are so poorly prepared that they should attempt a novel simply to grasp how a book is constructed. Yet if the knowledge of university scholars is defective, their prose is more so. Here the humanities profs pose the greatest risk. These "humanist intellectuals" have stirred Bellow's strong dislike through the years. He makes clear his feelings about them in *The Dean's December*. There he reasserts his dissatisfaction with the intellectual rigidity and parochialism of both scientists and humanists, but he is, as always, more bitter toward his humanities colleagues. Speaking through his hero, Albert Corde, Bellow indicates that he expects more of the humanists, culturally. But they "have flunked the course. They have no strength because they have no conception of what the main effort of the human mind has been for three centuries and what it has found."

What most annoys Bellow about these tenured humanists is that despite their ignorance they never suffer writer's block and are able always to supply literary articles so cheaply they have "all but wiped out...professional competitors." They want to wrench literature from writers and keep it for themselves. When such professors function as critics, they accumulate needless reading matter. Even more seriously, they redescribe basic texts—that is, major literary works—by relating them to myth, history, philosophy, or psychology; this redescription renders them "less accessible" to readers. It means, too, that for human emotion or response professors "substitute acts of comprehension." They are obsessed with meaning, especially hidden meaning. They are convinced fiction is not to be taken literally. What fervor academics can muster they devote not to creating imaginative literature but to "manufacturing 'intellectual history.'" But they consider seriously only books whose "attitudes, positions or fantasies" please them, for these works are now "their material, their capital." Taking from them what they need for their journalism or social critiques, they produce "hybrid works." Indeed, they reduce novels to cultural objects and dehumanized art.

Bellow does not deny the merit of proper literary study and analysis. But the "cultural bureaucrats" on campus shape things to their liking by ignoring all contradictions, aesthetic or social. They are bothered little, therefore, by gaps between their theories and practices. They have failed to find the will or the means to make their world a better place by applying their humanistic theories to their teaching or their society. For the writers among them the problems of relevance are compounded. Isolated in English departments, with little access to the sciences or other hard disciplines, they are unable or unwilling to formulate new literary ideas. Instead they follow the lit profs and merely restate "the Eliot view, the Joyce view, the Lawrence view." They also are satisfied merely to prepare students for an expanding culture's new power positions. In short, they wish to exploit only what is already there. So they rarely challenge the "modernist orthodoxy" dominating most English departments.

Sadly enough, insists Bellow, the universities want things this way. They do not hire these people to think creatively but only to turn students into professional writers and media intellectuals. The trouble is that writers (older and younger) have a feeble grasp of the social changes giving universities their new "revolutionary power." University-trained intellectuals dominate industry and education, politics and city planning. Yet their innocence impedes literature teachers and writers in making humanistic use of their students. Instead, these campus humanists fall prey to a studied but empty radicalism—one devoid of content and shaped by self-imposed postures. But then most American writers have little reason not to opt for the good life. Most are from this country's middle class, and it has shaped and justified their intellectual corruption and hypocrisy. It tells them they can enjoy all of society's good things while railing against them in their writings.

Bellow's point is that neither novelist nor poet should blame only the university for his moral confusion. For what happens on campus ultimately reflects what happens—or does not happen—off campus. Universities may be this nation's cultural "warehouses," says Bellow, but they do not sever anyone's moral ties to the community. Still, American intellectuals always imagine that their education removes them from ordinary events. This attitude is for Bellow "unjustifiably romantic." He argues that university people must adhere to their vaunted humanistic standards in community as well as faculty matters. Conversely, concludes Bellow, American society must be more generous to its writers.

None of this volume's contributors or the novelists they discuss is likely to disagree with Bellow's conclusion. Yet unlike those novelists, some writers do feel their universities have treated them fairly and even generously. Poet Theodore Weiss, playwright James Ragan, and novelists David Madden and Raymond Federman are among those who view their university teaching as an important adjunct, even stimulant, to their creative efforts. This is not to suggest they find their roles or functions within the academy to be without disadvantages or shortcomings. Each is keenly aware things could be better—indeed, much better—for the writer who teaches. But each has learned to accommodate his personal and aesthetic needs to the university's special demands or pressures—whether these pressures are exerted by administrators, academic colleagues, or students.

Theodore Weiss, for instance, has experienced most of the American university's changing attitudes toward creative writers and writing. His "forty years of college teaching," he points out, "have roughly coincided with the establishment and remarkable growth of creative writing in the university." His twenty years at Bard College and almost two decades at Princeton University as writer-in-residence and professor of English have provided an excellent vantage point. Some years ago Elizabeth Bowen summed up the prevailing British attitude toward modern teaching approaches when she confided to him: "Just between us I think teaching writing quite absurd.... But then I also consider it absurd to teach English literature at the university." Her point was that it long had been "taken quite for granted that a young man of good family, come to Oxford or Cambridge, would have read English literature, certainly modern things, at home." Weiss encountered a similar mind set at Oxford as late as 1963. "Victorian Literature was as modern an event with which its English department could be bothered." Recent poetry was not the concern of any academic department but "of the large—some one hundred members— sober Poetry Society."

The same attitude prevailed here. "Since American English departments copied English and German models," states Weiss, "modern literature in this country met similar resistance." Harvard University was among the schools strongly opposing a department of modern languages. Given the conservative attitudes "of those who regarded the university as a grand museum (its chief function being the preservation of the antiquities), this was not surprising." Indeed, granting "official status for an even more upstart subject, American literature, no doubt long continued to rankle. Still more barbaric and outrageous—after all, what studious length of years, what scholarship, research, rigors had hallowed it?—was the intrusion into the university of the creative writing workshop. With the Ivy League's inclination to regard the arts and writing as chiefly pastimes and hobbies, the writing workshop has naturally had a hard time at most old line insititutions." What was true at Harvard was equally true at Yale. Weiss recalls a prominent Yale English faculty member confiding to him "that his department was embarrassed by the whole matter of creative writing and did not know how to handle it." Early in his own teaching career, Weiss was assigned a writing course at Yale, "but I was firmly ordered not to encourage or accept any creative work."

Upon finishing college, in 1938, Weiss planned to concentrate on writing poetry. He could see that pursuing graduate work in English would be a "quixotic" choice. He was also advised of his additional academic burden: his being Jewish. Yet he stubbornly moved on to Columbia University's English graduate department. There he quickly learned the scholar's life was not for him. Fortunately, strong changes were overtaking academe, thanks primarily to the New Critics. These men generally were "of proper background in both education and station," and they were bidding for academic "place if not for power. And gradually, through their successes, it became possible to consider criticism a legitimate substitute for scholarship." Weiss found a series of teaching positions, and he and his wife started a magazine, the *Quarterly Review of Literature*, that prospered. He soon moved on to Bard College, "an experimental college still part of Columbia, and one more than willing to regard poetry as an adequate substitute for scholarly work."

At the same time, an even more surprising change was brought about, says Weiss, by many New Critics who were writing poetry as well as criticism. The key figure was T. S. Eliot, who impressed "the academy not only with his interpretations of past literature but also with his unusually erudite poems." These events suggested poetry writing was "a possible, if not yet a wholly respectable, undertaking for young men (if not young women!). The heroic dedication of the critic-poets Pound and Eliot, the work and devotion of poet-critics like Ransom, Tate, Winters, and Blackmur (especially since they were academy based), and the careers of important academic critics like Trilling and Levin...were all doing much to accelerate the presence of writing in the university." The criticism of poetry literally "swept the country."

Then at precisely the moment the New Critics were consolidating their triumph, says Weiss, "a larger revolution shook the university...poetry erupted. Dylan Thomas heralded this change...[as] minstrel, troubador, [and] pied piper." In fact, in the 1960s, "when the Beats took to the open road," they were following in Thomas's footsteps and producing a highly "exclamatory" poetry and enkindling "vast numbers of the young." In the revulsion these thousands of young people "felt at technology, with the sciences apparently in collusion with government, the military, and big business, the arts—for their encouragement of the individual—boomed." These young people "clamored for the arts' active presence in the university and, whatever their elders' reservations and dismay, the young prevailed."

One such "art" asserting itself on campus was creative writing, which often took hold in the most unlikely settings. "Under the skillful command of Paul Engle, creative writing had already established itself as an important enterprise at the University of Iowa. A way station for most of the promising young poets of the time, Iowa's workshops served as a pilot program... to the generations of workshops after." Before long many literature departments had "at least one writer...[and] the cultural revolution was on in full force." At Princeton, for instance, in a few years, the arts there grew "from one resident novelist and one poet, these usually on a one-year or two-year appointment...and one painter and one sculptor to twenty-three teachers." Creative arts programs increased steadily nationwide, but "some English faculty members continued to resent the presence of such unreliable, shady characters" as writing instructors. "Writers, many academics believed, were best when dead and fumigated and tidied up by time and scholarship."

Their attitude helps to explain why the arts had to settle for "a gradual, backdoor entrance into the university," says Weiss. "Then they did so in a fairly marginal way," first gaining acceptance at small progressive colleges like Bennington, Sarah Lawrence, and Bard. Slowly "the cultural experiments and educational innovations of progressive colleges found their way into the more orthodox schools. ... Today the arts occupy a prospering, if not prominent, place in university life." If the writers involved in creative activity obviously benefit, Weiss points out, so does the university. "Even as workshops often attract the liveliest, if not the best, students, so what goes on in them tends to overflow and color the more conventional offerings." Nonresident writers are invited to campus for readings and conferences. Consequently, "the university has become...the center of literary activity."

Weiss validates this claim by detailing some of his own methods of teaching poetry writing. But even so, he concedes, "one might ask what these several decades of poetry have accomplished." He does not think the final results are in, but then he does believe the university's role as "a major patron of the arts—the chief sanctuary for poets already well on their way—may be considered a positive happenstance." Indeed, as a teacher-publisher-editor of poetry (as well as a poet), he can testify "that the amount of poetry being written has grown prodigiously"—until today, "apparently there are many more writers of poetry than readers." This peculiar development suggests that America "may be breeding a new kind of poet: one who can write but not read." Yet on the positive side, the quality of today's poetry "generally far exceeds that of the home grown, amateurish efforts of twenty to thirty years ago." An Ezra Pound or Wallace Stevens may be rare, but for the first time in this country, concludes Weiss, "hundreds of able, dedicated poets are hard at work." In fact, with the possible exception of "historic periods in China, there has never before been so profuse a flowering of poets and poetry."

James Ragan shares Theodore Weiss's conviction that writing students should be more aware of language nuances and possibilities. Indeed Ragan, in his USC playwriting classes, devotes considerable time to enhancing his students' grasp of the power of metaphor. For he has grown acutely sensitive to a "falling out of love" with language not only by his literary contemporaries but also by his graduate writing students who are part of the "You know?" generation. These young people's "infatuation with media imagery," declares Ragan, has long been "replacing their love for the written word." From the 1960s to the present, the language of the masses has been "moving toward a popular illiteracy caused by public apathy to accurate communication." During these decades American society has literally lost any concern "for precision in words, spoken or written." The public's new "love affair...is with the media arts or any new forms of communication synthesized by the classical electronic media—radio and film. The 'New Mediaism'—television, video tapes and discs, audio books, personal computers, and the like...has replaced the written word as the nation's primary communication tool." This has resulted in what play-wright Edward Albee terms "a 'semantic collapse' of language in America today."

Unfortunately, says Ragan, he has witnessed the effects of this language decline in professional drama and in his playwriting classes. While he does not consider this an "irreversible" dilemma, he does think the linguistic decline poses a "most significant" classroom challenge. No one explanation "will cover this erosion of proper word usage," he cautions, but much of it may be attributed "to a post-Kennedy anti-intellectualism." For then this country's "new life...proved media-inspired, script-annotated, and sound-simplified, and suitable for television's instant broadcast and audience consumption." The result was a general "semantic disintegration. Like television's instant flashback, 'instant imaging' became the vehicle for instant truth and gratification." Hence Ragan has found it hard to convey his "concerns to a new generation of graduate writers...weaned on tele-vision and the computer sciences." For these young people "the technology

of 'instant imaging' has supplanted the multivalence of the written word."
This is hardly surprising, he notes sadly, as they belong to "the 'now'
generation that has popularized the acceptance of cliché, double-speak, no-
speak, the noncompleted simile 'like...' and the interjected 'You know?' as
norms of minimalist communication." These ambitious young writers
"literally have fallen in love with the technical virtuosity of the visual
'close-up' rather than with metaphor."

But their fondness for the new electronic technology does not move these
young people "to experiment and take chances." Instead, complains
Ragan, "their collective 'originality'" is more likely "to feed upon the worn
plots and characters culled from television or rock videos. Their plays (like
so many recent novels) are being written with a film or MOW (Movie of the
Week) foremost in their minds." Their role models or "writing heroes
generally are Judith Krantz and Jackie Collins, and their structural models
are action-spectacle dramas or musicals (*Cats*, *La Cage aux Folles*, or *42nd
Street*)." After all, these highly visible writers and their works "make it to
pay dirt—the miniseries or the great 'Broad Way.'" Most significantly, such
efforts are not so much meant "to disturb...as they are...to pacify."

What results, Ragan makes clear, is a greater tolerance of mediocrity and
the desire by writing students to embrace "instant success and gratification
without benefit of a *craft*." Instead of craftsmanship, many want to substitute tricks, "high concepts," or gimmickry. They would prefer "to achieve
their goals with as much expediency and as little creative pain as possible."
America's media society has convinced "would-be writers to believe that the
condensed or abbreviated version of anything is best." Such attitudes, says
Ragan, have formed the essence of his dilemma: "how to place metaphor
legitimately back on the written page and by performance back on the
stage."

This desire to improve the level of language among a new generation of
writers is what has kept Ragan and others of like mind teaching through the
years. Indeed, he feels this desire—as well as the usual economic motives—
has been the "dominant" reason why so many "conscientious" writers since
the 1960s have been driven into the academy. Yet these "nonmediaist"
writers, he concedes, contributed to the 1970s' "proliferation of writing
programs." But critics should realize that such programs are "perhaps the
last holdouts for true literary or 'premise' writing across America." Still he
is fully aware that the migration to campus resulted from more than "a
selfless desire by writers to protect the purity of language and the literary
crafts from the dollar-inspired pseudo-artistry hyped by television." He
realized quickly that this migration also was a direct "response to the...
emergence of an unlikely counterculture group called appropriately the
'leisure class.'" The interest of its members in the media and in inexpensive
paperbacks had sparked "the impetus for a book explosion unparalleled in

American letters. The clones of Rod McKuen and Leonard Cohen joined those of Jacqueline Susann and Harold Robbins to become the new interpreters and communicators of language and, indeed, of the entire New Mediaist culture."

By the 1980s "the campus version of this culture" had evolved, says Ragan, into "a matter of pure economics, as university writing programs proved the new 'in' subject in Yuppie career motivation." Those writers wishing to explore television and film were confronted by "an aesthetic dichotomy." Some chose to defend "the integrity of their art against the creeping Mediamania." Including themselves in this group, Ragan and his USC playwriting colleagues were quick "to deplore publicly the lack of subject-worthy plays on the nation's professional stages." Yet in the classroom this "worthy-subject idea" turned out to be merely "another pedagogic hurdle" as his students thought that any subject they found "interesting" merited dramatization. Few saw the value of a "moral premise or universal insight." Not surprisingly, their scenarios often were "flawed by a lack of originality and...artistic vision." Ragan's "solution" was to insist that each student develop a dramatic "premise" whereby he or she connected a personal experience to a more general one. Each was "to consummate aesthetically a marriage of the private to the public mythos" by striving for those themes "of human truth...[and] universality that have perplexed, mortified, or simply intrigued generations of playwrights and audiences."

Ragan holds that the university, by imposing a rational order amid "the pressures [of a] minimalist media" culture, offers "the artist his best chance of returning metaphor to the written page." He means that the classroom enables both teacher and student to recognize the power of metaphor by "an orderly reading of dramatic works." Taking his lead from the late poet-teacher Delmore Schwartz, Ragan argues that in a society given to ignoring the needs of its artists the academy provides "the most appropriate forum for the cultivation of aesthetic sensibility." He does not "deny the academy's intellectual and cultural shortcomings," but he does believe it helps the serious writer "to resolve the struggle with his psyche." Attempting to function in the present media-dominated performance world, that writer finds it nearly "impossible to deal aesthetically with...[its] chaotic societal elements." So he "struggles to reduce them to order within the confines of the academy."

Ragan recognizes that the blessings on campus are somewhat mixed. For creative writers encounter there "an order imposed by a bureaucratic overlay of workshops and curricula, formal lectures and faculty committees." In other words, its writers have chosen to place themselves amid "students in a classroom where limitations are placed on their own Dionysian impulses." Yet there the truly serious and talented writer "can strive to apprehend his world as he must rather than merely as he might have." But the presence in the university of so many writers—and their inevitable writing programs— has created a fierce all-out competition "for students to populate the class-rooms." To survive, these programs have "to extol the virtues and potentials of the New Mediaism." One sad result of this "hustle-hype" is that the American audience now accepts unquestioningly "less quality in its art."

This audience includes our creative young people. Ragan—paraphrasing Edward Albee—observes that America is the world's sole "democratic society whose youth...are not at the political-intellectual forefront." They have "been seduced by escapism and distortion, by instant gratification and minimalism." In short, these young people "have lost any sense of responsi-bility for precise communication." This negative situation, he insists, must be changed—and soon. "In the arts as in life," he declares, "the future lies with the coming generation of creative minds. Hence in drama the future belongs not to the children of the 'You know?' generation but to the child-ren of metaphor." To that end, concludes Ragan, the "primary message" he conveys to his student playwrights is "Live! Live! And Write!"

Whereas James Ragan insists on the importance of serious themes and subjects, David Madden opposes what he terms "theme mongering" or the overemphasis of subject matter in creative writing. Indeed, Madden also rejects the once widely held view that experience is the most essential element in writing fiction, a view advocated by, among others, Ernest Hemingway, James T. Farrell, and Norman Mailer. He sides instead with such diverse champions of the imagination as William Faulkner, John Barth, and James Michener. Yet even this conviction has come only with time, for early in his career Madden shared the popular "assumption that the serious writer must gather his raw material from real life." He accepted the assumption that realistic novels were based on "real life" and rendered in photographic detail. Such novels centered on life "in the fields or in the mean streets, in hard labor in an unjust system, in crime, drugs, sex, violence, political corruption, war, aimless travel, Life on the Road"; they definitely did not offer life "in a parlor in Amherst, Massachusetts." Accepting this idea, says Madden, leads one logically to charge that "Life in the university is not really real life." His own life, as well as his writing and teaching, he concedes, appear to contradict the very argument he wishes to develop here, but he still considers "both the assumption and the charge to be fallacious."

So if he rejects the "real life" approach, or makes occasional "contrary declarations about the writer in the university," he does not do so out of any lack of an event-filled life. "I have had plenty of experiences," Madden declares, "in both the real and the unreal worlds." He has known poverty, school suspensions, and thievery, while his brothers have seen the interiors of state and federal prisons. Hence his family and environment have provided him "with all the raw material that novels of realism thrive on." He drew on that material for his novels *Bijou* and *Pleasure Dome*. In fact, from age nine to nineteen he "held numerous dust-jacket jobs," tried the Greenwich Village life, and sailed as a merchant seaman. For that matter, his first novel, *The Beautiful Greed*, is a subject-dominated novel based on his own experiences. Even in more recent years his life has been filled with enough actions and events to provide all the material needed for his fiction. Yet what he has found important to his fiction is not whether real experiences are true to his life but whether they are true to his imagination. Most often his characters, Madden insists, are not "drawn directly from my real-life experiences." They, as well as their behavior and events, "are dreamed up, made up, imagined."

Where then did the aspiring young David Madden learn to write? He recalls that even fine teachers like Walter Van Tilburg Clark and John Gassner merely rephrased or reaffirmed what his own writing labors had taught him. Since then he has devoted his own life to teaching and writing. For if he was "no longer out there gathering experiences like a cosmic newspaper reporter," he still cultivated "an imagination, out of which came thirty-two books—novels, short stories, poems, stageplays, movie scripts, reviews, essays, critical books, and textbooks." What he has written may have been "engendered in a cloistered atmosphere," he states, but "none of it has remained in the files." All he has "merely imagined has proved relevant to the lives of readers out there in the workaday world." Numerous readers have made clear how important his fiction has been to their lives. In fact, whether his fiction derives from his "personal experience in the real world or [is] created almost entirely out of imagination, the responses are the same." He is told that he has caught and conveyed some meaningful aspect of their lives. "Ungrateful to real life," states Madden, "I declare that I owe it all to my imagination."

As a part-time teacher, Madden spends less time in academe's Ivy Tower than in the "Ivory Tower of Art." Intruding repairmen who enter "the gloom of...[his] book-congested study" wonder how he can stand being "cooped up" all day. He invariably is shocked to find they do not realize "that before they interrupted, I was having an intensely fantastic experience in the sunlight of imagination that would overshadow any experience that they or I could have just had out there somewhere in the actual sunlight." Thus for Madden the true "conflict is not between reality and imagination or facts and fantasy but the inclination to cultivate one to the diminishment or exclusion of the other." His problem then, as he sees it, "is how, in the creative process, to enable reality to stimulate my imagination and my imagination to transform reality as a continuous and simultaneous process." To him "the unimagined life is not worth living. The imagination is superior to real life." So he considers not *Bijou*, based on the facts of his thirteenth year, but *The Suicide's Wife*, "imagined and written in three weeks," as his "true autobiography."

How does teaching affect this imaginative process? Madden insists university teaching "neither poses problems for me as a writer nor nurtures my creative life." He believes that it is the "general assumptions about what fiction ought to be and do" that determine the "assumptions about the life of the writer as a teacher in the university." He thinks also that "life and literature" are what truly influence "a writer's imagination and the creative process with almost equal power, even in realistic, important issue-oriented novels." But the popular theory "that great writing must…be true to life, must tell the truth, must be subjectively honest, has persuaded many writers and teachers to promote several dominant literary fallacies." He rejects first the "subject-matter fallacy," which encourages "the preconception that certain raw-life subjects, such as sex, war, drugs, insanity, endow a novel with importance." He disdains also the idea that the serious writer must "deal with issues relevant to our contemporary problems," or that he should emphasize "the truth about life in general." Such pressures result in "the fallacy of theme mongering." Another premise closely related to that of "public relevance" is the one that insists the writer should reveal "his relevant personal feelings and depict his own experiences with an exemplary honesty and 'courage.'" This approach results in what Madden calls "the it-really-happened-to-me fallacy and in a fidelity in reporting one's life that is…just another form of journalism."

Still, when a writer leaves real life's "mean streets" to make his living in the university's "Ivy Tower," says Madden, he is likely to wonder how teaching will influence him and his work. For the university does assume he will "write and be published, or perish along with the scholar." He himself "has always had more than enough published to satisfy the assumption, in both imaginative and critical genres." Yet he has continued to believe "that excellence in teaching ought to be the main criterion for judging a teacher and that being published is good but not necessary." So despite the happy fact that he has "never had a problem as a writer or as the creator of a writing program with the [university] administration," states Madden, he has always harbored "the attitude of an alien," feeling that he is "on a prolonged tour of imposture through the groves of academe." He thinks "most writers feel that way." His campus experience causes him to reject other popular ideas. For example, he dismisses the claim that the university fosters "the life of the mind" thanks to the teachers there who "teach humanistic values." He rejects also the idea lying behind that assumption— "that writers share scholars' primary interest in ideas and issues, that they thrive on theme mongering when discussing literature. Many do; I don't."

Madden brushes aside also the view held by some writers that university teaching "offers a way of promoting one's career." He himself has chosen to go not to the "better" school but to "where the look of the landscape excites my imagination—not to Michigan State but to Appalachian State Teacher's College." Nor does he share the widespread opinion that a "writer's energy and creativity are dissipated in teaching." Adherents argue this is especially true for those "who bring to teaching the same creative energy and imagination they bring to their writing." What he has found is that teaching writing "is more time-consuming than teaching literature." In fact, he loves to teach writing so much, he admits, that he "must not do it." Instead, he prefers to give readings from his own fiction and merely talk about writing. In addition, his teaching has taught him "that while the most important things—talent and imagination—can not be acquired in a classroom, certain things—technique and the psychology of reading—can be. No writing program can create talent, but it can introduce a talented writer to the techniques that all writers share." But what is most significant or "most individual in a writer must be cultivated in solitude and developed out of an inner discipline."

Still the classroom does provide the writer-teacher with a stimulating setting. For teaching has moved Madden to explore all the creative possibilities inherent in that pedagogic process. When he does teach poetry, he realizes that "I tend to write more poems. When I teach drama or playwriting, I tend to write stageplays and screenplays." He has learned also to value "imagination over inspiration and raw material." In fact, he would like to see the term "creative writing course" replaced by "revision workshop," because he believes "that the limited role of inspiration and the teachableness of techniques in the service of imagination can best be demonstrated if we focus on the process of revision."

To the question whether writers or scholars prove more effective teachers of literature, Madden offers a clear response. Writers, he declares, "bring special perspectives and skills to the teaching of literature." For writers are better able than scholars to teach literature from the "authorial point of view." After all, their skills lie "in teaching a novel not only as a finished work but also as a work produced by this creative process."

David Madden, like Theodore Weiss and James Ragan, has found a satisfying role within the university. Many creative writers have done so. But very few of them, says Melvin Friedman, "have combined the academy and the creative life more happily or successfully than Raymond Federman. Certainly he would be the last to agree [with William Styron] that the academy offers the writer a 'living death.'" Indeed, Federman has made of the university a congenial setting from his undergraduate days to his present professorial ones. As a graduate student, he "developed a passion for Samuel Beckett, who became the subject of his doctoral dissertation. Since then Beckett has been the cornerstone of Federman's career," states

Friedman, "first as the special subject for his scholarly and critical investigations, later as the prime influence on his own fiction." In fact, his critical work on Beckett helped create "that first wave of commentary which determined the contours of all subsequent inquiry." Yet Federman differs from Beckett's other early critics, observes Friedman, in that "he used his critical skills as an entry to a career in fiction."

Even after establishing himself as a creative writer, Federman coauthored an "imposing bibliographic work" and coedited two other books on Beckett. Friedman finds it significant that "Federman went the way of Beckett" in that he wrote and published a volume of verse before he wrote his first novel. More to the point, Federman's secure position as a literary critic who writes within the tenured walls of the university has helped shape his novels; his narratives attempt to blur all distinctions between a sort of academic criticism and fiction. But even here Beckett's influence on Federman's fiction is clear. Federman even has coined the word "critifiction" to describe the process. Friedman points to the "early Beckett of *Murphy*, *More Pricks Than Kicks*, and *Echo's Bones and Other Precipitates*" as having "left its stamp" on the "critifictional phase of Federman's work." He refers to Federman's four full-length novels (*Double or Nothing*, *Take It or Leave It*, *The Twofold Vibration*, and *Smiles on Washington Square*), for these works "are remarkable storehouses of acquired wisdom and literary reference." Indeed, as Beckett's work has changed, so has Federman's. "The later Beckett, with his spare, accentless prose, clearly helped form...[Federman's] brief, unparagraphed, unpunctuated, bilingual *The Voice in the Closet*." Again in his *The Twofold Vibration*, Federman turned to Beckett for his title, storytelling technique, and frequent allusions. This novel, notes Friedman, like Federman's previous fiction, mixes "fiction, essay, and diary. The author parades before us his entire career as a writer and critic, never letting us forget that this career has been comfortably housed in the university."

Yet if he is "a novelist in every way committed to scholarship and the academic enterprise," Federman is also, says Friedman, "a novelist whose novels have virtually nothing to do with university life." In other words, Federman has positioned his career "squarely and crucially within academic parameters," but he has not "written directly about...[the university] and...it has never been the subject of his fiction." Instead, Beckett has provided that center. So when tracing the personal events shaping Raymond Federman's unusual career in fiction, Friedman points most specifically to his discovery as a graduate student of Samuel Beckett. For only then did Federman finally find "a congenial fictional manner to accommodate the twofold vibration he felt as Holocaust survivor and immigrant." Beckett has proved the ideal literary model in that by following his example Federman "has never ceased to be an experimental writer."

Surprisingly enough, "the university has proved for Federman a place to celebrate rather than denigrate." He offers sharp contrast then with those "academic contemporaries who have set their novels on college campuses... [and] generally concentrate on the ungenerous, unseemly aspects of university life." But the satirical approach, states Friedman, appears "to go against the grain of Federman's genuine and serious appreciation of his professorial commitment." He is grateful for what he looks upon as "a gilt-edged security" and the opportunity to write "noncommercial, 'non-nutritious'...fiction with no expectation of financial gain. He sees this as a 'freedom to write experimentally.'" He realizes he could gain "more ready access to commercial publishers if he would settle into the easy, safe, expected form of the academic novel. The splendid irony is that the university has supplied him with the financial security to avoid writing such fiction."

Federman's dedication to his professorial career, Friedman emphasizes, remains undiminished. He continues to write criticism, and he directs SUNY- Buffalo's Creative Writing Program. "Federman perceptively identifies two species of campus writer: 'The type who acts like a writer and therefore is looked upon and dealt with as though he were some kind of strange creature, some kind of *malade*. And the other type (I fit that category, I suppose) who acts like a professor, and therefore surprises people that he can also write good fiction.'" Friedman then expands this idea. "The former is a familiar presence in academic novels, and his restless, itinerant ways make him a short-term writer-in-residence at innumerable colleges. His allegiances are usually not to the university, which offers him, he feels, the convenience of a regular paycheck and little more. The second type is far less usual, although it includes such talented American contemporaries as William Gass, John Hawkes, John Barth, Ronald Sukenick, and Federman himself." Ironically enough, "with the possible exception of Barth, with his *The End of the Road*, none of these writers has published a conventional academic novel." Consisting exclusively of experimental writers, this "impressive roster of committed academics...appear[s] to reaffirm Federman's assertion that 'The university in a way gives me this freedom to write experimentally.'" He could be speaking for many writer-teachers when he concludes that "The university, as my refuge, as the place where I was able to study, think, reflect, experiment, question, made me the kind of writer I am." The sad truth is that not many writers are inclined to be as appreciative of the academic life as he.

### Notes

1. George Garrett, "Teaching Writing: A Letter to the Editor," in *Writers as Teachers, Teachers as Writers*, ed. Jonathan Baumbach (New York: Holt, Rinehart and Winston, 1970), pp. 62-63.

2. Leslie Fiedler, "The War against the Academy," *Wisconsin Studies in Contemporary Literature* 5, no. 1 (Winter–Spring 1964): 10-12.

# Novelists and the University
# CRITICAL VIEWS

# Desire, Hypocrisy,
# and
# Ambition in Academe
## JOYCE CAROL OATES'S
## *HUNGRY GHOSTS*

*Stanley Trachtenberg*

"THE difficulty with stories, even true ones," one of Joyce Carol Oates's characters complains, "is that they begin nowhere and end nowhere."[1] In place of recognizable structure, Oates has relied on just such narrative aimlessness to project the obsessive confusions troubling midcentury America; these include "a confusion of love and money, of the categories of public and private experience, of a demonic urge...an urge to violence as the answer to all problems, an urge to self-annihilation, suicide, the ultimate experience and the ultimate surrender."[2] Though Oates has claimed that violence is always an affirmation, she is disdainful of the isolated private figures commonly projected by the modernist imagination along with what she has called "the atrocious Id-pouring of much contemporary poetry."[3] The demonic struggles in her fiction are offered as hypothetical possibilities with which every artist must test reality and which must then be submitted to society for judgment.[4] Accordingly, Oates has been astonished when critics, who want to "linger lovingly over every image, every punctuation mark," refuse to recognize the essential cheerfulness of her characters, even the vicious ones. "Criminals," she has commented acidly, "have a right to happiness just as much as staunch, well-educated tax-paying reviewers and academics."[5]

At the same time, Oates has acknowledged that art may be limited to the ego's struggle to address a deeper self, a struggle serving as a means for purging the ghosts that haunt the writer's own consciousness.[6] This conflict between the artistic functions of private exorcism and public record is paralleled by contrasting roles Oates has alternately envisioned for the artist. These roles take the form of someone who shapes fantasies into an external structure that celebrates the life force and of a passive figure who transcribes the text rather than initiates it. Seldom, however, are those opposing roles or the fictive impulses to which they point allowed to contest each other in Oates's fiction. Instead, disembodied voices—shrill, insistent, terrified, urgent, dazed—rehearse the difficulty of making contact with others, of being understood, of understanding what is happening around them. Women sense obscurely sexual assaults, as much desired as feared, finally yielded to with erotic satisfaction. Men—more shadowy still— appear at once threatening and indifferent; their centers are fixed outside the fevered consciousnesses that attempt to imagine and so possess them. Oates's characters surface chiefly in indeterminate settings—cities that have no streets or buildings, countrysides with only empty fields, abandoned automobiles. Frequently given only first names, these figures are fundamentally generic rather than individual; they are identified chiefly as husbands, wives, parents, children, and defined chiefly within the web of family or, on its periphery, as lovers. Unspecified anxieties are announced in fairy-tale cadences, marked by the absence of thematic closure. The oppressive daily events, no less than the acts of sudden violence into which they erupt, appear blurred, even hallucinatory. These acts merge finally into a single texture that refuses to distinguish between what is important, what inconsequential.

Oates has been particularly sensitive to critical attempts to see in these menacing situations any correspondence with her own life. Writing of D. H. Lawrence, she has remarked that most critics "assume that their subjects are 'subjects' and not human beings, and that their works of art are somehow crimes for which they are on perpetual trial."[7] Similarly, she has seen John Berryman as the victim of the familiar attempt to associate the writer with fixed meanings in his work and so to isolate him from a sustaining social and literary culture. "When the writer believes his critics in such cases," she charges, "he has no course left but suicide."[8] Such suicidal ghosts are exorcised with satiric exaggeration in Oates's stories about academics.

Uniformly portrayed as egocentric villains, these academics are comically frustrated by their inability to impose a subjective vision upon the solidity of experience. Their single-minded efforts to do so result in joyless lives, shaped by the funneling of desire into an increasingly narrow vision. Malicious, petty, self-serving, pompous, frightened, they frequently conceal the shallowness of their thoughts behind inflated claims of importance for obscure literary figures with whom their scholarly reputations are linked. Few seem aware of the disparity between the manic intensity of their efforts and the worth of the advantages they seek. Fewer still evidence concern for the humanistic nature of their vocation; instead, they disguise mean self-interest by pious professions of concern for some ennobling ideal. Typically ineffectual, they find that their inability to control or even influence events only intensifies the anger that is their most authentic emotion.

In *The Hungry Ghosts*, a collection of seven short stories, each of which deals with some aspect of academic life, even the titles subtly suggest the lack of originality that characterizes the academic mind. Subtitled "allusive comedies," several were changed after initial publication in periodicals to echo works respectively by Bunyon, Nietzsche, Blake, Tocqueville, and Booker T. Washington. The satirical judgment implicit in these imitative titles is reinforced by the contrast between the furious motion of the characters and the uninflected tone Oates adopts toward it. The lives of her academics are consumed with longing. Oates explains the reference of the title in an epigraph. "A preta (ghost)," she writes, "is one who, in the ancient Buddhist cosmology, haunts the earth's surface, continually driven by hunger—that is, desire of one kind or another."⁹ In "Democracy in America," Ronald Pauli's desire is to publish his manuscript, a 385-page study of the twentieth-century criticism of the works of Tocqueville and Grattan. The bulk of the manuscript and the contrasting narrowness of its subject suggest a comic disproportion of effort and value that is emphasized by Ronald's admission that the work is not even meant to be interesting. Its publication will simply help him keep his job.

When a part-time copyeditor at the press that has accepted the work dies suddenly with the manuscript still in his possession, Ronald nervously rushes to the man's apartment to reclaim it. The earlier loss of the only copy—at one point Ronald will paranoiacally insist it was stolen—has increased his anxiety, and when he discovers no clue to where the manuscript may be in the copyeditor's filthy apartment, he nears hysteria. Markedly fastidious—he is at first most afraid of finding roaches—Ronald forces himself to plunge into the mess; he painstakingly begins to assemble his scattered pages buried among insurance forms, overdue library books, dirty clothes, half-eaten food, crumpled balls of paper, mimeographed notices, and pages ripped from a phone directory. That the manuscript is almost indistinguishable from all this junk confirms its lack of value; in addition, Ronald's desperate search suggests the indignity to which an academic will submit in attempting to advance his career.

In the midst of his search, Ronald discovers that a number of pages belong to someone else's manuscript, one written with greater assurance and authority. Confirming his worst fear, this discovery persuades the increasingly panic-stricken scholar of his own terrifying insubstantiality. As the manuscript grows more important as a surrogate for his own ego, each solid object in the room seemingly resists his efforts to assemble his work. A wall bed, a quilt, a lamp, a bathtub, even the copyeditor's clothes, prove almost willful obstacles. At one point, Ronald becomes convinced he is being haunted by a ghostly presence, perhaps the phantom writer of the other manuscript, perhaps the copyeditor, we are never sure which. In either case, the ghostly sensation ironically echoes his own condition. Miraculously, he does recover his entire manuscript, whose destruction he had come to equate with his own. "I'm still living," he whispers with relief. Once out of the room, however, he retreats in childlike terror when a sympathetic neighbor reaches to comfort him in a gesture obliquely sexual and at the same time reassuringly maternal.

Academic pressures similarly lead to the displacement of individual identity in "Pilgrim's Progress," when newly appointed lecturer Wanda Barnett arrives at Hilberry, a small Canadian university near the border, which serves as the locale for several of Oates's academic satires. Almost at once Wanda comes under the influence of Saul Bird, a charismatic instructor whose radical politics mask a preoccupation with his own career. Theatrical, abrasive, peremptory, intense, Saul is an academic bully able to experience pleasure only in the exercise of power. His wife, Susanna, also a teacher, serves as a physical as well as intellectual complement to her husband. Where Saul's face is mobile, his manner nervous and demanding, hers is blank, unsmiling, like "a stone with the moss of her dark hair around it." The metaphor, with its associations of dampness and concealment, qualifies Susanna's scholarly achievements and, by extension, that of all academics. More successful than her husband, she produced a book on Proust and their son Philip in the same year, a conjunction by which Oates slyly suggests the boy is merely another credit on her vita.

Though an English teacher, Saul has little interest in literature, and he contemptuously dismisses the value of scholarship. His obligation, he maintains, is to liberate students as human beings. Saul's political activism is brought into sharp relief by the myopic dedication to scholarship of Erasmus Hubben, a shy if somewhat clownish figure whose dissertation on Ernst Cassirer ran to 800 pages. Overwhelmed by Saul's intensity and exhilarated by the dramatic atmosphere into which he is drawn, Hubben, like Wanda, soon becomes part of a clique that surrounds their volatile colleague. Subsequently, Hubben agrees to take part in a campus demonstration that Saul organizes but in which he characteristically declines to participate. During a confrontation with campus police, Hubben has a breakdown and subsequently is institutionalized. To protest Saul's treatment by the university, Wanda resigns her job. Only then does she discover that Saul has found a new position and has abandoned his exploited disciples without a word. Their surrender of ego has brought these forlorn academics to the edge of violence, but without an ideological base of their own they are unable to find in their actions a cathartic release.

The inability even to recognize the destructive consequences of self-absorption becomes evident in "Up From Slavery." Frank Ambrose willingly trades on his blackness to obtain status in the liberal, white academic community. Sexually restless despite his success with students, Frank's apparent assimilation only intensifies his unease until his sense of loss becomes almost physical, "as if he were actually hungry for something without knowing what it was"(p. 64). Frank's hunger leads him to mistake the intentions of Molly Holt, a young teacher he is instrumental in hiring. A feminist who complains about being exploited as a woman and, at the same time, about the difficulty of getting her husband to continue child support, Molly sees in Frank only another victim of social prejudice and indignantly rejects his sexual overtures. In his anger, Frank drops his cultivated Eastern accent to revert to a richer ethnic idiom. "There's anything I hate," he tells her wildly, "it's a woman who talks too much." "Go back to your honky wife," Molly replies contemptuously.

At first Frank is rendered uncertain of his own judgment by this response, but he quickly reassures himself by persuading the sanctimonious chairman of the department that Molly's professional commitment is questionable. In a ballot taken hurriedly to allow the faculty members to make their next class, Molly is dismissed without any real chance to defend herself, or even to understand the vague charges leveled against her. Though she is the one fired, Frank, as her sponsor, is seen by his colleagues as the injured party. Frank feels no guilt at his vengeful deception. Instead he merely frames the incident in a self-satisfying melancholy that confirms his self-image of sensitivity.

Another departmental confrontation argued in terms of principle but resolved purely by self-interest occurs in "A Descriptive Catalog." Up for tenure with only minor publications to his credit, Reynold Mason responds to an unintended slight by Ron Blass, the departmental poet, by bringing charges of plagiarism against him. In contrast with the characteristically worried Mason, who paces the corridors before mail deliveries looking "distracted, anxious, ghostly," Blass is an affable and popular teacher. He is also the department's most frequently published member. His need to continue in that role long after he has anything to say has led him, however, to submit with only minor stylistic revisions the work of other poets. "It could be anything," he confesses miserably to a departmental committee, "because nobody reads it" (p. 94).

The work of the committee members, however, proves only slightly more substantial. The chairman lists on his *vita* mimeographed memos to the faculty senate, speeches made at local PTA meetings, and brief contributions to a highly specialized newsletter edited by his former students. Other committee members publish only brief notices attacking the discoveries of other scholars, or they confine themselves to feuding over inconsequential issues. When Ron confronts them with documented evidence of their own questionable practices, they abandon their pose of ethical concern to exonerate him. Forced to resign his own position, Mason has a breakdown. Neither he nor the incident leaves any lasting impression on the university. Academic integrity, Oates makes clear, constitutes only a pose of rectitude that masks a hypocritical venting of personal spite.

In "The Birth of Tragedy," Oates mixes ridicule with anger at pedantic faculty members who substitute exhausted scholarly concerns for vigorous commitment to their subjects and who use their tenured positions to tyrannize those attempting to enter the profession. At the last minute, an insecure Barry Sommer is hired at Hilberry as an assistant to Robinson Thayer, a senior professor whose lectures are repeated year after year without change, after having initially been copied from obscure literary sources. After unsuccessfully attempting to intimidate his terrified young assistant into spying for him on the indifferent students in his class, Thayer makes Barry the object of a shabby homosexual advance. When the overture is rejected, the professor drunkenly reveals the hypocrisy that pervades the administration. Along with other doctoral students, Barry has been admitted solely to maintain enrollment, though the university has long been planning to drop the Ph.D. program. Called upon to lecture on *Hamlet* to Thayer's class, Barry is led through his terror to the ecstatic truth that the meaning of tragedy is the exploitation of the living by the dead. Hamlet's problem, he decides, "was that he didn't run like hell to some other country when the ghost showed up" (p. 129). Like others haunted by the ghostly scholarship of hungry academics, Barry must free himself from its curse by accepting the challenge of life without an advanced degree. The sympathy with which Oates here views the need for individual fulfillment is seldom displayed in her writing. More commonly, the isolation of the individual from the community results only in tragedy. This isolation can be overcome only by a violent emotional reversal—that is, by witnessing the destruction of "self" and the breaking down of the barriers between human beings and the concomitant release of passion.[10]

No occasion parodies that release more than the carnival atmosphere generated in the university by the visit of professional writers who look to it for support. They become the subject of Oates's examination of desire in "Rewards of Fame." Now in his fifties, the poet Murray Licht has never fulfilled his early promise. With several ex-wives and a number of children, he leads an uncertain existence by means of a series of one-year, nonrenewable contracts, night courses, and lecture-readings whenever possible. At one of these readings, held at a small midwestern college, Murray finds faculty and students alike more interested in the reputation of the panelists than in the quality of their poetry. Oates leaves no doubt about Murray's stature both as a man and as a poet. His pocket change consists mostly of pennies. He is concerned about the fickle affections of his current mistress. Most of all, he is intimidated by the discovery that among the panelists will be Joachim Myer, a former schoolmate and rival, whose failed career as a poet was transformed into critical stardom by his *New York Review* essay on Marshall McLuhan.

For the increasingly dazed Murray, who imagines himself a ghostly figure, the numbing sameness of the poetry circuit takes on the quality of a nightmare. Only the surprisingly youthful-looking Myer, who arrives late, appears to have any substance in this spectral scene. Stringing together a senseless jumble of references to fashionable philosophers, meaningless statistics, and cant phrases, Myer cheerfully attacks both the work of his fellow panelists and the very idea of literacy. "I bring you freedom!" he cheerfully announces to an enthusiastic audience, "total liberation! and the flood of the polymorphous-perverse cosmos denied you by your parents and by our arch-oppressor, Poetry" (p. 169). Though Myer then leaves, viewing the entire proceeding as something of a joke, Murray is sustained, even transfigured, by a condescending reference the critic had made to him as once having been famous.

In "Angst," Oates makes clear that even the most casual involvement with academic pretensions is costly for a writer. Despite her anxiety about intimacy in any form, Bernadine Donovan is persuaded by her longtime suitor, Herman Geller, to attend a convention at which her finely crafted writing will be the subject of a seminar. Geller is an academic with the usual mixture of envy and self-serving praise for his colleagues. His interest in Bernadine's fiction, like theirs, derives exclusively from a desire for self-advancement. He does not even attend the session at which the humorless panelists distort Bernadine's intentions and meanings and even question her originality. After an embarrassing interruption during which Bernadine tries ineffectually to expose an attempt by a flamboyant graduate student to impersonate the author, she is left with only a near-mystical glimpse of the harsh realities of academe. Yet Bernadine's vision, like the frantic convention atmosphere, lies outside the scope of her imagination, and she is unable to use it even as a source of material for any future work she may do.

Oates has again written of Hilberry University in "The Transformation of Vincent Scoville" and in "The Liberation of Jake Hanley," both of which appear in her 1976 collection, *Crossing the Border*. Anxious to begin what he hopes will be a normal faculty life—one of love, friends, marriage— Vincent Scoville is given the opportunity to establish his reputation by editing a group of letters written by a distant relative by marriage of Rudyard Kipling and now owned by the university. He soon recognizes they are worthless as literary documents and, in fact, were donated by a wealthy widow in the hope of embarrassing her husband. Still, Vincent finds himself under pressure from a partially senile university president who sees in the letters a chance to vindicate his otherwise lackluster administration. Vincent desperately attempts to establish some connection, however tenuous, between the letters and the famous author. At first an embarrassment, the project becomes in time a consuming passion and ultimately his life's work. The once-balanced teacher is almost hypnotically transformed into an obsessive pedant, isolated not only from the world but also from the classroom he had earlier considered the last anchor of his sanity.

The seductive appeal of academic isolation similarly accounts for Jake Hanley's escape from the disorders of everyday life. Having impulsively confessed to his wife an affair with a former student, Jake is forced out of his house. He spends more and more time at his office, where he discovers an underground faculty that literally has taken to living there. Among its members is Frank Ambrose. Like Jake, Ambrose is separated from his family and finds in this unreal retreat a perfect atmosphere in which to indulge his recently awakened interest in scholarship, with its endless cross-referencing, archives, and special-collection rooms. Like Frank Ambrose, like Vincent Scoville, like Wanda Barnett—all of whom haunt the office corridors at night—Jake also moves into the office. After a time, he can no longer remember how he got there or that any other world exists. He is content at last.

In contrast with a satirical stance grown so broad in the later tales that it comes to border on fantasy, Oates's earlier stories with an academic setting rely on more subtly ironic, and even melodramatic modes to depict the shallowness of the university environment. In "The Expense of Spirit," she shows its shabby lives and failed ambitions, its lack of interest in ideas or in values, its exclusion of any life that might challenge its own intellectual pretensions. A young instructor's anxiety about his wife's leaving him causes him to pursue a beautiful undergraduate, whose vacuous social manner dissolves into near-hysteria when she accompanies him to a faculty party. The party proves a grotesquerie that shatters her naive fantasy of the graciousness of academic life. She finds only a strained attempt at non-conformity, marked by prepared expressions, facial tics, scatological references, and attempts to control conversations. No one is concerned about or even aware of anyone else except as an object of sex or envy. One instructor, Cowley, who is pointedly described as having come from the East, exemplifies Oates's contempt for the falseness of the university environment. Hiccuping violently, he drunkenly complains about the non-renewal of his contract while acknowledging that the indolence of campus life has so spoiled him for any regular work that he now longs only to write scholarly papers.

In "Archways," which appeared in *Upon the Sweeping Flood*, Oates's second collection of short fiction, Klein, a withdrawn graduate assistant, finds he is unable to interest his students in remedial composition or to convince them that he does not pose a threat to their career goals. The ruthless poverty of his own background, his social unease, his sense of the ugliness of his life, all drive him close to suicide. He is rescued from his depression when one of his students falls in love with him, despite—perhaps because of—her own insecurities, which mirror his. At first Klein, too, believes that he is in love, but the girl's wholehearted commitment to him triggers a feverish interest in scholarship, which leads him callously to abandon her. "He understood matters like that between the girl and himself happened often, perhaps daily at this great university."[11] Even Klein's ultimate discovery that he is only a mediocre teacher does not reveal to him the extent of his loss. He contentedly settles for an undistinguished career and the physical conveniences and satisfactions that signal a conventional existence.

The sterility of the university environment and the emotional rigidity it fosters result in more tragic consequences in "In the Region of Ice." Sister Irene is a woman in her early 30s with "hard gray eyes and a face waxen with thought." She is an instructor at a Catholic university where academic life is as anonymous as the inviolable convent rhythm to which she once dedicated herself. "Each day [was] dissociated from the rest with no necessary sense of unity among the teachers: they came and went separately and might for a year just miss a colleague who left his office five minutes before they arrived, and it did not matter."[12] The chilling sense that things do not matter, either to her cynical colleagues or to her indifferent students, leads Sister Irene to submerge her own personality in classroom attempts to communicate facts. When a mentally unstable Jewish student appeals for an intimate human relationship, she can make only a tentative response. The aggressive insensitivity of the boy's father causes her to back away even from this, and she withdraws into the safety of her academic routine. Only when she learns that the boy's unrelieved suffering has resulted in his suicide does she come to understand something of her own lack of feeling. So destructive is the effect of environment on her character, however, that Sister Irene realizes also that she is helpless to act upon her new insights. She retreats to a dreamlike self-absorption, more relieved than saddened by her experience.

An equally destructive self-indulgence takes the contrasting form of an excess of feeling in "Through the Looking Glass." Father Colton, a liberal seminarian, is a popular teacher on a small but crowded urban campus. Though he is exhilarated by his work and genuinely fond of his students, his concern for their welfare leads him to take over their conversations with his own monologues. In the unhappiness and suspicion of one student, Frieda Holman, the good-natured cleric sees a rare opportunity to test his own patience and humility. His obverse pride proves fateful. Giving up his vocation to marry her, he finds himself deserted when Frieda's indecision proves symptomatic of a serious neurosis. Father Colton is left without support of any kind. The experience, he recognizes, has led him to cross some border of the spirit into the loveless world. He can return only after the discipline of a self-imposed exile among the harmless distances of the Midwest.

Distance, then, rather than intimacy proves a necessary restraint upon the academic unwilling to acknowledge the hostile independence of the human personality. Loving or not, such figures struggle ineffectually for self-fulfillment in Oates's fiction. They are defeated by a life-denying aridity whether they reject the claims of humanity or attempt to respond to those claims. In "Accomplished Desires," the penalties for transforming the world into an instrument for the fulfillment of personal desires are distributed among all who attempt it. These include narcissistic Professor Mark Arber, his self-effacing wife Barbara, and the calculating student, Dorie, who becomes his mistress. Preoccupied with his career, Arber is unwilling to cancel his scheduled appearance on a panel even to drive Dorie to have an abortion. So completely has his wife submerged her own personality in his, however, that she is unable to resist the emotional needs of the younger woman and commits suicide to allow Dorie to marry her husband. Though Dorie thus accomplishes her desire, she finds herself excluded from Arber's life which, she comes to see, is governed by words "growing like weeds in his brain and his wit moving so rapidly through the brains of others that it was, itself, a kind of life."[13] Unable to escape the deadening domestic routine that follows her marriage to Arber, Dorie sits at a battered desk that reflects the condition of her own ego. She is trapped both by the existence she has manipulated others to bring about and by her emotional inability to deal with it.

Faculty wives are no more sympathetically viewed in Oates's fiction than are their husbands. Without the distractions of classes, campus politics, or even the pretense of literary scholarship, they find it difficult to cope with the stifling banality of academic life. In "Normal Love," the forty-year-old narrator remarks with unintended irony that, despite a rising crime rate in the quiet college town in which she and her family live, nothing has happened to them. The deadening routine of this environment translates into terror at any sign of her own mortality, and she begins to suspect a sinister design in the most casual social encounter. Even her family, perhaps her family most of all, exerts unbearable pressure on her to sustain its own routine; this pressure, triggered by the estrangement of her vacuous professor-husband, and coupled with his childlike dependence on her, leads to a breakdown.

The deadness of life in an academic community is also partially responsible for the collapse of Ilena Williams, in "The Dead," a loose reimagining of the well-known story in James Joyce's *Dubliners*. A part-time university teacher, Ilena becomes famous when she writes a novel about sex and drugs on campus. Though she is assured by her doctor that she is normal, Ilena is strongly attracted to death. Alienated in her marriage, Ilena finds even her love affairs have the grotesque, nightmarish quality of a Chagall painting. Though she has little professional commitment, she assures the loss of her job at a Catholic college by refusing to pass the examination of an obviously incompetent seminarian. The death of John F. Kennedy compels her interest more deeply than does anyone in her life. When one of her students dies of his heroin addiction rather than, as she had believed, in a Vietnam protest, she finds herself sexually stimulated. Her struggle with death, really the pull of self-effacement, finally proves overwhelming; at story's end she sits trembling, on the verge of a breakdown in a hotel room with her lover, as blank as the snow that begins to fall outside.

Oates has little sympathy for the difficulties many academics experience in choosing between the opposing pulls of freedom and safety. In "Magna Mater," Nora Drexler cultivates a potential for disaster by her inflexible personality. A meticulous scholar, Nora reveals Oates's view that a successful career is often the result of imitative scholarship. Though Nora professes her reluctance to publish critical reviews of her colleagues' work, she takes great satisfaction in the rise of her reputation at their expense. Her professed belief that art stems from a higher consciousness than routine emotional life proves to be simply a fear of change. "I have visions of the floodgates opening," she protests to a colleague,

> our universities vulgarized, destroyed...our programs infested with grotesque "literature" written by all kinds of people...even oral literature, even...even illiterate work.... Unless we're courageous and fight these issues at once, we'll be teaching Pawnee bear songs before we know it. [14]

Nora's snobbish emphasis on the background of people who should be allowed to write—as well as her restrictive view of the forms literature may take—reveals the prejudices that often underlie supposedly impartial academic judgments. One rather candid, if cheerfully sadistic, colleague admits both his lack of intellectual considerations and the pleasure he takes in the viciousness of his criticism. Ultimately, Nora is patronized and ridiculed by her friends and ignored by her father, a noted scholar himself, who is indifferent to, when not threatened by, his daughter's achievements. She is abandoned as well by her husband, an academic whose books are acclaimed as revolutionary and at once forgotten, and who, like Nora's father, resents her success. Only her nastily precocious son remains subject to her influence. Though he demands her attention, he has nightmares about being smothered by it. He pleases his mother only by pretending to accept the artificial scheme of order she desperately imposes on experience and by denying his fear of being abandoned. Nora's consequent reassurances to him expose not only the destructive cycle of need and dependence that underlies her relationships but also the general academic environment that fosters it.

Oates divides the narcissistic academic personality into two figures in "In the Autumn of the Year." Measured and deliberate, Eleanor Gerhardt attempts to control history; her more expansive, histrionic ex-lover, Edwin Holler, pretends to transcend its limits. Both present and past have become increasingly unreal to Eleanor, who remains convinced of her central importance in Holler's life and of the genuineness of his feeling for her long after their separation and his death. But from his son, now himself a professor, she receives a different view. A failed academic, Holler had been jealous of his colleagues and fearful of their contempt. He had tormented his wife and young son with operatic rages, during which he boasted of his many affairs. He justified his cruelty by attributing it to the passionate vitality of his nature. If less flamboyant, the son proves no kinder than the father. He vindictively confronts Eleanor with letters she had written imploring Holler to marry her. So threatening are they to the emotional shell that enabled Eleanor to cope with her rejection that she now denies, even to herself, ever having written the letters, even as one by one she burns them. The denial of the past allows her to deny as well her responsibility for the pain suffered by Holler's family. It enables her, finally, to cling to an idea of innocence that substitutes the rigid image of self for the shifting realities of experience.

The academic's fragile grip on reality, typically self-protective and marked by a professional immersion in language, dissolves completely in the ghostly "A Theory of Knowledge." Sinking into senility, retired professor Reuben Weber is haunted by his failure to organize into a definitive system his ideas on the nature of human knowledge. As his fragmented thoughts wander among old grievances, Weber is visited by a strangely silent boy from a neighboring farm. The professor finds himself both excited by these visits and increasingly fearful of what he suspects is mistreatment of the boy at his home. After repeatedly hearing what he thinks are cries for help, Weber makes a fantastic night journey to the boy's farm. There he finds him abandoned and cruelly tied up. In a gesture that suggests both his desire to liberate himself and to reclaim his own imaginary youth, Weber unties the boy. The gesture signals a complete break with the restraints imposed on the intellect by reality. Both the professor and the boy join in conspiratorial laughter, suggesting the madness such freedom may occasion.

Relevant here are Oates's comments on the attenuated process of consciousness in the works of Henry James and Virginia Woolf. Their writings, she claims, empty the natural world of much of the range of human experience as it is actually lived and people it instead solely with "spirits without personal bodies [who] inhabit time and space in a ghostly manner."[15] In contrast, Oates points to the more traditional novels of Fielding, Austen, or

Thackeray, for whom identity is defined in terms of social judgment. "Why must art be painful?" she asks. "And if it is deliberately conceived of as a negative human activity, how can its products be anything less than death-affirming, despairing, an unnatural distortion of one of the most joyful of all human adventures, the mysterious flowering of the imagination into conscious forms?"[16] Such objective forms are systematically reduced to nihilistic utterances by the academic refusal to accept mystery over reason. Academic ritual substitutes a desacralizing separation of incantation from sacrifice and so proves incapable of a healing violence. "I believe," Oates has observed, "that any truly felt lyric poem (not simply some Midwestern professor's attempt to write a Poem, to add to his bibliography for the Head of the English Department) can be expanded outward into a story—a novel—anything."[17] The geographical qualification "Midwestern" parochializes the academic's pretension to poetry; the capitalization of the word "Poem" suggests a condescending self-consciousness. Combined they limit the approach to imaginative literature within the clearly prescribed boundaries of pragmatic advantage.

Oates indicates how we are to understand and evaluate this conventional performance in her analysis of Shakespeare's *Troilus and Cressida*. At the play's center she finds a desire that never seems justified by the value of the objects toward which it is directed. Neither the dramatist nor the drama is thus able to arrive at any valid affirmation of values. The mockery is universal. Ambition—the assertion of self—is uniformly met not only by disappointment but also by the suspicion that all is hallucination. Those involved are unwilling to accept their fate even though it is the result of their character, perhaps because it is determined by character. We witness in tragedy the necessary submission of private ambition to public limits and so to universal good. Only in art can we realize the marvelous that we desire in life.[18] That academics refuse to realize this may be what Oates finds most disturbing about them. Like Hamlet, whose tragedy she claims is that he cannot accept appearances, they struggle against the obvious. But academics lack Hamlet's faith and only imitate Shakespeare's eloquence. Accordingly they convert delusion to farce.

Structured more as problem comedies than satires, then, Oates's stories with academic settings are never seen against a larger world of which they are satirical offshoots. Even Oates's narrative voice does not maintain its distance. It often enters the consciousness of her characters, shaping itself in terms of their hesitations and confusions. Accordingly, it cannot provide either sudden knowledge or even partial insights. Though Oates conveys an implied judgment of her typical academics, her voice generally sounds neither angry nor impatient with their Faustian intention. Instead, she seems merely troubled by the inability to balance loss of ego with loss of ego control.

Her professors, then, end up in much the same condition as they begin. Their small successes are not only seldom satisfying, but also always quickly overshadowed by the difficulties resulting from an exclusive reliance on intellect as a way of perceiving the world. These characters reduce experience to a projection of the self, with a correlative refusal to believe in the existence of others. Internalizing the rage that results from this isolation, they are unable to force into consciousness the perverse and often terrifying conditions that Oates sees informing our time. They are condemned to remain immobilized in the trance of self. This picture of the academic echoes the despair Oates has attributed to Sylvia Plath. In that doomed poet, Oates saw "a furious impatience with the limitations of the ego (which she called the 'mind'), a raging self-disgust that, had it not ended in suicide, might have cleansed her of those impurities of her era she had absorbed and allowed her the visionary experience she sensed was a human possibility."[19]

Despite, perhaps because of, her gravitation toward the visionary possibility, Oates offers in her academic fiction no hint of the complex educational or economic problems that currently beset the campus. Nor is there any suggestion in her fiction of how these problems affect or are affected by what was once innocently thought of as the life of the mind. Her academic tales lack characters struggling to develop their personalities in the recognizable fullness of human conflict; they offer no contrasting typological figures. There is in their narrow ironies no kindly if absent-minded professor or stern pedant who sharpens his students' minds by demanding an uncompromising intellectual rigor. There is no suggestion of the poignant self-assertion of Nabokov's Pnin, of the passionate devotion to teaching of Bernard Malamud's S. Levin, or of the rational decency of Lionel Trilling's John Laskell. Equally lacking is the nostalgic serenity with which Willa Cather's Gregory St. Peter thinks of his vocation or the naive idealism with which Saul Bellow's Moses Herzog plunges into the world of ideas as a refuge from his unstable personal relationships. Instability is an occupational hazard for Oates's academics, who refuse to acknowledge the murderous consequences of rationalizing their desires. The conflict between their inner compulsions and an unyielding reality often drives them beyond sanity. Comedy shrugs at this situation; irony indicates its disappointment from a position of superiority. Satire gets even. For academics who inflate their petty concerns into broad moral issues, Oates reserves a special comic punishment—that of ridicule.

She has described the central conflict in Chekhov's comedies of baffled expectation as a ghostly involvement in language divorced from both the images and realities that support it.[20] Writers, critics, and teachers in her own fiction similarly shape their fantasies into obsessive concerns that continue to haunt them even as they themselves victimize others. Writer, critic, and teacher herself, Oates seems haunted by these same controlling roles and by the hypocrisies and desires they project. To the degree that her characters' morbid passivity and violent frustrations are enacted in her fiction, she can exorcise these ghostly figures. At the same time, she takes revenge upon them for their attacks on man's knowledge of a shared, universal condition. No matter how ingenious or arrogant, the individual ego, Oates is convinced, can never erase the memory of that knowledge from our collective consciousness. In her fiction it seems to be in the academic nature never to stop trying.

### Notes

1. The *Assassins* (New York: Vanguard Press, 1975), p. 101. This and all other citations are to the writings of Joyce Carol Oates.

2. Remarks on accepting the National Book Award in fiction for *them*, repr. in Mary Kathryn Grant, *The Tragic Vision of Joyce Carol Oates* (Durham, N. C.: Duke University Press, 1978), p. 164.

3. Introduction to *The Edge of Impossibility: Tragic Forms in Literature* (New York: Vanguard Press, 1972), p. 6. See also "Transformations of Self: An Interview with Joyce Carol Oates," *Ohio Review* 15 (1973): 54.

4. "The Myth of the Isolated Artist," *Psychology Today* 6 (May 1973): 74.

5. "Transformations of Self," p. 58.

6. Ibid., p. 52.

7. "The Hostile Sun: The Poetry of D. H. Lawrence," in *New Heaven, New Earth: The Visionary Experience in Literature* (New York: Vanguard Press, 1974), pp. 45–46.

8. "Myth of the Isolated Artist," p. 75.

9. *The Hungry Ghosts: Seven Allusive Comedies* (Santa Barbara: Black Sparrow Press, 1978). Further references will be given in parentheses in the text.

10. "Forms of Tragic Literature," in *The Edge of Impossibility*, pp. 3–8.

11. "Archways," in *Upon the Sweeping Flood* (New York: Vanguard Press, 1966), p. 183.

12. "In the Region of Ice," in *The Wheel of Love* (New York: Vanguard Press, 1970), p. 32.

13. "Accomplished Desires," in *The Wheel of Love*, p. 145.

14. "Magna Mater," in *The Goddess* (New York: Vanguard Press, 1974), p. 206.

15. "The Art of Relationships: Henry James and Virginia Woolf," in *New Heaven, New Earth*, p. 11.

16. "The Hostile Sun," pp. 39–40.

17. "Transformations of Self," p. 54.

18. "The Tragedy of Existence: Shakespeare's *Troilus & Cressida*," in *The Edge of Impossibility*," pp. 11–36.

19. Preface to *New Heaven, New Earth*, p. 7.

20. "Chekhov and the Theatre of the Absurd," in *The Edge of Impossibility*, pp. 119–20.

# Academia and the Wasteland
## BERNARD MALAMUD'S *A NEW LIFE*
## AND HIS VIEWS OF THE UNIVERSITY

### *James M. Mellard*

BERNARD Malamud's *A New Life* (1961) has been labeled many things—a Western and a "travesty western," a proletarian and a frontier novel.[1] It may be read as any one of these types. Still, each reading has to be perceived through the frame provided by the book's most dominant generic form—that of the academic novel. Though the Great American Novel will probably never be an academic novel, *A New Life*, whatever else it may suggest, certainly belongs to that genre. But it may be argued that neither Malamud nor any other novelist sets out *merely* to write an academic novel.[2] The novelist has to consider many elements, including his need to provide a detailed context for characters, themes, and plots. If his academic novel is to achieve more than the genre itself can guarantee, he must bring his special qualities to it. Malamud does this in *A New Life,* as he works into the academic genre those elements of pastoral long identified with his fiction.[3] Thus, he expresses here his views of the university and its possibilities, but those views prove to belong within more pervasive concerns associated with pastoral archetypes.

### I

The academic or, more strictly, the college novel[4] displays an author's reactions to the college institution itself, its faculty, and the cycle of events linked to an academic calendar. As he did with the elements of *The Natural* (1952) and *The Assistant* (1957), and would do later with those of *The Fixer* (1967) and *The Tenants* (1971), Malamud draws these narrative elements through the alembic of pastoral archetypal conventions in *A New Life*. But here Malamud treats the pastoral conventions somewhat more ironically, for a major feature of this novel is the way an object within a pastoral iconography is likely to yield ambiguous meanings. To begin with, the college community Malamud portrays represents the antithetical possibilities of any landscape in his fiction: it may be a garden or a wasteland, or even both at once, depending upon the individual perspective. The college town is situated in a stunningly beautiful natural setting, between two mountain ranges (the Coastal to the west and the Cascades) and in an extraordinarily fertile valley. Seymour Levin (Malamud's protagonist) is drawn to this wonderland as he settles into his new home:

> He tramped for miles along dirt roads, wherever they led, usually from one farm to another. For weeks the blue sky was cloudless but lately huge white masses drifted in from the Pacific, floating toward the east.... A city boy let loose, Levin took in all the sights.... As he walked, he enjoyed surprises of landscape: the variety of green, yellow, brown and black fields, compositions with distant trees, the poetry of perspective.[5]

Beautiful and satisfying as is this landscape, its meanings are not as unequivocal as the conventions of pastoral might suggest. Levin will often momentarily misjudge the seasons, for example, because in the Pacific Northwest any time of year may bring days that resemble spring or autumn or winter. Another character tells Levin that "spring came sometimes in midwinter; autumn in the right mood might hang on till January, and at times spring lingered through summer" (p. 136). Thus, landscape and weather must be read within other contexts. They are not simple pastoral icons or signs. They take on deeper meaning and value within a human purview at each instant. So the newcomer should resist making too much of surface beauty and variableness.

Pauline Gilley tells Levin the day he arrives that "Nature here can be such an esthetic satisfaction that one slights others" (pp. 17–18). At the novel's end he and Pauline reaffirm this point:

> "Beautiful country."
> "If beauty isn't all that happens." (p. 335)

The purpose of a real education, Levin will realize, is to teach one that something conducive to humane pursuits results from any setting's natural beauty. For in itself a physical setting is merely a given, an accident of circumstance—not the end of one's existence. This idea is particularly evident in Malamud's handling of the college itself. His Cascadia College is located not in the ruggedly named Marathon, where Levin first alights in the state (also named Cascadia) but in the more gently dubbed Easchester. There are, he is told, people in town, "originally from the Plains states or the Midwest, who swear Easchester is paradise" (p. 22). But since what the place is will rest largely on individual perception, and that perception rests on one's values, Malamud's hero soon learns that Easchester and Cascadia

College are not paradise or Arcadia. In fact, from the realization derives the novel's theme of *et in Arcadia ego*. Levin must learn not only that sin already afflicts Cascadia, but also that he must take moral and political action toward its redemption.

Original sin, in terms provided by *A New Life*, is the separation of the human spirit from the material world, of humane values from our human acts. The Fall, as Malamud represents it in academia, occurs when the liberal arts are separated from the crafts, imaginative vision from practical application. When Levin arrived in Easchester, he did not know that original sin had already befallen the college. Gerald Gilley's capsule history of higher education in the state of Cascadia reveals it to him. Accepting the job offered him by Gilley, Levin had mistakenly assumed he would be teaching at a liberal arts college, where he could truly begin a new life in a setting that would guarantee it. Instead, he finds he is working at "a science and technology college" (p. 28). Cascadia once had taught the liberal arts, but, Gerald recounts, "We lost them shortly after the First World War," a result of "pitched battles for funds between us and our sister institution, Cascadia University at Gettysburg...our capital city, a hundred miles north of here, where they still rib us as 'southerners,' to say nothing of 'aggies' and 'hay palace'" (p. 28).

Levin's perception of Cascadia as an academic wasteland is reinforced by his gradual penetration to the real identities of his employers and friends. Like T. S. Eliot's *Wasteland* persona, Levin had not thought that death had undone so many. His inevitable disillusionment forces him into conflict with his colleagues, for their primary aim is not to redeem the arts, but to be good team players, cooperating, often enthusiastically, in carrying out the school's illiberal, antihumanistic curriculum. From Malamud's perspective, the faculty at Cascadia are all tragically benighted, however unwitting their subversion of humane values. Symbolizing the difficulty is President Marion Labhart, who has declared that "Plato, Shelley, and Emerson have done more harm than good to society." Still, according to Gilley, he should not be underrated: "This place has just about doubled in size and scope during his tenure. He's a first-rate organizer. As a student he paid his way through graduate school by founding and running a successful used-car business that his brother still carries on in Boise" (p. 264). Obviously, anyone who can run a successful used-car business can run a college, and if an automotive business ought to have a service division, a good college ought to have one, too. At Cascadia, the service division is called Liberal Arts.

The Liberal Arts Service Division, it happens, has a new dean. Lawrence Seagram, in the words of one professor, is someone "they dug up...from the cornfields of Iowa" (p. 116). Levin comes to hope that Seagram will bring a new humanistic spirit to Cascadia. It is he, indeed, who mandates a democratic election to determine the successor to Orville Fairchild, the head in

English, and it is he to whom Levin turns in hopes of accomplishing other reforms. But the new dean refuses to be Levin's hoped-for *deus ex machina*, for the school transforms the dean more than he it. Ironically, the change serves primarily to accentuate the humanity in Seagram, not the humanities in the college: "When Levin first saw him in September the dean was a clean-shaven youngish type; now he was middle-aged and wore a grizzled Van Dyke but at least looked human" (p. 226), if not to say *merely* human. Still, Levin finds Dean Seagram more open to the values of the humanities than his predecessor, Dean Feeney, would have been. Seagram does actuate one of Levin's ideas—a "Great Books Program" for all interested faculty members, but the circumstances surrounding his decision to do so are equivocal at best.

The leadership within Cascadia's English department, as Malamud portrays it, reflects the dismal pragmatism of the president and dean at their worst. Orville Fairchild and Gerald Gilley are cheerfully "philosophical" in their capitulation to the college's mandated view of the arts and humanities. "The first duty of a good leader," Fairchild tells Levin, "is to carry out orders." His "defense" is reminiscent of the "good" Germans who participated in the extermination of the Jews: "I did as I was ordered" (p. 54). The old man, on the verge of retirement—and death, too, though it catches him unawares—prides himself on having run "about the cheapest department on the Coast" (p. 54). The "main function" of his department, he says, "is to satisfy the needs of the professional schools on the campus with respect to written communication" (p. 41). Much to Levin's dismay, the old man considers literature to be distinctly secondary. Fairchild admits that the new dean may consider initiating an English major and more literature courses, but he does not accept those ideas. "We need foresters, farmers, engineers, agronomists, fish-and-game people, and every sort of extension agent," he tells Levin. "We need them—let's be frank—more than we need English majors. You can't fell a tree, run a four-lane highway over a mountain, or build a dam with poetry" (p. 41). If Fairchild has his way, the department will continue to offer only what Levin regards as "a glut of composition, bone-head grammar, and remedial reading, over about a dozen skimpy literature courses" (p. 40).

Fairchild's likely successor is Gerald Gilley, director of the composition program. But the professor (actually—and most crucially—only *associate* professor) who is expected to compete for the chair's job is C. D. Fabrikant, the department's most notable scholar. To some extent the philosophic conflict (more apparent than real) between the composition people and the literature people is reflected in the values of Gilley and Fabrikant. Gilley proves a virtual clone of Orville Fairchild. He has given up literature and its humane values for the more practical rigors of teaching "written communication." He once published a brief article on Howells in *PMLA*, but he has lost interest in literature, and the current focus of his "research" is a "picture book of American literature" (p. 33). Otherwise he engages in the many outdoor pleasures offered by the state of Cascadia—fishing (he's "the Fisher King" in the Wasteland myth[6] after all), hunting, and golf. Fabrikant makes much of his differences from Gilley. CD is known as a scholar, but what his research field is we do not really know. He is very secretive with his colleagues about his work, but he flaunts before them his Harvard education and presumably liberal values. Levin discovers, however, that the values of this scholar are only so much cant; the seedy CD fabricates them to hide his trite ambitions. He is determined to make full professor no matter what—even if it means abandoning Levin (as, two years earlier, he had betrayed Leo Duffy, another liberal idealist) and the liberal arts. Fabrikant will lie down with neither Leo the lion nor Levin the lamb if doing so jeopardizes his promotion. Though Levin gives up on CD later than he does on Gerald, he eventually realizes that one is no more to be relied upon than the other.

Malamud introduces us to a full range of academic types in *A New Life*, but virtually every single one fits the mold of Labhart, Fairchild, Gilley, or Fabrikant. Two others of some consequence are Avis Fliss—a female colleague—and George Bullock. Avis for awhile offers a romantic possibility for Levin, and Bullock seems to be the one colleague who might assist Levin in improving Cascadia's curriculum. Neither turns out as anticipated, however, and both eventually become Levin's adversaries. But one other consequential figure remains—Joe Bucket. Naturally, since Bucket seems at the outset the least likely to provide Levin with aid or comfort, he proves the only academic character in whom we and Levin have any faith.

Joe Bucket is a type to whom Levin can relate. Despite his long suffering, he is good humored and kindhearted, and he has a humility sufficient for sainthood. He is Malamud's Job. Like Job, he never curses God or others for his sufferings. These include, besides abject poverty, a (perhaps) never-to-be-finished, though many-times-revised dissertation on Sterne's *Tristram Shandy*; its title is "Disorder and Sorrow in Sterne," but, "in reality," says Bucket, it is "a study of his humor" (p. 62). Moreover, Joe Bucket is procreative—he has five children and a sixth on the way, "though they aren't Catholics" (p. 35). He is also productive with his hands. He is building his own house, though it appears as endless a project as the dissertation or the "building" of his family.

Above all, Joe Bucket knows and adheres to humanistic educational—and professional—values. He devotes much of his time to his students, trying to free them from their boundless provincial innocence. He refuses to lie to Levin merely to gain his good will, but instead he protects their mutual self-respect. A turning point for Levin comes when he gives Joe a draft of a scholarly essay to critique. Levin himself thought the essay "useless" (p. 246), but he became confused when C. D. Fabrikant praised it for its "illuminating insight" (p. 246). Joe Bucket, however, refuses to offer false praise; in fact, he says nothing at all. Levin, at first hurt and angry, comes to see that Bucket has done the right thing. Thus does Levin discover that "Humility is its own virtue, sweet, if true. I must be generous, kind, good" (p. 250). Joe Bucket, the college's least promising figure, turns out to be Levin's one cherished colleague. He is a redemptive saint in this academic wasteland. His recognition of the moral values manifest in Joe Bucket's life begins to redirect Levin's personal and professional life. Still, though Joe Bucket offers a fine moral exemplum, he is not sufficiently active to serve Levin as a political model. [7]

## II

Seymour Levin's growing disillusionment with his colleagues, crystallized by the episode with Joe Bucket, energizes the political plot line of *A New Life*. It prompts Levin to decide, however belatedly, that he must compete for the department chairmanship himself if liberal, humanistic values are to be promulgated there. He did not come to Cascadia College to be head of the English department. All he wanted was a college teaching job for a couple of years, several strong recommendations from the experience, and then an opportunity "to move on to a department where he could teach some literature" (p. 31), after beginning work toward his Ph.D. during the summers. True, he wanted to find "a new life" there, but he did not expect to become entangled in so many mysteries that would require solving before he could claim a new identity. He arrived at Cascadia as a thirty-year-old ex-drunkard and naive liberal idealist, who believed that things always are what they appear to be. He has since come to realize that few things at Cascadia are what they seem, least of all his own innocence. Hence his new life brings with it as much of the detective story as of traditional Western, or frontier, or proletarian plots. Levin becomes more shamus than Oedipus, a scruffy, overage Hardy boy solving mysteries of identity and morality in which he himself is somehow deeply implicated.

The mystery of identity is the darkest secret Levin must penetrate. If he is to have his new life, he must discover the most valid role models after whom to pattern himself. Roles and succession emerge as major elements of the novel. Dean Seagram has succeeded Dean Feeney. Gerald Gilley will succeed Orville Fairchild. George Bullock will succeed Gilley. *Professor* C. D. Fabrikant succeeds *Associate* Professor Fabrikant. If Joe Bucket is not quite the appropriate role model, whom will Sy Levin succeed? It will not be any of these. Gradually and reluctantly he rejects Gilley and Fabrikant (and with these Bullock). Levin must also reject Orville Fairchild. But Malamud does not depict the rejection primarily through actions Fairchild takes against Levin. Instead, he emphasizes Levin's reactions to a series of emblematic images suggesting the seductiveness of the academic life he seeks. On his first appearance to Levin, Fairchild might well be an angelic spirit. He carries then "a halo of sunlight ensnared in his bushy gray hair" (p. 39). After Fairchild outlines some of those views mentioned previously, however, Levin notices that his halo fades, perhaps just "a trick of some passing cloud" (p. 42). Later, in the same paternal discussion, as Fairchild welcomes Levin to the "beginning of a great career," Levin notes once more that the "sun flared in his hair and he looked like a saintly old man amid his books" (p. 53). At the discussion's end, Fairchild boasts he would change little in his life if he were able to live it over. Levin leaves with the old man "still talking, the light fading in his hair" (p. 54).

More cruelly ironical is the appearance the old man presents the final time Levin sees him alive. Orville Fairchild takes the paternal role seriously. He regards himself as a father to Gilley and the members of the English department. When he is rejected by one of them, he says, "I had built up some affection for the poor devil, perhaps thinking of him as sort of [a] prodigal son," except he "never returned to the parental fold" (pp. 48–49). The paternal role is of exaggerated importance to him, perhaps. His own father—a drunkard—had failed miserably in these duties, dying after a wasted life, apart from his family. "Many years later…I set out one summer in search of papa," Orville tells Levin, only to discover his father's death and, contrarily, "how to use" (pp. 52–53) his own life. Reacting to his father's alcoholism, Fairchild became a strict teetotaler. (He even laments Dean Seagram's name for its appellative associations.) But in the moments before the stroke that kills him, he appears to Levin a drunk out for a walk. "Does he secretly tipple from an office bottle," Levin wonders, "his father's fate long since caught up with him?" (p. 276). More ironical still, given our knowledge of the old man's love for grammar, are the reported last words Fairchild breathes. Following "The mys—mystery—of the…," he repeats "infin" three times. When Levin tries to finish the word—he guesses that it is "infinite"—old Orville corrects him: "In-fin-i-tive. Have—you considered—its possibilities? To be—." His last words before expiring, however, are "Poor papa" (p. 279). Being and paternity are not inconsequential subjects for ultimate wisdom. One's genesis and how to be—and not to be—those are the big questions of life and death. But Fairchild's universe is limited to correcting galley proofs of his book *The Elements* and musing upon the virtues of grammar. Dying he is—a dying god he is not. He is finally no more a role model for Levin than Gilley or Fabrikant or Bullock.

As he solves the simpler mysteries lying behind the surface appearances of Fairchild, Gilley, Fabrikant, Bullock, Joe Bucket, and others, Levin begins to untangle a mystery behind his own presence at Cascadia. Why was he the one chosen as the new English instructor? Why must *he* be sacrificed to restore the humanities and arts and thereby revivify the cultural wasteland he has begun to perceive? Joe Bucket has provided him with an element of professional identity. Yet in his efforts to bring new cultural life to Cascadia and Easchester, Levin has become enmeshed in mysteries of identity more primal than those of mere vocation. They focus upon the gradual unfolding of his psychosexual relationships with Pauline Gilley and Leo Duffy.

Leo Duffy represents the archetypal identity Levin seeks (or that seeks Levin). It seems plain Duffy is the double of Levin, the *archétrace* Levin's life seems destined to follow. Each time he learns something about Duffy, Levin soon realizes it will become a detail in his own life. Levin is being assigned to his departmental office when he first hears the name. "This office used to belong to someone by the name of Leo Duffy," Gilley says. "He was here for a year in '48–'49, a sort of disagreeable radical who made a lot of trouble. Among his wackinesses was the habit of breaking window panes.... When he first came here, Orville took a shine to him and assigned him this office. He treated him like a son and for all his pains got headaches. I was more than thoughtful to him too" (pp. 36–37). It appears that Duffy's major concern was to betray each confidence placed in him, according to Fairchild, who came to regard Leo as embodying both of academe's worst enemies—"the misfit who sneaks in to escape his inadequacy elsewhere" and "the aggressive pest whose one purpose is to upset other people's apple carts" (p. 42). He flouted the department's grading standards, schedules, textbook decisions, political assumptions, and sexual mores. For his transgressions, Duffy was called before the "entire staff" of the college and publicly denounced "as a fellow-traveling radical" and "a disgrace to the institution." He was cast out of Paradise, being informed that "his contract would not be renewed" (p. 47).

As his own experiences unfold at Cascadia, Levin learns that at every important turn Leo Duffy has (in Derridean language) "always already been there." Like Duffy (of East Chicago), Levin is from the East; like Duffy, Levin is a liberal who tries to change Cascadia's technocratic heart. A sexually impulsive man, Levin is also like Duffy in taking advantage of his coeds and in being loved by both Pauline Gilley and Avis Fliss. Again like Duffy, Levin becomes a member of the Freshman Comp Textbook Committee and is later fired from his instructorship ostensibly because of amatory indiscretions. As he sees his life follow in the tracks laid before him by Leo Duffy, Levin becomes aware that in some mysterious way he *is* Leo. At the same time, however, he must also see that his new life is not new at all. It has been mandated before his time, as if he is, "so to say, the extension of Duffy's ghost" (p. 298). Levin has chosen little. He has been chosen by the archetypal role he must play in this mythic rite of the sacrifice of the scapegoat. That he has accepted Duffy's role becomes clear when, after also being fired, he "put[s] his fist through Duffy's bloody window" (p. 317). Just as Duffy's old place in Humanities Hall had been given to Levin, so Leo's life had been granted Levin as an "office," too.

But as an office, that life—new or used—entails a source of power, authority, or motivatiion for the patterns of action Levin himself constantly sees doubled. Though Duffy had filled that literal and figurative office ahead of Levin, he is not the force that frames the fearful symmetry of the two lives. Pauline Gilley is—or at least represents—that force, which is the force of life itself. Typically, Malamud locates the primal force of material and spiritual life in a woman, the *right* woman. Pauline Gilley's real identity, however, like that of everyone else, is hidden behind a veil of appearances. When Levin first meets her upon his arrival at Marathon, she is merely a "tall, flat-chested woman in a white linen dress" (p. 7). She and Gerald take Levin to Easchester, where they promptly reclothe the new instructor in Gilley's trousers (after more than one accident befalls Sy) and settle him into the same boardinghouse room in which Gilley had lived some eighteen years earlier. The pattern of roles and succession with which we become familiar begins immediately to be asserted. Something has marked Levin's fate where the Gilleys are concerned, just as it has in connection with Duffy. But it is much later in the novel before Levin becomes aware of an attraction to Pauline. His awareness comes only after he has recognized Gerald, not as friend or double, but as his enemy (p. 168). Levin will not succeed Gilley in the departmental chair, then, but he will do so in the freshman director's marriage bed.

Typically (where Malamud's work is concerned), Levin has sought *the* woman elsewhere first. He has had brief, unsatisfactory interludes with Laverne (the waitress), Avis Fliss, and a student, Nadalee Hammerstad. The interlude with Laverne, one of the most comic in the novel, seems designed mainly to display Levin as a schlemiel of the highest order. For he proves a bumblingly incompetent seducer whose rival (an equally comic, but some-what more aggressive, Syrian graduate student) steals his clothes at a crucial moment in his bucolic assignation with the waitress in a farmer's barn. Levin's interlude with Avis Fliss suffers its interruptions as well. Gerald Gilley is the culprit this time, popping in on the breathless couple just as they are about to consummate their passion on the floor of Levin's office. They might have resumed successfully after Gilley's departure, but Levin discovers that Avis has just one good breast.[8] The other is sore from the removal of a fibroma: "He wavered indecisively" at this revelation, "then reached for his pants and drew them on" (p. 126).

The interlude with Nadalee, in a motel on the coast, at least results in Levin's actually getting in bed with the girl. She has become the goal of his parodic "heroic quest," in his used Hudson, over the mountains to the Pacific. He battles along a "perilous, tortuous road" against a "fiend," a "monster," who turns out to be a "pee wee driver with a snip of black mustache, more Chaplin than Hitler, offering a thumbed nose" (p. 137). Levin wanders through "pools of fog" (p. 141) that conceal a monster of another sort (a wayward mule), and the fog confuses him so that he drives miles and miles in the wrong direction. But since at heart Levin is a deeply moral person (as well as a timid worrier), he decides he must give up his relationship with Nadalee. He feels no more affection for her than he felt for Laverne or Avis. But he suffers nonetheless, and falls to the verge of an alcoholic's recidivism—"in iron desperation he concentrated on the sad golden beauty of a fifth of whiskey" (p. 155). He is "saved" by Pauline Gilley, by her "pair of brown eyes" staring at him through the glass of his back door.

Levin senses that something has happened at this moment. Pauline has shown up at his apartment to deliver, unasked, some cold medicine and to return his copy of Hardy's *The Woodlanders*.[9] He is not friendly. Yet, almost immediately, "He regretted not having said a kind word to her; but he felt like a man entering a new life and entered" (pp. 156–57). When he finally sees Pauline romantically, it is upon an enchanted evening, and she is across a crowded room. A "small veil floating before her eyes from a wisp of hat" creates for Levin "a mystery where none had been before" (p. 169). The imagery of the veil dances across the length of this momentous occasion, ending only when Levin tries to pluck it from her face much later as the two are alone in Gilley's house. There, Pauline Gilley makes an entreaty and a confession: "Mr. Levin," she says, "I entreat you to look after my poor babies," then adds, "I married a man with no seeds at all" (p. 179). When Levin and Pauline finally do make love, they do so in the Forestry School's forest, on a late January day that seems a "reasonable facsimile" (p. 181) of a day in March. In Pauline's primal gesture of sex, Levin sees "the mask unmasked" (p. 185). Ultimately, Levin will redeem Pauline's life, as well as his own, by getting her with child and taking on the responsibility for the two she and Gerald have adopted.

Pauline Gilley represents the force that lies behind Levin's new life. She provides Levin a means of attaining his primary goals: "Order, value, accomplishment, love" (p. 175). Once into the affair with Pauline, Levin begins to work toward other goals. Pauline brings him love, but for Levin to claim accomplishment he must exercise his sense of order and value. At the root of these rests his conviction that "the source of freedom is the human spirit" (p. 188). If the nominal leadership at Cascadia and in the English department will not foster that spirit in the curriculum and in the uses of authority, then Levin himself will try to do so. Giving up on Fairchild, Gilley, and Fabrikant, Levin decides to campaign for the department headship himself. In the meantime, Levin and Pauline weather various threats to their relationship. Initially, Levin pursues love as ardently as an adolescent, but guilt concerning Gilley (the "primal cheating" [p. 190]) and assorted other anxieties eventually cool down the physical passions of the lovers. Their physical dissatisfactions, along with the knowledge that their trysts are no longer secret, prompt Levin to break with Pauline: "Out of love he gave her up" (p. 232), Malamud explains, rather ambiguously. During this break in their relationship, Levin displaces his erotic drive with his campaign to find—or somehow to provide—a leadership for the department commensurate with his liberal, humanistic values.

## III

*A New Life* provides a view of sexual initiation, but it also traces the initiation of an extraordinarily innocent academic into the sad realities of college life. In true pastoral fashion, Seymour Levin is a complete naïf, albeit an urban one, when he arrives at Cascadia. He has a totally idealistic notion of academe. When Gilley tells him that the battle at Cascadia over who teaches the liberal arts is a "bread and butter proposition" (p. 29), Levin replies,

> "But that's fantastic...—ah—isn't it? How can we—if you'll excuse my making myself familiar—teach what the human spirit is, or may achieve, if a college limits itself to vocational and professional education? 'The liberal arts feed our hearts,' this old professor of mine used to say."

Levin's feeling is that "Democracy is in trouble" (p. 30) if the liberal arts are not taught in colleges. He is unwilling to accept Gilley's argument that a school like Cascadia must only give students a "'how to work' education" (pp. 29–30). Levin's idealism is sorely tested by the rigid pragmatism of the leadership in the college, but he does begin to perceive more clearly the true state of things. He tells Joe Bucket at a later time:

> "The way the world is now...I sometimes feel I'm engaged in a great irrelevancy, teaching people how to write who don't know what to write. I can give them subjects but not subject matter. I worry I'm not teaching how to keep civilization from destroying itself....I have the strongest urge to say they must understand what humanism means or they won't know when freedom no longer exists. And that they must either be the best—masters of ideas and of themselves—or choose the best to lead them; in either case democracy wins. (p. 109)

Levin finds that his values are truly tested when he must confront Gilley about the censorship of a particular story, Hemingway's "Ten Indians," to which an angry parent has objected. Though the "cracked glass" of Duffy's window looks like "forked lightning" while Levin debates the principles with Gilley, the latter seems to win the argument—since, again, it is "a question...of our bread and butter." But, we are later told, "After rereading Hemingway's innocent little story he felt faint, disgusted with himself for the ineffectuality of his protest" (p. 210).

By this point, Levin has begun to realize that Gerald Gilley will never be the champion of truly liberal values, so for a short time he turns to Fabrikant as a possible redeemer. But, as we have seen, Fabrikant falls far short of the necessary virtue. A fine talker about liberal ideas, he is a poor defender—as evidenced by his betrayal of Leo Duffy. Listening to Fabrikant lecture and aware of CD's betrayal of Leo, Levin questions his own commitment. He thinks: "The true liberal, in his moral fervor kept alive the visionary ideal, in the long run perhaps the decisive thing, and fought at every opportunity to translate it into a better life for people; but not Levin" (p. 211). Only after his encounter with Joe Bucket (and Joe's refusal to comment on that miserable essay) does Levin realize he must fight alone for his values against the *Realpolitik* of the department and college: "A man can find an ideal worth living for in the liberal arts. It might inspire him to work for a better society. It takes only one good man to make the world a little better." At this moment Levin thinks, "suppose *I* were head of the department?" (p. 253).

Bernard Malamud appears to focus his basic views of American university life in the final movement of *A New Life*. From the moment Levin decides to become a candidate for the headship, and Pauline becomes totally committed to regaining the man she calls "Lev," his personal and academic values coalesce within the still mysterious depths of pastoral archetypes. The havoc Levin's campaign raises within the English department ultimately causes some of his reforms to be initiated. Gerald Gilley, despite Levin's efforts, is elected department head, but in almost his first official act he abolishes Fairchild's textbook, *The Elements*, and its accompanying mind-numbing grammar workbooks for students. And Dean Seagram creates the Great Books program designed, presumably, as Levin had imagined it: to bring together mixed groups of "liberal arts people, scientists, technologists, and business school people" (p. 286) to read and discuss classics from literature, science, and the social sciences. The program will be credited to the dean and run by C. D. Fabrikant, but that makes no difference to Levin. The crucial matter is the restoration of the liberal arts and interest in and commitment to the humanities. One more of his goals is achieved: *instructors* without the Ph.D. will teach an occasional literature class. Gilley apparently will adopt this policy Levin had so strongly endorsed.

In his personal life, Levin makes a commitment to Pauline Gilley that similarly displays his values in action. He will assume responsibility for her and her children, even if it means loving Pauline merely "on principle" (p. 319) and despite Gerald's dire catalog of his wife's many limitations. He must also promise Gerald to give up college teaching to have Pauline. Most humbling of all, he learns why he was able to come to Cascadia at all: he *was* chosen, chosen by Pauline Gilley, not for himself, or even for Leo Duffy, but because he reminded her "of a Jewish-boy [she] knew in college who was very kind" (p. 331) to her during a trying time in her life. "So I was chosen," Levin says, acknowledging his relationship just this one time to an ethnic heritage.[10] At the same time Malamud seemingly acknowledges his hero's role in a still broader archetypal ambiance. Bringing new life to a wasteland—academic or otherwise—is heavy going, but somebody has to do it. If many are called, few are chosen. Seymour Levin is one of the chosen.

## Notes

1. Leslie A. Fiedler speaks of the novel as, among other things, a "Western, or more accurately a neo- or meta-Western, which is to say, a Western written by an author (typically in a university, where such literature is studied) aware of the tradition, the genre, and therefore a book about that genre as well as about life in the West." See his "Malamud's Travesty Western," *Novel* 10 (1977): 212–19. In "Bernard Malamud's Mythic Proletarians," in *Radical Sophistication: Studies in Contemporary Jewish-American Novelists* (Athens: Ohio University Press, 1969), pp. 56–68, Max F. Schulz applies the term "proletarian" to *A New Life*. John A. Barsness puts the novel into the framework of frontier fiction in "*A New Life*: The Frontier Myth in Perspective," *Western American Literature* 3 (1969): 297–302.

2. In this context, one should note that Malamud told the Fields that *A New Life* represented "the simple act of writing a novel out of my experience. The 'academic novel,' as such simply doesn't interest me" ("An Interview with Bernard Malamud," in *Bernard Malamud: A Collection of Critical Essays*, ed. Leslie A. Field and Joyce W. Field [Englewood Cliffs, N.J.: Prentice-Hall, 1975], p. 10).

3. For example, see James M. Mellard, "Malamud's Novels: Four Versions of Pastoral," *Critique* 9, no. 2 (1967): 5–19, an essay reprinted in *Bernard Malamud and the Critics*, ed. with an introduction by Leslie A. Field and Joyce W. Field (New York: New York University Press, 1970), pp. 67–83.

4. The most useful essay on the academic elements in *A New Life* is that written by a former professor at Oregon State University, where Malamud taught from 1949 to 1961: Richard Astro, "In the Heart of the Valley: Bernard Malamud's *A New Life*," in *Bernard Malamud: A Collection of Critical Essays*, pp. 143–55. On the college novel generally, one should see John E. Kramer, Jr., *The American College Novel: An Annotated Bibliography* (New York: Garland, 1982) and John O. Lyons, *The College Novel in America* (Carbondale: Southern Illinois University Press, 1962); for Lyons' brief comments on *A New Life*, see pp. 161–62. Astro and Jackson J. Benson have edited a very useful essay collection, *The Fiction of Bernard Malamud* (Corvallis: Oregon State University Press, 1977), that adds considerably to our understanding of Malamud as an academic.

5. Bernard Malamud, *A New Life* (New York: Dell, 1970), p. 58. All subsequent quotations from this novel will be cited by page numbers within parentheses in my text.

6. Various critics have commented upon Malamud's use of mythic elements related to grail quests and the restoration of the Wasteland. See, for example, Edwin M. Eigner, "Malamud's Use of the Quest Romance," *Genre* 1, no. 1 (January 1968): 55–74, and Mellard's "Malamud's Novels: Four Versions of Pastoral," cited above. Both essays are reprinted in *Bernard Malamud and the Critics*.

7. I do not quite agree with Edwin Eigner's suggestion that Levin is too much the saint to revitalize society or that "the more social conception of the hero is better realized in... *The Fixer*" (Eigner, "Use of the Quest Romance," in *Bernard Malamud and the Critics*, p. 100).

8. Malamud's habit is to associate women who are false goddesses with their having damaged or "sick" or tiny breasts, though diseased breasts are more problematic than merely small ones, as the example of Pauline will indicate: a vigorous "hero" can restore life to her. See Mellard's "Malamud's Novels," in *Bernard Malamud and the Critics*, p. 74.

9. Edwin Eigner points out that Malamud did a master's thesis on Hardy, and that he highly valorizes Hardy's work: "As we might expect, Pauline has read and reread *The Return of the Native*, and as nature goddess she tries to live out *Under the Greenwood Tree* and *The Woodlanders*. She does not mention *Jude the Obscure*, but surely, as a woman in a university novel, she is modeled in large part after Sue Bridehead" ("Use of the Quest Romance," in *Bernard Malamud and the Critics*, p. 99).

10. Leslie Fiedler, in "Malamud's Travesty Western," makes much of Levin's calling himself "Sam" at the novel's end, suggesting the likelihood that he is finally to be acknowledged as a Jew, to be associated with "Samuel," first of the Hebrew Prophets. In this vein, one can play with "Pauline," nee "Josephson," and the conciliation of New Testament Christianity and Old Testament Hebrew traditions in the belated couple formed by Levin and Pauline. Pagan elements are also reconciled with these biblical ones, as there is a pointed allusion to "Chief Joseph" (in a "Mt." Chief Joseph) at the novel's beginning that must be assimilated into the general pattern of emphasis on Joseph, Christ, and St. Paul.

# The Gnomes of Academe
## PHILIP ROTH AND THE UNIVERSITY

### Eric Solomon

I

"HONORED Members of Literature 341," says Philip Roth's professor of desire, David Kepesh. These words, in Roth's ninth novel, suggest that a protagonist finally is making his intellectual and emotional peace with the university. Inspired by Franz Kafka—not to mention Chekhov and Flaubert, Mann and Dostoevski and Conrad—Professor Kepesh is integrating the two worlds that usually split Roth's protagonists into schizoid halves. These "worlds" include life and literature, society and the academy, reality and books, sexual rage and intellectual order, Jewish *Angst* and American assimilation, and passion and control. For this sexually obsessed SUNY comparative literature teacher on leave in Prague, the "veneer of donnish satire" (*PD*, p. 171)[1] dissolves as he prepares the lecture that he hopes will both free him from fixations on satyriasis and release him from immaturity. For Kepesh (as for his predecessor, Professor Peter Tarnopol in *My Life as a Man*), talking about great works of fiction may finally enable him to comprehend the meaning of his own life. This professor's desire is to discuss books *and* "the intimate facts of my personal life." He wishes also to break down the professorial strictures that squeeze emotion out of classrooms dedicated to the New Criticism or deconstruction and to such code terms as "structure," "form," "symbol," and "non-referential," or "epiphany," "persona," and "existential." Instead, he wants to deal directly with Tolstoy, Mann, and Flaubert, as well as with inner reality and "solitude, illness, longing, loss, suffering, delusion, hope, passion, love, terror, corruption, calamity, and death" (*PD*, pp. 171–74).

That Philip Roth is, in Joseph Conrad's term, one of us (an academic to his marrow) has been clear from his earliest fiction. His pages inevitably echo the literature professor's analyses of great novels. His literary references are Joycean in quantity, and many of his characters are writers and readers. Yet Roth's major resonance has appeared—certainly to his negative critics—the opposite of academic order. Such critics view his writing as wild, childish, obsessive, whining, Jewish (or anti-Jewish), Freudian, and, of course, hysterically sex-obsessed. But from the start, when he presented life and the university in conflict, until finally (through Chekhov, Kafka, and the others) his literature professors conjoin their worlds of passion and control, Roth has been an intensely academic novelist.

Indeed, Philip Roth has long been a man of the university. His 1954 election to Phi Beta Kappa from Bucknell, his M.A. in 1955 from the University of Chicago, his return to Chicago after the army to become a doctoral candidate and composition and literature instructor there, all emphasize that Roth's academic career, in its essential outline, is indistinguishable from that of thousands of others. Even after he diverged, rejected the Ph.D. for life and writing, "Professor Roth" has remained close to the university. In 1960 he was on the faculty of the Iowa Writers' Workshop. In 1962 he became writer-in-residence at Princeton. Since 1964 he has been a part-time professor at the University of Pennsylvania. Still, Philip Roth has resisted the obvious. He will not write the traditional academic novel. Thus he has insisted in his fiction that the dual worlds of academy and society remain distinct. But oh those subtexts, those references, quotations, explications! Did Roth ever not believe that "what a church is to the true believer, a classroom is to me"? (*PD*, p. 175).

In his superb self-criticism, Roth declares that at the University of Chicago he was "as transfixed by [Henry] James's linguistic tact and moral scrupulosity as...[he] had ever been by the coarseness, recklessness, and vulgar, aggressive clowning" of his own youthful friends (*RMO*, p. 82). Torn between worlds made up of English departments and/or urban Jewish families, split as a person between (in Philip Rahv's terms) paleface and redskin, Roth becomes, ultimately, a "redface" (*RMO*, p. 83). He then strives to write—like his master Flaubert—of extreme behavior in ordinary situations, trying to control life so the work can be impassioned. Roth uses this tension fruitfully in his early work. But he finally resolves the strain in his crucial academic novel, *The Professor of Desire*; in it his hero, David Kepesh, moves from Addison's description of "a rake among scholars, a scholar among rakes" to the self-acceptance of "I love teaching literature. I am rarely ever so contented as when I am here with my pages of notes, and my marked-up texts" (p. 14) and with students.

In other words, Kepesh achieves the ability to carry out E. M. Forster's dictum and "only connect" by teaching and living the professor's life. He then does what Philip Roth the novelist does. Like Tolstoy and Mann, Chekhov and Kafka before him, Roth tells of the invented, certainly, but also authentic, life of the author. Having reached this point, Roth then can truly start his Zuckerman books—orderly, shorter narratives joining the worlds of literature and life. In words that parody Freud, Kepesh (like Roth and his major characters) has too often been trapped between two worlds. These are not like Arnold's religious crisis in which one world is dead, the other powerless to be born. Rather, his dilemmas cause a passionate crisis: "where physical rapture should be, there logical (and illogical) discourse is instead" (*PD*, p. 20). In Roth's terms, Kepesh seeks to find "the means to be true to these seemingly inimical realms of experience that I am strongly attached to by temperament and training—the aggressive, the crude, and the obscene, at one extreme, and something a good deal more subtle, and, in every sense, refined at the other" (*RMO*, p. 82).

## II

Roth treats university life and motifs peripherally in *Goodbye, Columbus* (1959). He attacks the grimness of teaching and learning in *Letting Go* (1961). He laments the absence of scholarly interests in the characters of *When She Was Good* (1966). He deflects his protagonist's intellectual drive in *Portnoy's Complaint* (1969). Only then does Philip Roth approach his basic materials and themes in *The Breast* (1972). In this "prequel" to *The Professor of Desire*—which will appear five years later—Roth gives us his ill-fated professor of comparative literature, David Kepesh. Later Roth will display him trapped between the university's literary order and the world's sexual disorder. Now, like Kafka's great fictional creation Gregor Samsa, whose body followed his guilts and obsessions to his metamorphosis as a cockroach, David Kepesh metamorphoses from a guiltily sex-obsessed professor to a massive female breast. He is a breast, fortunately, who retains the power of speech—speech with readers, with his father, his psychiatrist, mistress, and dean; it is speech that establishes a connection between the academic study of literature and the novelistic creation of fantasy. This eighty-five-page novella provides a comic model for Roth's ultimate combining of his two worlds of literature and life, of the grotesqueness of art and the disorder of sexuality.

David Kepesh's opening words here are recognizably those of a university professor. He feels the need to define "odd" after declaring that "It began oddly" (*TB*, p. 3). Perspective, reflection, consideration are his key words. His setting is now a hospital bed, but it was the university. The tingling in his groin first appeared "in the men's room adjacent to my office in the humanities building." His hectic day was that of the academic—"teaching and conferences, and commuting, and dining out" (*TB*, p. 5). But David Kepesh's trauma centers in his penis, that Rothian appendage of pleasure and pain, imagination and reality.

Roth, then, imagines the penile-fascinated literature professor turning into a breast. Having established this literary trope, Roth joins comic excess (Kepesh's absurd state) to critical exegesis (his comments on the intertexuality of books and life). Paranoid about his condition and in fear of television monitors, Kepesh bewails the substitution of the hospital for the campus. For the latter was "where the social constraint practiced by and large by the educated classes provided me with genuine aesthetic and ethical satisfactions" (*TB*, p. 22). His frustrations are intellectual, for (like Job) Kepesh cannot comprehend his punishment, and sensual, since he needs to be masturbated continually.

His comforters (father, psychiatrist, mistress, hopital staffers) are objects of his lectures. So are the readers: Kepesh tells us how to read the tale. Freud is out: "No, the victim does not subscribe to the wish-fulfillment theory, and I advise you not to.... Reality is grander than that." Literary motifs are in: "Reality has more style. There. For those of you who cannot live without one, a moral to the tale." Close our Freud, open our Swift. "'Reality has style,' concludes the embittered professor who became a female breast. 'Go you sleek, self-satisfied Houyhnhnms, and moralize on that!'" (*TB*, p. 37). Reality indeed has style, Swift's style—satire, mockery, reflexiveness, polemic; above all there is a savage indignation, the ordered rhetoric of the preacher-lecturer—and an imagination sufficiently vivid to advise readers to eat babies and believe in giants.

We listen to this professorial breast, formerly Professor Kepesh. The university world he has left now represents a different kind of absurdity, and Kepesh sketches it 'from his time at Stanford as a Ph.D. student to his present position at Stony Brook. He has followed Arthur Schonbrunn, at one time Kepesh's thesis director, then his department chairman, now his dean. Through Kepesh's analysis of this type of university success, Roth indulges briefly in a staple of the academic novel: a wickedly satirical vignette of the professor-on-the-make. Arthur Schonbrunn is one of us. He is "one of those academics (often enough deans and provosts, occasionally just drunks) who produce a work of intellectual distinction in their early thirties—in his case, a sharp little book on the ficton of Robert Musil...and then are never heard from again; the second book (Arthur's was to have been on Heinrich von Kleist), the one they are writing summers and weekends and plan to finish 'on sabbatical,' is alluded to for about a decade, until at last the author has risen so high in university circles that it is impossible to imagine he has an existence outside of the committee room." He has an ambitious wife, and he has "confidence with men" and "power over an audience of two or two thousand!" (*TB*, pp. 47–49). Professors of literature everywhere may well breathe sighs of relief that Professor Roth of the University of Pennsylvania has not committed himself to depicting fully the life of the writer in the university. Given his satirical knowledge, his academic novel undoubtedly would have made those of Mary McCarthy, Randall Jarrell, John Barth, or David Lodge seem sentimental and forgiving.

Kepesh wants to hang on to his university connection, even as a breast. "Back at Stanford I had been a 'reader' for one of the enormous sophomore classes that...[Schonbrunn] lectured in—'Masterpieces of Western Literature'—couldn't I perform such secondary function again?" (*TB*, p. 50). But Western masterpieces and years of academic and administrative self-discipline cannot restrain Schonbrunn's hilarity. To laugh at Job, at Gregor, is—in literature and life—an unspeakable act. Despite Schonbrunn's beautiful letter of apology and his wife's useful gift of Olivier's *Hamlet* recording, Kepesh is furious at the dean's breach of decorum. As a literature professor should, he tries many drafts of his angry letter. His shifts of tone are by turn "gracious, eloquent, forgiving, light-hearted, grave, hangdog, literary, noncommittal, businesslike, arch, angry, vehement, vicious, wild, snide, dadaesque." In the end, Kepesh the sensual man reduces his outrage to simpler words for his dean: "vain, narcissistic, dandified prick." So much for professorial understanding and support from this friend and mentor who has revealed himself as functioning "beyond the perils of human nature" (*TB*, pp. 52–53, 59).

Parody, yes. But through his protagonist Roth also emphasizes the realistic values for a writer of the professorial role. First, form: "Sometimes teaching one hears oneself speaking in perfect cadences, with just the right emphasis and timing, developing ideas into rounded sentences and then combining them in paragraphs full to brimming, and it is hard then to believe that the fellow now addressing his hushed students with a golden tongue and great decisiveness was confusing them just the hour before with the most unconvincing literary speculation delivered    forth in rags and tatters" (*TB*, p. 58). The *Modern Language Association Professor's Handbook*, if such existed, couldn't better have sung the praises of the academic role. Roth establishes a professorial stance of clear thought, and Kepesh tries to transfer this intellectual mode to the irrational world of (sur) reality, where he lies prone, in bed, a talking breast.

Second, content—and the last quarter of the novel is brilliantly sustained literary criticism of texts crucial to Philip Roth and to the modern writer-teacher's sensibility and syllabus. Kepesh even teaches his own doctor how to diagnose "from fiction" this weird condition. Indeed, the etiology of his illness may not be psychological or sexual but literary, he explains, and directly derived from "my European Literature course. Teaching Gogol and Kafka every year—teaching 'The Nose' and 'Metamorphosis.'" His psychiatrist objects that others teach these books. Kepesh's response is that of the egocentric and ironical university professor: "not with so much conviction as I do." Kepesh believes that what happens in the books he teaches can happen grotesquely (for the books are grotesque) to the professor-patient because of the "power over my imagination of Kafka, or of Gogol...or of Swift.... I'm thinking of *Gulliver's Travels*, which I've also been teaching for years" (*TB*, pp. 60, 62). Beautifully joining form and content, Philip Roth now presents a mini-academic story. In it the form of Kepesh's lecture melds with the content of the great books to comment on an imagined situation for an imaginary character. Hence form and content reflect on the idea of the academy *and* the object of its production, *The Breast*, while simultaneously yoking humor and terror to comment on a professor's nightmare vision: to teach *Metamorphosis* is to become Gregor Samsa. Although the doctor thinks such views are clinically naive, especially for a Dostoevski reader, any professor reading *The Breast* may well shudder.

In his attempt to survive as a person, Kepesh tries to resume his university role. He imagines himself returning to his classes, "teaching Gogol and Kafka rather than experiencing vicariously the unnatural transformations these writers had imagined for the characters in their famous fictions." In other words, this character in Roth's fiction wants to return to a bifurcated world view where books belong to the classroom and reality is linked to daily life. Thus Kepesh lectures his father on Kafka and Gogol, on their fantasies of physical transformation. And in seeking a medical answer, Kepesh carries out the professor's task of scholarly investigation, of, indeed, literary criticism. "What whirling chaos of desire and fear had erupted in this primitive identification with *the* object of infantile veneration? What unfulfilled appetites or ancient confusions?" The answers could appear in a literature and psychology course. But there are two worlds, and his pragmatic father is not of the academy. He is moved to ask: "You teach this stuff, in a college?" (*TB*, pp. 65–66).

Is there hope for a professor-breast? Seemingly there is not, except in literature itself. But in what text? Why, back to the classics, there to purge the guilt that stirs in all professors of "modern literature." Kepesh accepts the gift of Shakespeare records. He returns to the works we all want to restudy as one of those cultural endeavors that would be good for us. At first he is lost in the syntax and the sense. But then he enlists his mistress's help. (Claire looks up words in the footnotes and reads him long-forgotten Elizabethan meanings.) Kepesh strives for nothing less than an English professor's rebirth. His psyche's return is to "The Shakespeare text that I used in college—Neilson and Hill...bound in blue linen worn thin in places by my earnest undergraduate grip and heavily underlined by me then for wisdom" (*TB*, p. 79).

What Kepesh must purge is the contemporary academic's sin of over-specialization, the removal of literature from life, so as to *use* the texts in class. "As a student, then a professor, my experience of literature was

necessarily contaminated by self-consciousness and the burden of verbaliza-
tion; either I was learning or I was teaching." He has let the university
teaching and the practice of literary criticism kill his spirit as dead as that of
any dryasdust scholar. Fiction has felled the professor in his attempts to be
a Kafka, a Gogol, a Swift, those worthies who could envision the great
transformations since they were creative artists. Thus, rationalizes the
professor, they possessed the language and the obsessive fictional brains.
But he, Kepesh, in order properly to read and teach, lived the thing, made
the leap beyond sublimation, "Out Kafkaed Kafka." His obsession? "I had
the artistic longing without the necessary detachment. I loved the extreme in
literature, idolized those who made it, was facinated by its imagery and
suggestiveness" (*TB*, pp. 79–81).

The final questions—Why Kepesh? Why Kafka?—are not answered. But
for Roth the dangers of extremity can be as real and distorting in university
teaching as in sexual activity. His two worlds prove equally threatening.
Roth creates Kepesh's last surreal plan: he will escape from the hospital and
Shakespeare to sex—with young girls licking his nipple before thousands in
Shea Stadium. Still leaning on literary props, Kepesh recalls Gulliver
walking on maidservants' nipples. But Gulliver didn't enjoy it because he
was a "humane English physician...a child of the Age of Reason." But
Kepesh is a modern American teacher, and he is tired of listening to
recordings of plays that contain all the ordered rationality of "Sophocles,
Sheridan, Aristophanes, Shaw, Synge, Racine" (*TB*, pp. 83–84).

Wildness and escape are not the final words here. David Kepesh reminds
us that strong as his desires for fame and sensuality may be, he remains a
university professor. "Let me conclude the lecture by quoting the esteemed
German modernist poet Rainier Maria Rilke. You all know how fond we
impassioned and well-meaning literature professors are of ending the hour
with something *moving* for the students to carry from the pure-hearted
classroom out into the fallen world of dormitories and dope." This
"defrocked teacher" still dreams of bringing great poetry to "enormous
flocks of sheep." And he hopes his story will "at the very least illuminate
Rilke's great lines for you in a fresh way, particularly his concluding
admonition." As in *Portnoy's Complaint* (and Joyce's *Ulysses*), Roth ends
with a beginning. "Yes, let us proceed with our education, one and all."
Professors Roth and Kepesh, however, leave the readers more to do. Properly to understand *The Breast*, as well as "The Nose" and *Metamorphosis*,
we must read critically and with special attention the ending of Rilke's
"Archaic Torso of Apollo." For as we depart the classroom of this short
novel, we do so with Rilke's last line in mind: "You must change your life"
(*TB*, pp. 84, 86–87).

## III

In his *The Great American Novel* (1973), Roth parodies some major American writers. In his collected essays, *Reading Myself and Others* (1975), he establishes his credentials as a Jamesian critic of his own and others' works. In addition, his subsequent fictions are filled with critical perceptions and conclusions. His *My Life as a Man* offers noteworthy examples. Here Roth creates his trilogy hero, Nathan Zuckerman, to tell the tale of a writer-teacher destroyed by predatory women; this he does in the first part of the book, "Useful Fictions." He then reworks the professor-woman situation in "My True Story"—the "autobiography" of Peter Tarnopol, who is the author of the two previous useful fictions. Writing as Zuckerman or Tarnopol, Roth employs his ur-plots and settings. Two stories make up "Useful Fictions"; they are "Salad Days" and "Courting Disaster." These recount the boy-parent-wives-mistresses routines, and they are filled with ethnic love and sexual excitements. "My True Story," however, presents a deeper and darker version.

In "Salad Days," young English major Nathan Zuckerman turns on his mother for her imprecise language. He also changes his attitude toward "Life" at "Bass College" because of Thomas Wolfe's *Of Time and the River*, and he stars as one of three Jewish intellectual powerhouses in the college's English honors seminar. There he is the chosen of the chosen. He has tea with his civilized teacher to whom he reads his paper "Subdued Hysteria: A Study of the Undercurrent of Agony in Some Novels of Virginia Woolf." Very much a product of 1950s repressions and the New Criticism's textual disciplines, Zuckerman believes in order. His critical catchwords are "irony," "values," "fate," "will," "vision," "authenticity," and "human." His dream is the dream of all good 1950s English majors: to visit Poet's Corner in Westminster Abbey, or John Donne's churches, or the Lake District, Austen's Bath, Yeats's Abbey Theatre, or Joyce's River Liffey. But the ultimate expectation is to "live to be a professor of literature some day, with a D. Litt. from Oxford or Cambridge and a house of his own cozy with fireplaces and walled with books" (*MLM*, p. 21). That is his world of academe.

The other world, the real one, is the army (where he fears violence and death) and sex—where this "student of English letters" shares unspeakable delights and perversions with the pampered middle-class daughter of Al "the Zipper King" Shatzy. Roth plainly splits his two worlds. The army is illiterate; Sharon's obscene words entrance and repel the "votary not only of *Mrs. Dalloway*...but also of *Madame Bovary* and *The Ambassadors*" (*MLM*, p. 23). His parameters are clear: boredom vs. beauty, crude pronunciation vs. "the H. L. Mencken of Bass College," and "extraordinary lay" vs. the photograph of Virginia Woolf. This story of youth, told in the third person, closes abruptly as the self-conscious narrator criticizes his own technique and calls for a darker sense of irony. He now feels the need for "a grave and pensive voice to replace the amused, Olympian point of view" (*MLM*, pp. 28–29). So he tries again in "Courting Disaster (or, Serious in the Fifties)." This story proves to be another Zuckerman tale, with different family occupations and siblings and told in the first person. If the academic reader catches the connection with William Faulkner's obsessive need in *The Sound and the Fury* to keep telling his story, with changed narrators, why, all the better for Professor Roth's own seminar in narrative technique.

The second story unfolds the painful account of Zuckerman's unwise marriage to a lost and corrupted Lydia Ketterer, whom he meets, of course, in his English composition class. He is now a confident M.A. at the University of Chicago, working for his Ph.D. Zuckerman is a good boy still, just as he was as a sophomore who read Tate on the sublime and Leavis on Matthew Arnold with his breakfast cereal (*MLM*, p. 40). He believes that one should be "attentive, methodical, thoroughly punctual, and persevering...orderly, patient, self-disciplined, undiscourageable, and industrious—and of course, intelligent. And that was it. What could be simpler?" (*MLM*, p. 47). This is an unarguably fine set of qualities for an English teacher (or "Professor," as his parents call him), qualities found also in the syllabus of brief quotations from Aristotle, Browne, Pater, Swift. These are the qualities he and his assigned authors extol in his three classes that meet for an hour each, five days a week. Here is literary authority, the "good-humored seriousness of the pedagogical exchange." Here is personal order: the afternoon writing fiction, the solitary dinner in the commons where he relishes not only the stews and salisbury steaks, but also the taste for "intellectual dignity" satisfied by the "dark wood tones of the paneled hall, and the portraits of the university's distinguished dead hanging above the refectory tables." Best of all are the books, which he loves and collects. Indeed, he finds exciting merely owning "a slightly soiled copy of Empson's *Seven Types of Ambiguity* in the original English edition." Always there is class preparation; this may include beer in the graduate-student hangout, and filling gaps by reading and underlining a "major work of European literature"—fifty pages a night. He deems himself rich in spiritual goods and undeserving of even the meager financial rewards of this pleasant world. He should be paying the university for the privilege of leading such "a full, independent, and honorable life" (*MLM*, pp. 44–51).

As narrator, Zuckerman misses the irony. He also does not understand the cause of his headaches. They started in the army, but he considers them similar to the necessary illnesses of such literary figures as Milly Theale, Hans Castorp, Arthur Dimmesdale, and Gregor Samsa. A thoroughly dedicated academic, Zuckerman writes a critical article on Virginia Woolf for a *Modern Fiction Studies* issue dedicated entirely to her works. The migraines suggest not merely a need to imitate Woolf, but also an as yet unconsidered dissatisfaction with his withdrawn university world. For even he concedes that teaching freshmen to write clear and logical sentences is "not always an enchanting experience." Yet his chosen war is against the philistines who appear in public life, and so he accepts the university and its neighborhood, Hyde Park, as his Bloomsbury. Hyde Park then becomes a "community of the faithful, observing the sacraments of literacy, benevolence, good taste, and social concern" (*MLM*, pp. 58–59). It is a place he need never leave. After all, he is a good boy. He refuses to take a sexual interest in his students. He addresses the Senate of the Faculty. He rewrites a story four times to get it right. And he is restless.

In fact, he leaves his secure niche at the University of Chicago to teach "Creative Writing" at the downtown division. This is a dangerous deviation from the ordered course in which he has taken such pride. His introductory lecture takes him a week to prepare. Entitled "The Strategies and Intentions of Fiction," it is replete, he concedes, "with the right quotations from Aristotle, Flaubert, Dostoevsky, James—correspondence, diaries, prefaces." It offers his bemused students justifications for a serene, ordered art, exemplified best by Conrad's Preface to *The Nigger of the Narcissus* (*MLM*, pp. 61–62). But after twenty-five pages of lecture, he elicits only one question; it comes from a black woman who asks how to entitle a letter to a little girl. Here he meets Lydia Ketterer, the most sensible writer in the class; at least she uses details, not symbols. Roth parodies night-class exotics: the elderly Russian émigré who creates "Ribald Classics"; the cop who writes O. Henry gutter stories; the "ex-newspaperman" who talks about "Max Perkins" and "Tom Wolfe"; the housewife with fine legs who wants to seduce the professor (*MLM*, p. 65). Roth offers marvelously comic dialogues in the form of arguments about whether a story is "universal" or a character is "sympathetic." He also details the controversies over realism versus prose poetry and symbolism.

Most significantly, and despite personal and professional qualms, Zuckerman seduces Lydia Ketterer. Farewell safe university world, hello dangerous interpersonal world. What he learns about life is in sharp contrast with the orderliness of the university. Yet his actions provide the subject matter for fiction, *this* fiction. As time passes, Zuckerman seeks redemption by loving Lydia despite his realization that for him love no longer exists, and that the emotion essentially results from his literary studies. He blames his plight on the university world; "where Emma Bovary had read too many romances of her period, it would seem I had read too much of the criticism of mine." Zuckerman fails to unite the academy and the larger world. He realizes that his life resembles a text upon which literary critics of his era can vent their ingenuity. In fact his new world can be reduced to a different senior honors thesis: "Christian Temptations in a Jewish Life: A

Study in the Ironies of 'Courting Disaster'" (*MLM*, pp. 72–73).

The narrative is all richly humorous, thoroughly Rothian, and similar to the bad moments of *Letting Go*. Zuckerman must cope with the jealous, unappealing Lydia, with her ghastly daughter, and her awful husband. But he remains the *teacher* while telling his 1950s tale and imitating a favorite gambit of that period's inner-directed novels: the reflexive discussion of the form itself. Hence he explains his subtitle, argues his story's plausibility, and adds university details of lectures and parties. But all this he does only to make his readers believe the text—even though he knows that "to call up such memories in order to make the affair more credible as he taught his students would actually be to mislead the reader." His is now an anti-university life, and one "*without moral content.*" Although he tells his readers that a shift in tone might be possible, he remains true to his chosen decorous and orderly form as a reflection of the decade. As his "comic" tale, seriously told, unfolds, Zuckerman becomes the familiar Jewish schlemiel. Filled with desire for his wife's adolescent daughter, he flees with her to Italy. This he does after his wife's death has made him a "scandalous" figure and "no longer...a member in good standing of that eminently decent and humane university community" (*MLM*, pp. 81–82).

Here is imagining Peter Tarnopol imagining Nathan Zuckerman. Roth-Tarnopol conceives Zuckerman as freed from his dreadful wife and living in Italy like an Aschenbach or a Vronsky—with Lolita. No longer "an earnest young academic," he is still a writer of short stories and the subject of some journal articles, as well as a teacher of literature at an Italian university. Zuckerman is then a somewhat familiar literary figure: the exile who wants to go home again. But he can't, and he blames literature and his social humiliation; his two worlds join, but wrongly. "It seems that either literature too strongly influences my ideas about life, or that I am able to make no connection at all between its wisdom and my existence" (*MLM*, p. 87). He may not be Joseph K. in Kafka's *The Trial*, but he feels equally shamed. He dreams of his previous university life when he read the European masters in his bachelor bed. Still governed by literary abstractions like Perversity or Chivalry, or "Innocence" or even the "Art of Fiction," he fears he has squandered both his manhood and his career.

So much for Nathan Zuckerman. Now Roth again recounts a marital war, but this time in the guise of Peter Tarnopol. Doffing his literary gloves, Tarnopol declares this narrative segment to be "My True Story." It is a tale, he makes clear, replete with savage passion, fierce sex, brutal sadism. Tarnopol begins with a vita that is a duplication of Zuckerman's invented life. He, too, is a literature and creative writing teacher, but formerly at Wisconsin and now at Hofstra University. He is also in the throes of a publicized divorce and of a long-term analysis with Alexander Portnoy's therapist, Dr. Spielvogel. The basic events here are similar to those of the earlier stories, but the action (inner and outer) is more extreme. Now the wife, Maureen, is mad, and she drags the domestic world into the university, silencing Tarnopol's address to a Brooklyn College workshop on the art of fiction by her appearance, just as she had at Wisconsin when she interrupted his seminar on *Death in Venice*. He quits his teaching jobs rather than have Maureen scream "filthy liar" at him as he is about to quote Flaubert or Henry James. His two worlds join, but in a truly painful fashion.

As a teacher, Tarnopol is thus stymied. As author of the novel about his marriage, he is again blocked. Even his supportive brother Morris, a Columbia sociology professor and tough pragmatist, cannot help him. Tarnopol sends his sister copies of the stories about Zuckerman that he has written (and we have read), but she criticizes their lack of realism: they are not true to life because they project his wife's death. This analysis not only predicts the ending of this story but also of Philip Roth's most recent work. His publisher, Tarnopol states, asks whether he plans to "continue to write Zuckerman variations until you have constructed a kind of full-length fictional figure?" (*MLM*, p. 115). Indeed he does. And his sister wonders— as do all Roth's critics—whether he has no source for his art other than his guilty conscience. She includes a letter from her editor questioning Tarnopol-Roth's art that is in the mode of *Commentary* attacks: "the work of a gifted literature student straitjacketed by the idea that fiction is the means for proving righteousness and displaying intelligence." Such 1950s modes, declares this editor, are appropriate only "for English departments located in the upper reaches of the Himalayas" (*MLM*, p. 118).

Roth is having fun with his own work and his critics. Tarnopol's *A Jewish Father* is Roth's own *Portnoy's Complaint*. Tarnopol's present work, he is told, is "a disguised critical essay by Tarnopol on his own overrated first book" (*MLM*, p. 119). His brother Morris, the liberal social scientist full of Eugene Debs and George Orwell, Leon Trotsky and Dwight Macdonald, plays a tough-minded William James to Tarnopol's soft-thinking Henry James. Morris questions current Jewish authors' dependence on *shiksa* castrators—like Bellow's Madeline Herzog or Mailer's Deborah Rojak, or Malamud and Arthur Miller's unpredictable women. Roth's novel then *is* academic in its pervasive literary criticism and its onion-like peeling of its own reflexive technique.

Always life and the academy join to create Tarnopol's disasters. (Maureen is furious because Tarnopol has an affair with a creative writing student.) She is the reality instructor (according to her analysis) freeing him from a childish academia: Maureen drives home the point that "The world didn't turn out to be the sixth-grade classroom at P.S. 3" (*MLM*, p. 128). She also drives him from his university positions by harassment and emotional crippling. Not even his affair with the compliant Susan, an adult who has never been his student, saves him from this estranged wife. Maureen

denies him a divorce and demands huge support payments—all in the
name of making him grow up. Tarnopol is in hell. ("Oh, if I were Dante"
[*MLM*, p. 138]). Incidentally, Susan too fears the university. Her adored
father had been a professor of classics at Princeton, and her own breakdown
had occurred during her freshman year at Wellesley. Tarnopol "saves" her
by sending the wealthy, bored, exploited lady back to the university. He
sends her not to Columbia (where she likely would enroll for night courses,
do all the work, then drop out before she had to speak in class) but to
CCNY, the place where she survives. His belief in the university world is in
tact. If no longer for him, it will prove therapeutic for her. He knows it is
"better to be a full-time student at City College than a matriculated
customer at Bergdorf's" (*MLM*, p. 167). His two worlds continue to
diverge, however. For Tarnopol can teach Susan how to complete courses in
the classroom, but not how to have an orgasm in the bedroom. Still he
*must* teach.

Perhaps the best explanation of the academic tension in much of Philip
Roth's fiction comes midway through *My Life as a Man*. Peter Tarnopol
recounts once more his now-familiar personal story. This time he claims to
have dropped out of the University of Chicago Ph.D. program, "a casualty
of 'Bibliography' and 'Anglo-Saxon,'" to become a novelist. He then quotes
a key phrase from that model of ordered writers, Flaubert: "Be regular and
orderly in your life like a bourgeois, so that you may be violent and original
in your work" (*MLM*, pp. 177–78). Philip Roth, the quiet privatist who is
also a university professor, achieves this aim. But he writes violent and
original novels about erratics like Peter Tarnopol, David Kepesh, and
Nathan Zuckerman who fail to achieve such a balance.

Tarnopol remains a literary scholar despite all. He also remains
unworldly. Maureen tricks him into marriage by the old faked pregnancy
gambit. He believes her because he reads and teaches literature too seriously. Maureen is for him a character out of soap operas or naturalistic novels.
He thinks she has put him into a situation out of Mann or Conrad, James
or Dostoevski. Alas, poor Tarnopol has read not wisely but too well. He has
fallen too much in love with "these complicated fictions of moral anguish."
He depends too much on "teachers and books," and he remains too
"susceptible to a literary education." He has made a crucial mistake in
marrying a true bitch, but his basic error derives from the literature class.
He has mixed genres: "instead of the intractability of serious fiction, I got
the intractability of soap opera. Resistant enough, but the wrong genre"
(pp. 197–99).

Some readers may find Peter Tarnopol an unreliable narrator, a weak
madman who has destroyed Maureen by his own egocentric immaturity.
But the preponderance of evidence convinces the reader of the opposite. Dr.
Spielvogel would agree, even though Tarnopol soon questions the doctor's

value as his therapist. For the latter publishes in an obscure scientific journal a faintly disguised version of Tarnopol's case. Following his literary training, Tarnopol naturally casts the analytic sessions into classic paradigms out of Hawthorne and Tolstoy. Also unhappy in his own way, Tarnopol weeps and weeps until Spielvogel asks, "Are you finished?" (*MLM*, pp. 207–08). Thus Roth entraps his readers in a Proustian world that echoes from one of his books to another: we are hearing a reversal of Spielvogel's first words to Alex Portnoy about "beginning." And when Tarnopol confesses his pursuit and seduction of the student Karen, Roth is reminding us once again of the yoking of two worlds: "classroom/sex; literature/life" (*MLM*, p. 211).

By such means does Philip Roth turn novelistic and university conventions against themselves in comic self-parodies. His Peter Tarnopol imagines others writing about the first two stories, and he is very funny with one student's supposed paper for "English 312, M & F 1:00–2:20 (assignations by appointment)." He catches the style of an undergraduate essay (that earns an A +): he moves from the opening title, "The Uses of the Useful Fictions: Or, Professor Tarnopol Withdraws Somewhat From his Feelings" (*MLM*, p. 221), to the quotes from Sartre and de Beauvoir, to the inflated literary terminology. He captures not only the inherent humor, but also a fine juxtaposition of his own sexual activity and the familiar form of university literary criticism. His comments on the student's paper continue the joke. After gently reproving her grand style and weighty epigraphs, he writes a mock comment in which he blames himself, employs his arsenal of literary references, and rejects his own education and teaching. This "comment" material centers attention on Roth's academic novel as an art form and on the questions his narrative suggests: Can Flaubert's advice hold when "personal experience" is shaped by "aesthetic detachment"? How does the true academic blend the ivory tower and daily life? What about form? Should the author get rid of the "I" and go back to "Zuckermanizing myself?" What of the critics? What will *Commentary*'s reviewer make of all this? (*MLM*, pp. 234–36). As Philip Roth deconstructs his own ficton, the scaffolding of "sublimation and high art" cannot conceal the cry of pain and low mimesis.

Even under the pressures of his ex-wife's lawsuits, his neurotic ladyfriend's demands, his analyst's queries, Tarnopol holds together partly because of the necessary routines of his Hofstra professorship. Teaching creative writing in a psychedelic age may be unrewarding, but he continues to flourish in the honors seminar that he teaches, and that helps him reject his own condition. His subject is "transgression and punishment," and his texts are the customary Roth books. Tarnopol, like his creator, comes to realize just how much he owes to *The Brothers Karamazov*, *The Scarlet Letter*, *The Trial*, *Death in Venice*, *Anna Karenina*, and Kleist's *Michael*

*Kohlhaas*. Rambling through New York, Tarnopol believes that he is strongly similar to "that great paranoid victim and avenger of injustice in the Kleist novella that I taught with such passion at Hofstra" (*MLM*, p. 241). And he *is* his own previously published novel, a copy of which he discovers in a secondhand bookstore alphabetically shelved between Sterne, Styron, Swift, and Thackeray, Thurber, Trollope. When one faces loss of identity, the book saves: Tarnopol is, if nothing else, his novel. The world of books exists both at Hofstra University and at a Second Avenue bookstore.

Flaubert, however, is the writer who most clarifies Roth's double vision. The great novelist warned against excessive emotion or too much hatred. Yet Flaubert, "this genius who had done so much to form my literary conscience," offers a mixed message. "Art, like the Jewish God, wallows in sacrifice." Again, "In art...the creative impulse is essentially fanatic." The great masters whom Tarnopol and Kepesh and Roth admire all write to excess and mostly about themselves. If his own major novels take the form of autobiographies, that is the master's lesson Philip Roth encodes in his fiction and criticism: "His *self* is to many a novelist what his own physiognomy is to a painter of portraits: the closest subject at hand demanding scrutiny, a problem for his art to solve" (*MLM*, pp. 244–45). Yet Tarnopol the professor cannot convince Spielvogel the scientific writer that fiction is not mere fact or autobiography but rather "a rumination on the real" (*MLM*, p. 256). The novelist's function, he argues, is to make private life public. That the professor-novelist also makes public life (great novels) meaningful to his own and his students' private concerns is indicated by all of Philip Roth's books about university professors.

## IV

The joining of the worlds in *My Life as a Man* at times may seem forced, but this work proves Philip Roth's most literary, most technically intricate novel. It hovers between art and artifice. His next novel, *The Professor of Desire* (1977), however, is ultimately a fully successful bringing together of the university's detached life and personal passion. In it Roth traces David Kepesh's growth from a Roth-like lad (this time in a Catskill hotel) to a "sober, solitary, rather refined young man dedicated to European literature and languages" (*PD*, p. 9). Kepesh is an intense individual in both worlds. In fact, he is the most sexually obsessed and sexually active of all Roth's protagonists. In addition, he is an active, publishing scholar, not merely another of Roth's blocked novelists.

From the start, David Kepesh strives to link his two selves. For him the reading room of the Syracuse University library is "a place comparable to the runway of a burlesque house in its power to stimulate and focus my desire" (*PD*, p. 19). Academic propriety and sexual lust are mutually supportive. Miserable in the scholarly constraints of his London Fulbright research into Arthurian legends, Kepesh takes not Galahad but Maupassant as his idol. He discovers Soho and the two Swedish girls with whom he will play out the sensual games that become a permanent part of his lust-guilt memories. Even when pursuing his rakish desires, Kepesh casts himself in scholarly garments: he crosses the city like Raskolnikov played by Pudd'nhead Wilson. Indeed, Kepesh's character splits between Dostoevskian guilt and Twainian naiveté.

Eventually Swedish sex succumbs to Stanford Ph.D. studies, and the twenty-four-year-old scholar's academic sensuality moves into its second phase when he meets his Helen. She is Helen Baird, an exotic world wanderer ("out of the novels of Conrad"). Their long marital struggle commences as a love affair in which Kepesh-as-critic tries to discover reality. "Is the unbelievable character Helen in her diamond-stud earrings or is it the dutiful graduate teaching assistant in his wash-and-dry seersucker suit?" These two intellectual opposites are wonderfully paired physically. But the worldly Helen hates David's academic side. He will not become with her "a *cum laude* student of real life" because his information about the real world was learned "at Tolstoy's feet." She is bored by *Anna Karenina*, and she rejects Kepesh's claim that books exist that deal with real life (*The Ambassadors*) or with Helen and her friends (*The Sun Also Rises*). The battle lines are drawn quickly: "I hate libraries; I hate books, and I hate schools," cries Helen. She pinpoints the true culprits—the professors, the David Kepeshes. "It's those poor innocent theoretical bookworms who do the teaching who turn it all into something worse" (*PD*, pp. 51, 54).

As his characters' arguments grow more fierce, Roth is tempted to present another traditional slice of academic life. Helen's complaint about the learned professors and their peppy, dowdy wives is funny, but it is the stuff of familiar university fiction: "I'm not clever enough to bake banana and carrot bread and raise my own bean sprouts and 'audit' seminars and 'head up' committees to outlaw war for all time." She flees to Hong Kong, and Kepesh must follow to rescue her from jail rather than stay at home to finish his book. There is a lovely academic in joke here as Kepesh and his retrieved wife fly from the mysterious East, Conrad's world. Kepesh gets through "the million remaining hours of the flight" much like Joseph Conrad's Marlow, who is saved by routine work: he has "these examination papers to hang on to." Since the professor has his schoolwork, he doesn't strangle his wife—as someone in a Browning poem might do. Kepesh puts worldly melodrama aside to correct every comma fault or dangling modifier and to fill the margins with commentary and questions. Is Kepesh saved or lost by his dependence on the university, on "'finals'; my marking pen and my paper clips"? In short, is he saved by being "a literature professor and not a policeman"? (*PD*, pp. 76, 85–86).

This first section of *The Professor of Desire* ends with David Kepesh weeping for Helen, for himself, and for a chubby Jewish student with whom he, as professor, has somehow succeeded. For he has moved her to where she can compose a grim and lovely lament that summarizes Chekhov's philosophy of life. He raises the questions all teachers of literature face: How can the two worlds join? How can we, through literature, teach students about life when we, like Kepesh, are only just beginning to learn? Chekhov's lesson—rephrased by the student—will be Kepesh's text, and its implications are those he must grasp through the remainder of the novel: "We are born innocent...we suffer terrible disillusionment before we can gain knowledge, and then we fear death—and we are granted only fragmentary happiness to offset the pain" (*PD*, p. 87).

In addition to his psychiatrist (now Dr. Klinger), David Kepesh has as a "savior" during his divorce Arthur Schonbrunn, his thesis adviser. Schonbrunn takes Kepesh with him to the "State University of New York on Long Island" to teach comparative literature. Kepesh's therapy includes his attempt to deal with the guilt of being *merely* a scholar, one who likes to read and write and teach about books. The solution for such a professor is not "to teach great books to the girls at the University of Tahiti," or to return to his earlier sexual antics. Always the critic, Kepesh has learned from Chekhov's "The Duel" about "the libidinous fallacy." His choices are negative—to be a pimp or an associate professor who teaches the master-works of disillusionment and renunciation. His therapy takes the form of a debate wherein Shakespeare and Dostoevski are his "literary reserves" who help defend his fascination with moral delinquency (*PD*, pp. 93–94, 96). His actual colleagues are little help. Arthur Schonbrunn is the total academic politician. Ralph Baumgarten is the doomed (to be denied tenure is academic death) raunchy poet. The first advises him to work on his book. The second recommends more street activity and less irony or complexity. "Save your subtlety for your critical articles." The sex-obsessed poet knows how to communicate with Kepesh in a language he truly understands: "You remember your James, Kepesh—'Dramatize, dramatize'" (*PD*, p. 117). But the latter has no woman, and his Chekhov book consists merely of drafts.

Roth is here coming close to writing an academic novel, a version, say, of John Barth's *End of the Road*. Academic jokes abound: Kepesh finds Helen's picture among his lecture notes on Francois Mauriac, and the reader must smile with recognition at mention of the misogynist author. Kepesh defines anxiety in terms of a student handing in a plagiarized paper, or he rereads Kafka's "A Hunger Artist" after observing a crude eater. Roth tries also to outcritique his critics. Thus Baumgarten and Kepesh have an intense discussion about Kepesh's family. Then Baumgarten launches a marvelous critical attack that could be leveled against Roth's own novels from *Columbus* to *Zuckerman*. Begging to be spared the subject of the

Jewish family and its travails, Baumgarten wonders how one can still get worked up over sons and daughters and mothers and fathers driving each other crazy. "All that loving, all that hating; all those meals...and baffled quest for dignity. Oh, and the goodness. I understand somebody has just published a whole book on our Jewish literature of goodness." This, he avers, would be like an Irish critic writing on conviviality in Joyce. The dialogue is long and very funny. All Kepesh-Roth's idols are impaled on the shaft of the rowdy poet's wit. So is literary criticism. Hence that "cunning Yiddish theater" known as "Literary Criticism" is the product of "middle-aged Jewish sons, with their rituals of rebellion and atonement." But Baumgarten's anger exceeds the mockery familiar to academic novels, for he is satirizing the problem that obsesses Philip Roth in his university fiction. Throughout academe esteemed but hypocritical professors dwell in two worlds: they call for moral literature while "sticking it into some graduate student"; that is the truth behind the Sunday *New York Times* book reviews that pretend to guard the sacred flame. It also is what serves to gain kudos from the "Brandeis Kollege of Musical Knowledge" (*PD*, pp. 129–31). Despite Baumgarten's scurrilous attacks on the moral hypoc-risies of the literary scene, he himself reduces literature to a tool for seduction. He haunts bookstores and preys on girls who purchase Hardy's *Tess of the D'Urbervilles* or Brontë's *Jane Eyre*. This poet-professor is the Conradian double (or "secret sharer") of any critic-professor. He simply joins the worlds of art and sex on a lower level.

Only when David Kepesh falls in love with Claire Ovington does he start to integrate his worlds. He returns to society and to his study of Chekhov. He saves five of his many pages on romantic disillusionment. Then, in domestic calm with Claire, he studies, rereads, and creates a forty-thousand-word "essay on license and restraint in Chekhov's world." This proves to be his first book of criticism, *Man in a Shell*. It deals with Chekhov and Kepesh himself—and with "longings fulfilled, pleasures denied" (*PD*, p. 149).

The novel's final section returns to another Roth literary obsession, the life and work of Franz Kafka. Employing fiction more directly than he did in his earlier Kafka pieces, Roth sends his Professor Kepesh on an appro-priate academic mission. Having taught the Kafka course at his university, Kepesh flies to Prague to present a paper on Kafka and spiritual starvation. He quotes his examination question that asked his students to deal with the paradox of Kafka's letter to his father. There Kafka claims that his father determined the direction of his writing—and the opposite. Kafka's problem, like those of Roth's protagonists, is personal. He, too, is obsessed with melding his family travails and his aesthetic imagination. How does "a fantasist as entangled as Kafka was in daily existence," asks Kepesh, transform "into fable his everyday struggle?" (*PD*, p. 157).

Kepesh and Claire tour Prague in the manner of ordinary academic tourists, and he learns that Kafka is to his countrymen a realist, that they view his fictional world as a prediction of present actuality. With a sounder grasp of Kafka, Kepesh is able to link that writer's blocked figures to his own sexual blockage. "To each abstracted citizen," he muses, "his own Kafka" (*PD*, p. 164). Ever the professor, he prepares for his next year's comparative literature class. Being now ready to join life and literature, he will organize the class "around the subject of erotic desire." Indeed, he will start with "disquieting contemporary novels dealing with prurient and iniquitous sexuality." Can anyone doubt that several Philip Roth novels will be included? For they will be novels "in which the author is himself pointedly implicated in what is morally most alarming." The course will end, predictably, with such Roth staples as *Madame Bovary*, *Anna Karenina*, and *Death in Venice*, for in them the assault of illicit and ungovernable passion is made by other means (*PD*, pp. 164, 169). Kepesh is not yet finished. He has to observe the city's whores and to write his imitation of Kafka's "Report to an Academy." This lecture is his letter to the real world. He wants with all his heart to deliver it, not in September but at that very moment, to prostitutes in Kafka's homeland. For there the professor, his lecture, and the sensual, disordered world make a single unity.

The lecture itself, derived from the heart of Europe, contains the heart of Philip Roth's belief. Considering the art of fiction to be real, Roth rejects as false the New Criticism and nonreferentiality. Hence he resents a professor who contrasts literary criticism with real life to underscore his own fictional-critical, professor-novelist concerns. This lecture then is the vital center of Roth's own form and content. It organizes and pinpoints his fascination with separate worlds, in this novel as well as in his canon. Finally, it proves to be his answer—for his created literature professor and for his own dual role as professor and novelist. Indeed, the lecture explicates the title of the book: Kepesh is himself the first of the semester's texts, the professor of desire. The distilled world is "in this bright and barren little room" (*PD*, p. 174) where he confronts and teaches life. As a footnote to this climactic moment, Philip Roth creates, as only he can, a wildly absurd and disgusting dream scene. In it Kepesh meets Kafka's old whore. Still mentally talking to his literature class, he wonders whether he is real, as he acts out fiction in dream reality. "Students of literature," he declares, "you must conquer your squeamishness once and for all" (*PD*, p. 181) and touch the pubic hair of Kafka's whore. Thus does Kepesh-Roth blend Imagination, Reality, Art, Life, Dream, Fiction—and Final Exam.

Back in America, in the Catskill world of his childhood, David Kepesh brings his worlds together. His materials include Claire, his aging father, his father's friend who has survived a death camp, his ex-wife, and his two spiral notebooks: one will become a book on Kafka (by the literature professor), and the other is his lecture on his own life (by the fiction writer). He reads Colette and prepares his course (now known as Desire 341). He is now indeed the professor of desire who can not only list his novels but also cope with reality when invaders from his genuine past interrupt his intellectual concentration. There is a comic coda. His father gives Kepesh a grotesquely expensive gift of thirty-two Shakespeare medallions; each bears a scene from a play on one side and a quotation on the other. Yet like one of Shakespeare's comic subplots, the absurd gift supports the serious theme—the joining of university and real life. His father proudly announces: "And he can take it to school too.... That's what so useful. It's something not just for the home" (*PD*, p. 226). Also, being silver, the medals are a hedge against inflation—a clear indication of literature's true "value" in the real world.

Finally, Kepesh opens his mail from the university, composes a mock recommendation letter for Baumgarten, and tries to imagine happiness with Claire as in a Chekhov story. But he realizes that whereas Gogol truly exists for all time, he, David Kepesh, may well end up alone and in therapy despite his newly gained strength and idyllic relationships.

That Philip Roth closes *The Professor of Desire* on the traditional literary note of dramatic irony typifies his fictional credo. Readers of Roth know, as David Kepesh does not, that the professor's moment of stability (wherein his two worlds are one and he possesses both his literature and his sexuality) is fleeting: Kepesh will lose his balance, and his realistic fiction will give way to mad fantasy. For Chekhov will be replaced by Gogol, and Kepesh will become a female breast. For Philip Roth, however, who is neither character nor reader, the balancing act he finally achieves in *The Professor of Desire* releases him to write openly—with full seriocomic control—three short novels and an epilogue about that same writer-teacher who started these academic fictions, Nathan Zuckerman. Indeed, Philip Roth now appears to be free of the academy, free to live the examined life in that world of reality where the writer fantasizes for himself, not for his students in a university.

## Note

1. Quotations from Philip Roth's works are cited parenthetically in the text using the following abbreviations:

*PD*: Philip Roth, *The Professor of Desire* (1977; reprint, New York: Bantam, 1978).

*MLM*: Philip Roth, *My Life as a Man* (1974; reprint, New York: Bantam, 1985).

*RMO*: Philip Roth, *Reading Myself and Others* (New York; Farrar, Straus & Giroux, 1975).

*TB*: Philip Roth, *The Breast* (New York: Holt, Rinehart and Winston, 1972).

# John Barth, the University, and the Absurd
## A STUDY OF *THE END OF THE ROAD*
## AND
### *GILES GOAT-BOY*

### *Elaine Safer*

CRITICS have examined many aspects of Barth's novels, including his employment of multiple frames for telling the story, different genres (like the epistolary novel and the epic), comic nihilism, and parodies of societal myths.[1] A recurring subject in the novels, not heretofore stressed, is what Barth calls the "spectacle of these enormous universities."[2] Barth satirizes the grand academies of education that frustrate both the pursuit of reason and the advancement of knowledge.

John Barth, who has spent most of his adult years teaching in the university, manages to incorporate many of his own experiences as teacher and writer into his satirical novels. In this respect he is in the tradition of contemporary academic writers like Mary McCarthy, in *The Groves of Academe*; Randall Jarrell, in *Pictures from an Institution*; Philip Roth, in *Letting Go*; and Saul Bellow, in *The Dean's December*.[3] Barth's novels, like the works of these authors, show a strong preoccupation with the frailties of university teachers and students. In two of his novels—*The End of the Road* and *Giles Goat-Boy*—the action takes place on a university campus. In all of his novels, Barth gives the academic background for the major characters, and, in addition, draws upon his own experiences in the university for particulars. Largely, the setting for the novels is the Eastern Shore of Maryland (where he was brought up), Johns Hopkins (where he received B.A. and M.A. degrees and is now Alumni Centennial Professor of English), and Penn State (where he taught for many years).

Barth's method ranges from using the university as a setting—as in *Giles Goat-Boy*, with its East Campus and West Campus involved in a cold war— to employing merely the trappings of academia. In his most recent novel, *Sabbatical*,[4] Susan Seckler, an associate professor of literature and creative writing at Washington College, is on leave for a year. Susan is unsure if she will return to teaching and accept a tenured position at Swarthmore. Fenwick, her husband, likewise has to decide if he will accept an adjunct professorship at the University of Delaware. In Barth's first novel, *The Floating Opera*, the protagonist, Tod Andrews, is an undergraduate at Johns Hopkins; Jacob Horner, of *The End of the Road*, completes his master's examination at Johns Hopkins and immediately enters a state of gross motivational decline. Upon his recovery, he obtains a position as instructor of English at Wicomico State Teachers College, on Maryland's Eastern Shore. George, who is Giles Goat-Boy, leaves his tutor Max to matriculate at New Tammany College, which has many geographical similarities to Penn State, including a goat farm.[5] Ebenezer Cook, of *The Sot-Weed Factor*, leaves Cambridge and then completes his education in the wilderness of Maryland. Scheherazade, in *Chimera*, makes reference to her early training at Banu Sasan University. Later, in the palace of the Shahryar, she has her own special tutor in creative writing: a baldheaded genie with glasses, a twentieth-century time traveler and writer of tales, who resembles John Barth.[6] In *Letters*, most of the characters are academicians from Barth's previous novels. So, too, is the principal new character, Germaine Pitt, the acting provost of Marshyhope State University in Maryland.

Barth, indeed, is writing for an audience of mainly academicians. He satirizes educational practices and the theoretical suppositions that lie behind them. On the one hand, the reader often cannot become involved with characters like Jake Horner and Giles Goat-Boy because of their foolish actions. On the other hand, the reader—particularly if he is an academician—recognizes in the situations truths about the profession, the university community, and himself. Humor collides with a more painful tone, and the reader, because of his similar experiences, becomes strangely affected by the tales.

In *The End of the Road* and *Giles Goat-Boy*—novels that focus on the university—Barth's comic vision is developed by ironical allusions to traditional ideals of education. In this respect, Ralph Waldo Emerson's "The American Scholar" (his Phi Beta Kappa address at Harvard College in 1837) can serve as a paradigm for the American educational ideal. Barth does not allude to "The American Scholar" directly. Nevertheless, the work is a repository for many of the notions that encompass the American ideal of teacher and scholar. An examination of it will help establish a traditional framework for American visions of education, to which Barth develops ironical counterparts in *The End of the Road* and *Giles Goat-Boy*.

Oliver Wendell Holmes acclaimed "The American Scholar" oration as "our intellectual Declaration of Independence," and James Russell Lowell praised it as being "an event without any former parallel in our literary annals."[7] In the oration, Emerson characterizes the scholar as "Man Thinking"[8] and actively reasoning as he moves toward basic truths. He is an observer of nature, a reader of books of the past, as well as a creator of new books. He also is a man of action, who serves society as teacher and leader: "Him Nature solicits...him the past instructs; him the future invites" (*Works* 1:84).

As an observer of nature, the scholar classifies phenomena, "perceiving that these objects are not chaotic, and are not foreign, but have a law which is also a law of the human mind." For the scholar it is important to reduce "all strange constitutions, all new powers, to their class and their law...[to go] on forever to animate the last fibre of organization, the outskirts of nature, by insight." The scholar appreciates that books "are the best type of the influence of the past." Emerson does show some skepticism, however, when he points out that people should not worship books; they should not "stop with some past utterance of genius." The main purpose of books should be "to inspire," to promote the progressive thinking of the scholar, who will brood on the material, connect it to the present, and actively create his own knowledge. "Each age," Emerson insists, "must write its own books." The true scholar turns "dead fact" into "quick thought." His "active soul" is aflame with life and creative energy (*Works* 1:85–90).

Emerson ridicules the "notion that the scholar should be a recluse, a valetudinarian,—as unfit for any handiwork or public labor as a penknife for an axe." The scholar has duties in this world. "He is the world's eye" and "the world's heart." The thinking man, Emerson explains, is able to see through the pretension of the world. He is capable of pursuing "the ultimate reason" of things, the "one design [that] unites and animates the farthest pinnacle and the lowest trench" (*Works* 1:94, 101, 111–12). The scholar leads men toward the truth because he is able to encourage them to rely on the "universal soul" instead of the dictates of society.

The conception of the scholar-teacher is of utmost importance to Emerson. It is evident in the Phi Beta Kappa oration and also in an "Address on Education" presented two months earlier in Providence, Rhode Island.[9] In the earlier address, Emerson emphasizes the need to reform education so that instead of creating "accountants, attornies, [*sic*] engineers," scholars will help to "form heroes and saints." The teachers and leaders of colleges, churches, and schools comprise a "priesthood." These people foster the best in man and remind him of the "symbolical character of things." Teachers, "whether in the pulpit or in the Academy," have to exert their vision in order to prevent a people from perishing (*Early Lectures* 2:199, 202).

Emerson's celebration of the instructors and leaders in colleges is reminiscent of Cotton Mather's praise of the early Puritan divines who founded our country. In *Magnalia Christi Americana*, the ecclesiastical history so popular in seventeenth-century America, Mather devotes an entire book to the history of Harvard College and the exemplary Puritan divines who taught there. The *Magnalia*, as a whole, educates the reader by presenting the lives of great Puritan teachers such as John Winthrop, John Cotton, and Thomas Hooker. Mather compares these saints with biblical leaders like Moses and John the Baptist who helped their people toward salvation. Like John the Baptist, these American divines—because of their vision—turned a wasteland into a new Paradise. Their "errand in the wilderness" was to educate the people to return to God. Before the arrival of these men, America was a "hell of darkness," but after their leadership was felt, it became "a place full of light and glory"[10] that could provide a model for all to follow. Mather continually shows the esteem in which he holds the university and educational leaders. It is to such ideals about American education—beliefs held by Mather and by Emerson—that the satirist John Barth develops an ironical counterpart.

*The End of the Road* burlesques the Emersonian educational ideal of "Man Thinking" and reasoning by having as protagonists two university professors who represent the extremes of super-rationality and unreason. Joe Morgan, professor of history, is a rigid thinker. Jake Horner, instructor of English, is the epitome of unreason. Joe thinks he can learn how to cope with life's problems just by using his great mind. Jake views decision making as a completely arbitrary process. He follows the advice of the Doctor: "If the alternatives are side by side, choose the one on the left; if they're consecutive in time, choose the earlier. If neither of these applies, choose the alternative whose name begins with the earlier letter of the alphabet."[11] The emphasis on purposeless movement parodies the Emersonian concern for meaningful action—that is, the education of the scholar by action. "Inaction is cowardice," says Emerson, but he significantly adds, "there can be no scholar without the heroic mind" (*Works* 1:94). The mindlessness of Jake's actions provides an ironical contrast to this concept.[12]

The fact that Jake and the Doctor categorize examples of thoughtless decision making extends the farce: "These are the principles of Sinistrality, Antecedence, and Alphabetical Priority—there are others, and they're *arbitrary*, but useful" (*End*, p. 85; italics added). The belief in the senselessness of the categories contrasts with the traditional notion that categories are caused by a "unifying instinct," one that enables men "to discover meaning in accumulations of phenomena." Emerson explains: "What is classification but the perceiving that these objects are not chaotic, and are not foreign, but have a law which is also a law of the human mind" (*Works* 1:85–86).

Jake, who should be focusing on reason, having just passed his master's examination at Johns Hopkins University, is more receptive to the Doctor's ideas of unreason than to the logical method espoused in university teaching. When faced with decision making and thinking, Jake finds that his eyes, which should be filled with the sublime fire of a scholar, are "sightless, gazing on eternity, fixed on ultimacy." Jake is afflicted with the "malady *cosmopsis*, the cosmic view." "When one has it," he observes, "one is frozen like the bullfrog when the hunter's light strikes him full in the eyes" (*End*, p. 74). The stance of this modern scholar is similar to that of Swift's Laputan scientists who have one eye "turned inward, and the other directly up to the Zenith."[13]

Barth signals the humorous discrepancy between the educational ideal and its loss by using such key words as "reason," "light," "eyes," "eternity," "ultimacy," "the cosmic view." These, in traditional tracts, would evoke affirmation of right reason, by which man could move toward the light of God, the light that Emerson connects with "the ultimate reason" of things. For Jake, however, the light is a bright glare in a world denuded of reason and order and meaning. Jake's graduate education at Johns Hopkins seems to have resulted in a loss of reasoning powers: "There was no reason to go to Cincinnati, Ohio. There was no reason to go to Crestline, Ohio. Or Dayton, Ohio; or Lima, Ohio. There was no reason, either, to go back to the apartment hotel, or for that matter to go anywhere. There was no reason to do anything" (*End*, p. 74).

Each aspect of the Doctor's educational therapy for Jake gains its comic quality by being an ironical contrast to the life of reason, as stipulated by traditional thinkers like Emerson and Cotton Mather. The Doctor suggests that Jake engage in Mythotherapy, a method requiring a man to choose his myths and ideologies anew in each situation. Man, like an actor engaged in various performances, is most successful if he is able to adapt himself to "changing scripts as often as necessary" (*End*, p. 88). If one mask does not work, another should be tried. Jake should not be concerned about general truths; he should just act the role most appropriate in each setting.

Fulfilling the role of an anti-Emersonian, the Doctor carefully regulates Jake's reading habits and his actions so that he will avoid having to do any thinking at all. Whereas Emerson speaks of the importance of books to inspire the active soul, the Doctor advises Jake to read "no novels or non fiction." The safe book—one that will cause no thinking—is the "World Almanac"; that is to be his "breviary" (*End*, p. 85). The safe job, according to the Doctor, is a university professorship in "prescriptive grammar" (*End*, p. 5), a position that calls for no reasoning on the part of the teacher, "no optional situations" to encounter. "Don't let yourself get stuck between alternatives, or you're lost" (*End*, p. 85), he advises.

This depiction of the university instructor as nonthinker is an ironical reversal of the educational ideal of scholar-teacher. The contrast is the butt of many humorous episodes in *The End of the Road*, including Jake's interview at Wicomico State Teachers College. At the interview, Jake plays the role of enthusiastic teacher for a panel of professors, who take great pride in the position of scholar-teacher. The scene mocks not only the conception of the individual instructor—Jake Horner—but also the academy itself with its professors who speak of the educational ideal without having the intelligence to practice it. Jake tries to impress the board at Wicomico State College with his interest in teaching: "You take a boy—bright kid, alert kid, you see it at once, but never been exposed *to thinking*. ... You see a fresh young mind that's never had a chance *to flex its muscles* [last italics added], so to speak." The audience is receptive. Jake continues:

> So you start him off. Parts of speech! Subjects and verbs! Modifiers! *Complements!* And after a while, rhetoric. Subordination! Coherence! Euphone! You drill and drill, and talk yourself blue in the face. ... And then, just when you're ready to chuck the whole thing—"I know!" Miss Banning breathed. ... "That's what we're here for!" Dr. Schott said quietly, with some pride. "That's what we all live for. A little thing, isn't it?" ... "And then you can't hold him back!" Dr. Schott laughed. ... "He's like a horse that smells the stable up the lane!" (*End*, pp. 17–18)

Humor is developed by means of the numerous incongruities in the situation: Jake's enthusiastic speech versus his inner apathy; the strong interest he seems to take in developing the art of reasoning in his students versus his own desire to choose a job that involves no reasoning for the teacher; the great egos of the teachers on the panel, in contrast with the humble status of their teachers college with its low salaries; the exuberance expressed over teaching prescriptive grammar, as opposed to its uninspiring nature. What is particularly hilarious is Barth's description of teachers who use incongruous metaphors, like a mind "flexing its muscles," and derogatory and inappropriate analogies, like that between a student who finally is ignited and a horse that "smells the stable up the lane."

That Barth should base his comedy on the disparity between the scholarly ideal and its gross manifestation in the teachers of the academy shows his hostility toward educator "types" who have been his colleagues for years. In fact, Barth seems to find the professors of English—his own field— particularly comic. Jake, who obtains the job of instructor of English, experiences a sense of confusion and chaos that precludes an appreciation of his own identity. He merely can observe: "In a sense, I am Jacob Horner" (*End*, p. 1). He suffers from having no inner self, no moods, no "weather." Even his dreams reflect this problem, for he recalls one dream in particular in which he tried to learn the weather prediction for the next day— searching the newspapers, dialing the weather number, calling the Weather Bureau directly, only to be told: "There isn't going to be any weather tomorrow. ... All our instruments agree. No weather." Jake explains: "That was the end of the dream" (*End*, p. 35).

The history professor, Joe Morgan, in contrast with Jake, relies solely on his mental powers, even though they may be in conflict with his emotions. When he was a college student concerned about whether to get into a serious relationship with Rennie, he convinced her to take off two days from work so that they could discuss their suitability for each other. "We talked about it almost steadily for two days and two nights," Rennie explains, "and all that time he wouldn't touch me or let me touch him. I didn't go to work and he didn't go to class, because we both knew this was more important than anything else we'd ever done." The absurdity of depending on reason alone is underlined by the contrast between Joe's high seriousness and the crude language that characterizes his philosophic observations: "The world is full of tons and tons of horseshit, and without any purpose" (*End*, p. 61).

The farce increases through a series of incongruities: the importance of the problem is very great, yet Joe simplistically thinks that they indeed can reach an answer in two days; they can do this, he believes, by isolating reason from emotion. Rennie explains that they intended to compare their "ideas absolutely, impersonally," as if such a thing were possible. In addition, Rennie, who believes she finally is becoming a thinking person, reveals a total lack of self-reliance. She states: "We agreed that on every single subject, no matter how small or apparently trivial, we'd compare our ideas absolutely impersonally and examine them as sharply as we could, at least for the first few years, and he warned me that until I got into the habit of articulating very clearly all the time—until I learned *how* to do that— most of the more reasonable-sounding ideas would be his" (*End*, p. 61). Rennie, a worshiper of Joe's intellect, does not realize that by adopting his "reasonable-sounding ideas," she fails to do any creative thinking herself. Postulates—such as "Man Thinking" and being self-reliant—seem preposterous in relation to the university professors in *The End of the Road*. The connection between the scholarly life and the productive life for the individual and society, so paramount for Emerson, is acted out as farce in this novel of the absurd.

In *Giles Goat-Boy*, Barth creates nostalgia for an educational ideal and then frustrates the reader's expectation by developing a contrast to the standard model of excellence. The narrator signals the disparity between present practices at spring registration at Tammany College and traditional ones when he explains: "Few who participated in these festivities were aware of their original significance, any more than they recognized *Carnival* as coming from the Remusian 'farewell to flesh' that preceded any period of fasting" (*Goat-Boy*, p. 298). He indicates that these revelers on West Campus— at the outset of their university career—grasp eagerly the promises of easy graduation, and would gladly accept a diploma with no work expected. They lack the educational and moral standards of early scholars.

Barth criticizes a university community whose actions are in direct contradition to the three major tenets that Emerson emphasized for the scholar: to be an observer of nature, a reader and creator of books, and a thinker who has duties in the world. At Tammany College, professors pursue abstract theories and talk nonsense. The scientist Eblis Eierkopf is an egghead who is preoccupied with measuring the exact points of "Tick" and "Tock" in a complicated university clock project (*Goat-Boy*, p. 481). So completely engrossed is he with his complex optical equipment—telescopes, watch glasses, binoculars, and his own gigantic eyeglass lenses—that he fails to be involved in everyday life.[14] He cannot take care of his own bodily functions without the aid of a servant, Croaker, who feeds Eierkopf and carries him astride on his shoulders.

Barth's description of Eierkopf, who is separated from his natural surroundings and dependent on another for help, is reminiscent of Swift's treatment of the mad gazers of astronomy in *Gulliver's Travels*, who "are so taken up with intense Speculations" (*Prose* 11:143) that they need Flappers to rouse them to attention. Eierkopf also reminds us of Swift's professors in the school of political projectors in the Grand Academy of Lagado, who are "wholly out of their Senses" and continually creating schemes that are "wild impossible Chimaeras." We recall that Swift has Gulliver say that "there is nothing so extravagant and irrational which some Philosophers have not maintained for Truth" (*Prose* 11:171).

Dr. Kennard Sear is another mad theoretician who uses modern technology in a way that estranges him from the natural world. For him, fluoroscopes, one-way mirrors, and optical prisms are means of studying unusual and unnatural sexual activity. His wife is concerned that he has lost interest in ordinary coupling and only wishes to watch others. She "could interest him only by masturbating before the fluoroscope" (*Goat-Boy*, p. 399). Drs. Sear and Eierkopf accomplish little that is worthwhile with their complex scientific equipment. The educational ideal of being an observer of nature is in direct contrast not only with the impractical research activities of Drs. Eierkopf and Sear, but also with the actions of many other members of the university community, who show unquestioning respect for all new scientific theories. The narrator tells us that theories like Max Spielman's Cyclic Correspondence have been "dogmatized by the Chancellor, taped by the Chief Programmer, and devoured by [the computer] WESCAC" (*Goat-Boy*, pp. 43–44).

Barth mocks the corruption of training in the contemporary university by using scatological imagery. One of Spielman's laws states that "the 'sphincter's riddle' and the mystery of the University" are the same. "*Ontogeny recapitulates cosmogeny*—what is it but to say that proctoscopy repeats hagiography?" (*Goat-Boy*, p. 43). We could observe that the reduction of the heroic (Oedipus's solving of the Sphinx's riddle) to the

ribald and comic (the anal sphincter's riddle to be examined with a proc-
toscope) typifies how far educational pursuits have fallen. The theory also
casts a comical light on the role of saints' lives as a model for instruction.
Instead of Foxe's *Book of Martyrs*, so popular in seventeenth-century
England and in colonial America, or Cotton Mather's *Magnalia*, we have
Barth's *Giles Goat-Boy* with its ironical models: Giles, who is a rather
confused Grand Tutor, and Max Spielman, who has left the university for
the goat farm. In Barth's academic travesty, the heroes are "saints" of the
absurd, far fallen from the exemplary lives described by Foxe and Mather.

Giles looks to the university—New Tammany College[15]—as a place
that will help him to progress toward the truth, in the Emersonian sense.
The futile confrontation between Giles's serious desire to gain knowledge
during his stay at college and the frivolous attitude of the student body
creates more frustration. This disparity in academic interest is made obvious
to the reader by the narrator's description of spring registration. He sets the
tone by explaining that "few who participated in these festivities were
aware of their original significance" (*Goat-Boy*, p. 298). He compares the
attitude of students during spring registration in the twentieth century with
that of the past when education was a sacred endeavor, leading the
candidate toward salvation. Using allusions to ritual and religion, the
narrator observes that the tradition originated "in ancient agronomical
ceremonies and [was] modified by the Enochist Fraternity to celebrate the
Expulsion of Enos Enoch, His promotion of the Old-Syllabus Emeritus
Profs from the Nether Campus, and His triumphal Reinstatement" (*Goat-
Boy*, p. 297). These details cause the reader to think of Christ's expulsion of
the money changers from the temple, His Crucifixion, and His preaching to
the Old Testament patriarchs during the harrowing of hell, in order to
provide for their salvation. Enos Enoch's triumphal reinstatement suggests
the Resurrection on the third day after the Crucifixion. That is when Christ
appeared to the Apostles and "five hundred brethren at once" (1 Cor. 15:6)
and to the eleven disciples in Galilee, requesting that they "teach all nations,
baptizing them" (Matt. 28:19).

The narrator connects (by analogy) the spring initiation into the academic
life (which begins at dawn) to the Easter service at dawn, when serious
candidates for baptism (catechumens) were initiated into the Church. The
catechumens had to pursue a stringent three-year training period. They
studied Holy Scripture, were tutored in the principles of Christian life, and
memorized the Apostles' Creed and the Lord's Prayer.[16] At Tammany
College, however, no lengthy preparation is necessary, either for admission
to the institution of higher learning or for graduation. The strict matriculation requirements and religious instruction of bygone days are abandoned.
The Spring Carnival—the annual celebration of student registration—ends
with the gates to New Tammany Mall opened to admit, indiscriminately,

the qualified and unqualified. Students flock around the antischolar Harold Bray, who parodies Christ's words as he promises easy graduation: "Dear Tutees...Trial-by-Turnstile will begin in one minute....Remember: Except ye believe in me, ye shall not pass....So be it" (*Goat-Boy*, p. 391).[17]

All aspects of university life are subject to ridicule in *Giles Goat-Boy*. This is done from the perspective of Giles the goat-boy, who has left the farm to attend the great institution of higher learning. Giles strives to affirm order and meaning as he studies to be a Grand Tutor at Tammany College. He descends into the belly of the computer WESCAC three times, works out the seven assignments of his Pat-card with its PASS ALL / FAIL ALL mystery, and finally completes the revision of the New Syllabus. However, at the end of his studies, Giles concludes: "Passage *was* Failure, and Failure Passage; yet Passage was Passage, Failure Failure! Equally true, none was the Answer...my eyes were opened; I was delivered" (*Goat-Boy*, pp. 708–9). This novel of black humor shows the inversion of traditional standards of educational excellence; disorder, rather than unity and meaning, emerges at the end of Giles's instruction at the academy.

Not only does Barth emphasize the futility of the pedagogic process in the academy, but also he seems to doubt whether even the best instruction can actually help man to use reason to understand an illogical world. In *The Sot-Weed Factor*, Burlingame, the tutor for Ebenezer and his twin sister Anna, schools his pupils in readings that include the world's great myths, legends, and epics. He makes learning an exciting game, directing the children through adventures in history, philosophy, and geography. "The result of this education," explains the narrator, "was that the twins grew quite enamored of the world."[18] Yet, in spite of such excellent early training, as well as the later years at Cambridge, followed by Burlingame's continued guidance in his adult years, Ebenezer remains incapable of coping with the world's diversity.

Barth seems to reach beyond the characters in all his novels in order to educate the reader. He seems to be asking the reader to question his own basic assumptions, including notions about national history and genealogy. In *The Sot-Weed Factor*, for example, Barth develops allusions to the heroic figures Captain John Smith and Pocahontas, as well as to other early settlers of our great nation, people for whom courage and the moral dictates of Puritanism were so important. Captain Smith, the courageous, gallant explorer, is—in Barth's novel—preoccupied with "conquests and feats of love," and "fancieth him selfe a Master of Venereall Art" (*Sot-Weed*, pp. 162–63). Pocahontas, celebrated as being the noble princess who "hazarded the beating out of her own braines to save" Smith's life,[19] is a girl of sixteen who wishes to find a man capable of deflowering her (*Sot-Weed*, p. 791). Also demythologized are the early settlers, who are depicted as gamblers, prostitutes, and profligates. Barth creates an ironical counterpart to expectations based on the reader's traditional learning, and he gently laughs at the reader's disappointment. He also satirizes "a certain stodgy variety of squint-minded antiquarians" (*Sot-Weed*, p. 805) who would criticize his treatment of traditional history.

Barth derides the reader for relying on societal myths (and the educational researchers for contributing information that helps to form these myths). His particular method of mocking the researchers is to focus on their concern for narrowly specialized material, that which is associated with the work of recluses, valetudinarians, and "squint-minded antiquarians" in the university. Such people, he (like Emerson) indicates, are unfit for public labor in the academy. Ironies, therefore, abound when we appreciate that the author himself, Professor John Barth, is preoccupied with his own type of esoterica. *The Sot-Weed Factor* offers a prime example. In this novel, the chapter headings, digressive and interpolated stories, and authorial intrusions call attention to Barth's antiquarian interest in an eighteenth-century Fieldingesque style. In addition, there is Barth's choice of the 1708 poem "The Sot-Weed Factor" (written in Hudibrastics by Ebenezer Cook) as title and subject for his novel. Barth even has Ebenezer and Burlingame compete with each other in composing Hudibrastics, the jangling octosyllabic couplets that Samuel Butler made famous in the late seventeenth century and Jonathan Swift used in the eighteenth century. In fact, when Barth was questioned about the difficulty in keeping to an eighteenth-century style in *The Sot-Weed Factor*, he quipped: "The difficulty was just the opposite. It was to stop writing letters that way.... Once you get in the spirit of writing in Hudibrastic couplets, say, then you start to think in Hudibrastic couplets and talk on the telephone in Hudibrastic couplets."[20]

It is noteworthy that even though Barth criticizes academia, he gains his primary readership from university teachers and students. Even he puzzles over this: "Do you know what I think is interesting.... It's the spectacle of these enormous universities we have now, all over the place, teaching courses in *us*.... Now that means that a born loser like *The Sot-Weed Factor* might even be gotten away with, because 2,000 kids in northeast Nebraska or somewhere have to read it in a Modern Novel course. Alarming.... God knows what we're up to."[21]

## Notes

1. See Cynthia Davis, "'The Key to the Treasure': Narrative Movements and Effects in *Chimera*," in *Critical Essays on John Barth*, ed. Joseph J. Waldmeir (Boston: G.K. Hall, 1980), pp. 217–27; Campbell Tatham, "John Barth and the Aesthetics of Artifice," in *Critical Essays*, pp. 43–54; Russell H. Miller, "*The Sot-Weed Factor*: A Contemporary Mock Epic," *Critique* 8 (Winter 1965–66): 88–100; Gordon E. Slethaug, "Barth's Refutation of the Idea of Progress," *Critique* 13

(1972): 11–29; Richard Boyd Hauck, *A Cheerful Nihilism* (Bloomington: Indiana University Press, 1971); Daniel Majdiak, "Barth and the Representation of Life," *Criticism* 12 (Winter 1970): 51–67; Elaine B. Safer, "The Allusive Mode and Black Humor in Barth's *Sot-Weed Factor*," *Studies in the Novel* 13 (1981): 424–38; Charles B. Harris, "John Barth and the Critics: An Overview," in *Critical Essays*, pp. 3–13.

2. John J. Enck, "John Barth," *The Contemporary Writer*, ed. L.S. Dembo and Cyrena N. Pondrom (Madison: University of Wisconsin Press, 1972; original interview conducted on 17 April 1964), p. 21.

3. See also John O. Lyons, *The College Novel in America* (Carbondale: Southern Illinois University Press, 1962); Mortimer R. Proctor, *The English University Novel* (1957; reprint, New York: Arno Press, 1977).

4. *Sabbatical: A Romance* (New York: G.P. Putnam's Sons, 1982).

5. Visitors to the campus of Penn State often are shown particular landmarks mentioned in the novel. *Giles Goat-Boy* (1966; reprint, New York: Fawcett, 1968). Parenthetical text references to Goat-Boy are to this edition.

6. *Chimera* (New York: Random House, 1972), p. 12.

7. Bliss Perry mentions this in *The Praise of Folly and Other Papers* (Boston: Houghton Mifflin, 1923), pp. 95–96.

8. Edward Waldo Emerson, ed., *Works of Ralph Waldo Emerson* (Boston and New York: Houghton Mifflin Co., 1903), 1:84. Parenthetical text references are to this edition.

9. Stephen E. Whicher, Robert E. Spiller, and Wallace E. Williams, *The Early Lectures of Ralph Waldo Emerson* (Cambridge: Harvard University Press, 1964), 2:195–204. Parenthetical text references are to this edition. Cotton Mather, *Magnalia Christi Americana*, ed. Thomas Robbins (Hartford: Silas Andrus & Son, 1853), 1:246. The account of Harvard College is in vol. 2, bk. 4.

11. *The End of the Road* (1958; reprint, New York: Bantam, 1969), p. 85; italics added. Parenthetical text references are to this edition.

12. The Doctor relates Mythotherapy specifically to Sartre and his concern about action: "Why don't you read Sartre and become an existentialist? It will keep you moving" (*End*, pp. 84–85). Indirectly, however, Barth also is burlesquing the traditional belief that "action is...essential" for the scholar (Emerson, *Works* 1:94).

13. Herbert Davis, ed., *The Prose Works of Jonathan Swift*, (Oxford: Blackwell, 1939–68), 11:143. Parenthetical text references are to this edition.

14. Dr. Eierkopf's only involvement with the world is that of a voyeur. He uses his night-glass for such pleasures as watching a coed undress in her room a quarter-mile away (*Goat-Boy*, p. 364).

15. The name of the college is particularly ironical because it is a blatant allusion to the corruption in Tammany Hall in New York City.

16. See Rev. Josef A. Jungmann, S.J., *Public Worship*, trans. Rev. Clifford Howell, S.J. (Collegeville, Minn.: The Liturgical Press, 1957), p. 73.

17. Barth, as scholar-teacher, develops much of his humor by substituting academic terminology for biblical, as in the following examples:

| *Bible* | *Giles Goat-Boy* |
| --- | --- |
| Verily, verily, I say unto you, He that heareth my word, and believeth on him that sent me...is passed from death unto life" (John 5:24). | "Except ye believe in me, ye shall not pass" (p. 391). |

| | |
|---|---|
| "A prophet is not without honor, but in his own country" (Mark 6:4). | "A proph-prof is never cum laude in his own quad" (p. 690). |
| "for many be called, but few chosen" (Matt. 20:16). | "Many are Registered but few are Qualified" (p. 296). |
| "Thou shalt love thy neighbor as thyself" (Matt. 22:39). | "Love thy classmate as thyself, or flunked be" (p. 424). |
| "Whosoever shall not receive the kingdom of God as a little child, he shall not enter therein" (Mark 10:15). | "Except ye become as a kindergartener, ye shall not pass" (p. 390). |

18. *The Sot-Weed Factor* (1960; reprint, New York: Bantam, 1969), p. 8. Parenthetical text references are to this edition.

19. John Smith, *Travels and Works of Captain John Smith*, ed. Edward Arber (Edinburgh: John Grant, 1910), vol. 2, *Generall Historie*, p. 531.

20. Enck, "John Barth," p. 22.

21. Ibid., p. 21.

# Joseph Heller and the Academy

## *James Nagel*

THE biography of Joseph Heller is a tale of the rise from rags to riches, of the cultivation of talent and sensibility, and of university education as a vehicle for both socioeconomic advancement and self-discovery. Heller was born in Brooklyn in 1923, the youngest of three children, and grew up in Coney Island. Upon graduation from high school, he went to work as a file clerk in an insurance office for sixty dollars a month, a position he retained until he enlisted in the Army Air Corps at nineteen. Trained as a bombardier, he flew sixty missions in World War II before being sent home. Financing his university training with the G.I. Bill, he enrolled briefly at the University of Southern California before transferring to New York University, where he studied creative writing, published a series of short stories, and received his B.A. in 1948. He took his M.A. from Columbia the following year, writing a thesis on "The Pulitzer Prize Plays: 1917–1935," and then studied for a year at Oxford on a Fulbright scholarship. He taught composition at Pennsylvania State University from 1950 to 1952 before returning to New York to work in advertising, a career he pursued until the publication of *Catch-22* in 1961. Since then he has returned often to the academy, teaching writing at various times at Yale, the University of Pennsylvania, and City College, and lecturing on campuses throughout the United States. In short, far from being an antagonist of the academy, Heller is very much a product of it. As his letters indicate, he took no small satisfaction in the fact that *Catch-22* quickly made its way into American literature courses at major universities.

There is a satisfying symmetry to Heller's career in that he began writing in a university and has returned in glory to the scene of his earliest artistic striving. As a gifted undergraduate, Heller wrote stories published in *Esquire* and the *Atlantic Monthly*, stories that reflect a young writer's

"Joseph Heller and the Academy" appeared originally as "Joseph Heller and the University" in *College Literature* 10 (1983): 16–27. It has been revised and expanded for inclusion here. Reprinted by permission of *College Literature* and the author.

101

growing sense of craft. Several of them echo the tone and plots of Ernest Hemingway's short fiction: "Nothing To Be Done" is about a college student who is about to be beaten or killed by a local thug.[1] The tone of stoical resignation is reminiscent of "The Killers." The emotional emptiness of the veteran in "I Don't Love You Any More" recalls "Soldier's Home," as "World Full of Great Cities" in some respects resembles *To Have And Have Not*.[2] The other stories either feature college students as characters (in, for instance, "Bookies, Beware!") or parents and relatives who dream of the opportunities of college for younger children, as in "Castle of Snow."[3] These are not remarkable creative efforts; however, they have a definite retrospective value, for they hint at what was to become a continuing motif in Heller's more significant fiction: a preoccupation with universities and education, with educational background as a means of defining character, and with related themes of assimilation and social justice, of snobbery and exclusion, of access and denial. These concepts form an important and persistently overlooked subtext in Heller's most notable works, *Catch-22*, *Something Happened*, and *Good As Gold*.

*Catch-22* has been examined from nearly every conceivable angle, yet no one has thus far observed that virtually every major character in the novel is identified in terms of institutional affiliation and that socio-academic status is a central element in the method of establishing character.[4] What becomes clear is that education in *Catch-22* is not so much a vehicle of social mobility for the disadvantaged as an emblem of prestige and privilege for the rich. In the world of Pianosa, it might be argued, moral virtue is inversely proportionate to the amount and prestige of collegiate training. The more educated a character is, the less sensitive he is likely to be to the prerogatives and feelings and very existence of others; the more prestigious the institution he attended, the more likely that the character will become obsessed with defending an insensitive capitalistic system and with issues of exclusion and class distinction. Within the ethical structure of the novel, the better educated a character is, the less he is likely to understand.

Clevinger is a case in point. Before the war he had been a Harvard undergraduate who is described as a "genius," as a "gangling, gawky, feverish, famish-eyed brain" who is certain to be an academic success. Indeed, in the planning stage of the novel Heller had written on a note card that Clevinger was an "honor student at Harvard," a detail he omitted from the novel.[5] Heller deleted a similar concept from the manuscript, a passage that read:

> Clevinger knew it all because Clevinger was a genius of sorts with a pounding heart and blanching face who had been the first person to be graduated summa cum laude from Harvard since the last one.[6]

Lest genius begin to imply some measure of practical intelligence, however, the narrator is quick to add that "Clevinger was one of those people with lots of intelligence and no brains.... In short, he was a dope." Yossarian thinks of him as a cubist portrait with both eyes on one side of his face, an image "generated by Clevinger's predilection for staring fixedly at one side of a question and never seeing the other side at all." Even his literary propensities are assailed on these grounds, for Clevinger is said to know "everything about literature except how to enjoy it" (*C*, pp. 67–68).

There is more than just pointless satire here, for it is precisely Clevinger's obtuse myopia that leads him to refuse to argue about flying extra missions over Bologna if Cathcart wants him to (*C*, p. 121); that sets him in contention with Yossarian's growing disenchantment with the military establishment; and that leads to Clevinger's shocking discovery in his trial that of all the people on earth who hate him, his own superior officers hate him the most (*C*, p. 80). In the published novel, Clevinger is not only an excellent student at Harvard but also an activist who attempts to defend dismissed faculty members (*C*, p. 67). In the manuscript there is a deleted passage that goes on to indicate that the professors were fired

> for such assorted transgressions as sodomy, espionage, fornication and bastardy, intelligence, failure to publish, copping the Fifth on reasons of principle, and grieving above a whisper over the murder of democracy in Spain by Franco and his gangsters with the assistance and approval of other hoodlum members of the international crime syndicate.[7]

In a related passage, also deleted, Heller explains how Clevinger became involved in the war:

> Clevinger was diligently at work on his PhD when someone tapped him on the shoulder one day and told him he was at war, and even those instructors to whose defense he had never found it necessary to spring with such zealous impotence agreed that Clevinger was a person of exceptional intellect and impeccable character who was certain to go far in the academic world.[8]

There is so little substance to Clevinger that it is not surprising that on the way back from the Parma mission his plane disappears in a cloud off the coast of Elba leaving no debris or trace behind (*C*, p. 103).

These basic ideas are extended into the lives of the other characters. Scheisskopf's nymphomaniac wife, who entertains her husband's troops in an extremely generous manner, is described in the manuscript as a graduate of the Harvard School of Business[9] but in the published novel as a "crazy mathematics major from the Wharton School of Business" (*C*, pp. 67–70). Heller deleted from the manuscript a rather more general satirical gibe at higher education in a passage about Lieutenant Scheisskopf himself:

Meanwhile, he [Lieutenant Scheisskopf] kept amassing marching data steadily and soon had more marching data amassed than everyone else. He found himself with enough marching data amassed to have done a doctoral dissertation on the subject that would have been accepted by any university in the land, since it would have fulfilled the primary requirement of making an original contribution of nothing new to a subject of no importance.[10]

Another passage deleted from the manuscript explains why Chief White Halfoat and his family were never allowed to settle in one location for more than a day or two:

"Some experts in New York with a Harvard education had figured out that we could more than triple our oil production if they kept us moving all the time, and that's just what they did."[11]

In the manuscript Colonel Cathcart had once been a pretentious student at Harvard who strolled the campus with a long cigarette holder—a passage that may have been deleted on the premise that Harvard had already received more than its fair share of attention.[12] In the published novel General Peckem is said to have an "Ivy League background" that impresses Colonel Cathcart, and this may in part account for Peckem's success in having Special Services take control of combat operations by the end of the novel (C, p. 211). The Texan, whose inane gregariousness quickly drives all the malingerers out of the hospital, is described merely as "educated," a status that may be related to his view that "people of means—decent folk—should be given more votes than drifters, whores, criminals, degenerates, atheists, and indecent folk—people without means" (C, p. 9). At the end of the novel it is Major Danby, a "university professor with a highly developed sense of right and wrong" (C, p. 434), who tries to convince Yossarian to accept a deal that will send him home but require the other men to fly additional missions. Aarfy, perhaps the most morally insensitive of a bad lot, is said in Heller's preliminary notes to have "enjoyed hazing as fraternity man at Midwestern College."[13] He is a college graduate who asks other people what school they went to and who insists that Nately, scion of an Eastern Brahmin, should date a proper Red Cross nurse from Smith and forget the elusive whore of his dreams (C, pp. 62, 282–83). Indeed, Nately's plan is to marry the whore and to send her kid sister to Smith, Radcliffe, or Bryn Mawr (C, p. 350).

The social implications of the academic theme are everywhere apparent, as in the juxtaposition of Dunbar, whose father worked hard but could never make enough money to send his children to college, with the "dashing young fighter captain" who cheated his way through prep school and college and whose inherited fortune will give him advantages for the rest of his life (C, p. 169). Cathcart has contempt for Colonel Korn because Korn enrolled at a state university (*C*, p. 187), a dire fate also endured by Major Major, who was not only an American literature student but also was suspected of being a Communist (*C*, p. 84). Indeed, there is a good deal about Major Major and the academy deleted from the typescript of the novel:

> His education over, Major Major had joined the faculty of an insignificant university, where he alienated every one of his colleagues <in record time> by refusing to bear false witness against any of the others and where his teaching career was shattered beyond repair four years later by a senior member of the department who wrote appreciations of Henry James. Major Major had been cautioned against just such a fate only the year before by a beery old bum at the Modern Language Association convention who came reeling out from behind a potted palm in the hotel lobby and stopped him as he was hurrying to attend a seminar on Thomas Love Peacock. The beery old bum wore a Phi Beta Kappa key and had a gray beard and a glittering bloodshot eye. He prattled acrimoniously about better days gone by and then rasped out his warning.
> "Never trust a man who says he likes Henry James," he intoned in a husky voice. "He's either a liar or nuts."
> When the Henry James faction finally seized control of the English Department with the aid of an insurgent splinter group from the Metaphysical Poets party, Major Major was out in the cold, for he had never declared for either side. No defense was imaginable, for he was oblivious to what had occurred. Even when the intramural shooting had died down, he was not aware there had been any. Returning to the farm was out of the question, for his father and the bad-tempered girl from the A&P were sponsoring teenage sex orgies there each weekend and did not want the children around.[14]

Doc Daneeka has obviously had an opportunity to take a medical degree, yet he has no regard for his profession and even less for his patients; he views the war primarily as a fiscal inconvenience that has taken him away from his practice at an extremely infelicitous moment. Daneeka complains to Yossarian, "I don't want to make sacrifices. I want to make dough" (*C*, p. 32). It is ironically appropriate, therefore, that Daneeka suffers his bureaucratic "death" in McWatt's plane by being on the flight log so that he can collect extra pay. As Chief White Halfoat solemnly reflects, while standing next to Daneeka on the ground, Daneeka was "killed by his own greed" (*C*, p. 342).

A key passage for the academic theme in the world of *Catch-22* did not appear in the published form of the novel, although it is part of the manuscript and was published later as a short story entitled "Love, Dad." It is an epistolary section dealing with Nately and his father, who wears Brooks Brothers suits and gives no quarter to those he considers inferior. Indeed,

when he sends Nately to Andover he counsels his son that the social
climbers who go to Exeter, Choate, Hotchkiss, and Groton will presume to
address him as equals, which they surely are not. When Nately enters
Harvard, his father offers a similarly restrained assessment:

> "Harvard is more than just a good school; Harvard is also a good place
> at which to get an education, should you decide that you do want an
> education. Columbia University, New York University, and the City
> College of New York in the city of New York are other good places at
> which to get an education, but they are not good schools. Universities
> such as Princeton, Yale, Dartmouth and bungalows in the Amherst-
> Williams complex are, of course, neither good schools nor good places at
> which to get an education and are never to be compared with Harvard."[15]

In view of sentiments like these it is clear that Nately's father was cast as
one of the principal villains of the novel, directly in conflict with the ethical
thrust of Heller's anticapitalistic themes. Similarly, Nately, fresh out of prep
school and two listless years at Harvard, is no intellectual match for the
grizzly old man of the whorehouse, who has no apparent education
whatever but manages to negate logically Nately's most cherished bromides.
Nately is a mere child at disputation in comparison with the old man, who
scoffs at religion, patriotism, and bourgeois morality, and Nately wishes the
old man would shave and put on a Brooks Brothers shirt and a tweed jacket
and stop asking so many questions (*C*, pp. 236–45). Yossarian must be said
to be of indeterminate educative background (although his frame of reference suggests extensive literary training), but it is significant that as he feels
his way through the complex social and moral issues of the world he lives in,
he emerges at a point almost identical to that of the hedonistic old man.[16]

*Something Happened*, Heller's second novel, is much less significant in its
development of the academic theme. Yet always in the swirl of Bob
Slocum's neurotic introspection there is an awareness of education, of
institutional status, of culture and intellectual cultivation.[17] Like Yossarian,
Slocum is of uncertain background: it is clear that he graduated from high
school at seventeen and went immediately to work for an insurance
company (*SH*, p. 15). He would seem not to have had time subsequently for
a college career, although at one juncture he reflects that he is better
educated than Green, who represents to him "vulgar good breeding" (*SH*,
p. 45). Whatever the case, the central point is that for all the depth of his
elaborate and unrelenting examination of his own thoughts and feelings,
Slocum thinks of other people only rather superficially, often in terms of
their university affiliations, as he does in recalling that painful sexual
encounter with an "uninteresting Ann Arbor dropout" who made fun of
him in his garters (*SH*, p. 447). Indeed, Slocum's habits of mind often lead
him to think of things in terms of their impact on campus: when he ponders

abortion he surmises that modern undergraduates will all have had at least one abortion, and graduate students two (*SH*, p. 556); as he reflects on the state of the American economy, it occurs to him that "colleges are going into bankruptcy" (*SH*, p. 482); and as he considers the spread of the use of marijuana, he concludes that "even Ivy League fraternity boys on the executive level at the company smoke it now" (*SH*, p. 181).

There is more than gratuitous academic preoccupation here, for Slocum's torturous reverie is primarily a quest in self-discovery, an exercise in formulating and revealing himself, in fixing his identity and that of the people around him. From Slocum's perspective, identity is often an extension of, or at least related to, education. He thinks often of his daughter as a future college student[18] and of her young man as a "college graduate" rather than in any other formulation (*SH*, p. 456). Significantly, he never thinks of his normal son as being in college, a fact related to his foreboding of the early demise of his favorite child. When Slocum remembers his sister-in-law, it is always as the girl who "got knocked up as a college kid," the important point of the pregnancy presumably being the termination of education and not the inception of life (*SH*, p. 377).

On another level, Slocum is very much aware of the educational backgrounds of the people in his office. It is not lost on him, for instance, that Philip Reeves went to Yale (*SH*, p. 44) and that Andy Kagle did not go to college at all, a fact that Slocum thinks accounts for Kagle's social awkwardness (*SH*, p. 47). During one of his midday amours, Slocum thinks of Jane, she of the art department in his company, as being "just a few years out of college, where she majored in fine arts" (*SH*, p. 23). But his most persistent subject of reflection and lament is Virginia Markowitz, who worked in his office at his first job and who committed suicide while he was in the army. What torments him most is that he never made love to her, never, for want of logistic sophistication, seized the moment to rent a room in a hotel and consummate his most tantalizing flirtation. Related to this preoccupation with the room not taken is her background at Duke University, not so much that she had to leave Duke when her father committed suicide, although the implications of that event haunt him, but more that she once made love with a young man in a canoe (even though she would not later make love with Slocum on the stairs or in the storeroom) and even entertained five members of the football team in a dormitory room (*SH*, pp. 83, 387). The result of his fixation on these scenes is that he not only dreams of himself as a college student but also on three occasions pretends to others to have been a student at Duke himself.[19] Although *Something Happened* is in no sense an "academic novel," it is also true that this remarkably personal study, perhaps the most agonizingly introspective novel in American literature, presents "identity" consistently in educational terms.

Heller's most extensive treatment of the university theme comes in *Good as Gold* (1979), a novel that not only features an English professor as protagonist but also has him working a good deal of the time on an essay entitled "Education and Truth or Truth in Education." [20] In terms of background, Bruce Gold grew up in Coney Island and later took his B.A. and Ph.D. at Columbia. At one point he spent a summer session at Wisconsin. Now, at forty-eight, he has a son, Noah, at Yale, another son, Barry, at Choate, and a younger daughter at home who goes to private day school. Gold obviously wants a prestigious education for each of his children, and he is very aware of the educational backgrounds of his friends and associates, yet his philosophic views would suggest another rationale: he writes in his essay that "education is the third greatest cause of human misery in the world. The first, of course, is life" (*GG*, p. 140). He shows little interest in his field (literature) and spends almost no time thinking about it or the profession. He hates teaching and longs for a position in government. [21] In fact, some aspects of his position strain credulity: he holds the rank of professor, yet he seems to do no scholarly work and writes only familiar essays; despite his rank, he is untenured and appears not to understand tenure:

> His job was secure. He was esteemed by his colleagues and did not like that. He soon would be given tenure and didn't want it. He would rather feel at liberty. (*GG*, p. 138)

He seems to feel that tenure would bind him to the institution rather than the institution to him. Despite his professorial role, he patently does not believe in academic freedom (*GG*, p. 73). And, although he is in residence teaching throughout the novel, he rarely attends class, never prepares, and only groans at the thought of the term papers about to come due.

In a few matters, however, he would seem to show considered professional judgment, especially in that he avoids faculty meetings, spends as little time on campus as possible, and prays for an endowed chair (*GG*, pp. 135, 137). His principal value to his department would seem to be his skill in writing course descriptions that lure students into classes, descriptions for such courses as "Through Hell and High Water with Hemingway, Hesse, Hume, Hobbes, Hinduism and Others: A Shortcut to India" and "The Role of Women, Blacks, and Drugs in Sex and Religion in World and American Film and Literature." Although his strategy may lack a little something in integrity, it does not want for success, and the English program swells:

> It was now possible...for a student to graduate as an English major after spending all four years of academic study watching foreign motion pictures in a darkened classroom without being exposed for even one moment to any other light but that of a movie projector. (*GG*, p. 138)

A secondary impact of the popularity of these courses is that the English department now provides classes to be taught by professors of programs in decline, with the result that "professors of German [are] teaching remedial English to natives of Hong Kong and Puerto Rico" (*GG*, p. 138).

Although much of this may sound distressingly familiar, "Professor Gold" is more a satirical construct than a believable human being, as are most of the other characters. Indeed, few of them, and few of the prestigious institutions in America, are spared Heller's satirical bite. This impulse is well represented when Gold gets a

> note of genial accolade from a nonagenarian in Massachusetts who said he had not read a book or a poem, looked at a painting, or given thought to anything but his income and his health since graduating from Williams seventy-eight years earlier and had not in that time suffered a second's regret or sense of loss. (*GG*, p. 145)

Another dimension is suggested by Lieberman, who vowed in his youth, "'When I grow up…I'm gonna fuck a girl.' Instead he went to college" (*GG*, p. 63). Gold's putative intended, Andrea Biddle Conover, is another satirical figure. Her educational progression begins with two prep schools and admission to Sarah Lawrence, where she does not finish. She does not finish at Bennington either but adds to her burgeoning credentials an affair with an art professor, a background that serves her well at Smith, where she slips under the sheets with the fathers of her closest friends (*GG*, p. 392). Despite this impressive dossier, her ultimate educational record is one of impossible degrees: a B.A. from Smith, an M.S. from Yale, a Ph.D. from Harvard, and a lectureship at Cambridge, all in home economics (*GG*, p. 143).

As there was in *Catch-22*, there is in *Good as Gold* an acute sensitivity to the educational backgrounds of even minor characters, with the added dimension of references to actual people. Gold ponders the fact that Nelson Rockefeller went to Dartmouth, that David Eisenhower, despite being a hopeless simpleton, "was probably the outstanding Amherst alumnus of his generation" (*GG*, p. 43), and that Henry Kissinger, arch knave and principal object of satire of the novel, is a professor at Harvard.[22] Heller's satire of people from the "real" world is made all the more bitter by virtue of the fact that he uses their own public statements to reveal their intellectual and moral limitations.

The purely fictional characters are spared that indignity but are exposed in much the same terms: education associated with wealth and prestige is not only empty but also a source of villainous insensitivity to social issues. Ralph Newsome, for example, joined Gold in graduate school at Columbia after his undergraduate work at Princeton. He got his Ph.D. by copying Gold's papers and has become the epitome of double-think and bureaucratic equivocation in his government job in Washington. Harris Rosenblatt went to a prep school in Manhattan and graduated from Columbia with honors, but he is later thought by Gold to have "inanimate powers of concentration and no ability at thought" (*GG*, p. 66). The inversion of this pattern, the rise of a bright student from a poor family by virtue of intelligence and diligent application, is represented by both Gold himself and by his friend Murray Weinrock. "Murshie" Weinrock grew up in Gold's neighborhood in Coney Island and took night courses for six years, until the beginning of World War II. At that point the army, needing medical staff, sent him to Swarthmore for his senior year and then to Harvard Medical School to complete his training. At the time of the action of the novel he is a successful internist in New York (*GG*, pp. 69–70). A variation of the poverty-education concept is the story of Gold's brother, Sid, who did not have money enough for college but who grew sufficiently wealthy in the laundry business to help his father in retirement and Bruce with his education (*GG*, p. 66). All his life, however, he regrets having missed college.

*Good as Gold* is a useful point of conclusion for the university theme in that it combines the two major lines of development of this concept in Heller's fiction. The first is the satirical deflation of institutions of prestige on the grounds of their social insensitivity and lack of substance beneath the ivy walls. This attitude is evident in Ralph Newsome's explanation to Gold as to why the government needs Gold in Washington:

> "You see, Bruce, we have a very big need for college professors, and we can't go back to Harvard after all they've done. The country wouldn't stand for it."
> "How's Columbia?"
> "Still clean. I don't think anyone here associates Columbia with anything intellectual." (*GG*, p. 52)

In a subsequent conversation Gold is quoted as having commented that "Harvard and West Point together have afflicted civilization with a greater number of harmful blockheads than all other institutions in the history of the world, combined," to which Ralph responds, "throw in the whole Yale graduate body and you've got it just about right" (*GG*, p. 265).

The second line of thematic thrust has an even more explicitly social edge: it is becoming increasingly difficult to move upward in American society, increasingly difficult to get the requisite education. But Gold's older friends and relatives still have confidence in education as a vehicle of social mobility: "They like education, the larger the amount, the better the effects" (*GG*, p. 45). Pugh Biddle Conover inadvertently shows how education can overcome ethnic prejudice when he asserts that he wants nothing to do with Jews except, of course, for his "doctor, lawyer, dentist, accountant, book-keeper, secretary, broker, butcher, travel agent, tailor, business partner, realtor, banker, financial manager, best friend, and spiritual adviser" (*GG*, p. 370). Much of Gold's bitterness about education derives from his awareness that the traditional opportunities have broken down, that the lower classes, especially the ethnic minorities, have almost no chance. As he concludes on his visit to his old Coney Island neighborhood, "assimilation was impossible, upward mobility a fantasy" (*GG*, p. 326). The culprit, shades of *Catch-22*, is clearly an insensitive and inhumanly bureaucratic system of government, one well represented by the state senator who calls Gold seeking support for an "education bill denying financial aid to any community in New York containing poor people" (*GG*, p. 145).

Ultimately the portrayal of universities and of education in Heller's work must be regarded as an instrument of social satire directly analogous to his treatment of the military in *Catch-22*. However, the university theme is a deeper satirical vein in that it runs throughout the Heller canon, linking and enriching the novels and stories along the way. Viewed in terms of a coherent theme, it is possible to trace the treatment of education as a progression of attitudes from the early short stories through *Good As Gold*. The early stories, written while Heller was himself a student, portray relatively unsophisticated characters in a world in which education offers hope, amelioration of social injustice, a vehicle of self-discovery. Whatever the grim circumstances of the protagonist, some optimism is justified by the possibility of socioeconomic mobility and intellectual advance as a result of further education.

*Catch-22*, written after the completion of Heller's graduate training and a stint as a composition teacher in central Pennsylvania, presents characters in educative stasis. Although the thematic center of the novel rests on Yossarian's moral growth, his development is free from, perhaps even opposed to, the formal structure of higher education. The educational experiences of the other characters, with the exception of the chaplain, exemplify their true natures rather than change them. Whatever hope is sustained through the conclusion of the novel resides in a resistance to formal institutions and the people who embody their values, not in their utilization. Yossarian finds no solace in the ivy polish of his superiors, and not the slightest suggestion that appeals to social conscience or principle will persuade Colonel Cathcart to allow him to save his own life without risking the lives of others. The Sweden he runs to at the end of the novel is Huck Finn's territory of innocence and moral freedom, not the world of professional and social progress that the characters dream of in the early short stories.

Bob Slocum's world in *Something Happened* is a blend of two earlier streams: in one Slocum observes the dismal consequences of the educational backgrounds of his peers, and in the other he hopes for the self-realization of his children through education. In this novel these themes are informed by Heller's considerable experience in the corporate jungle of New York—an environment he apparently preferred to even the most bucolic of academic groves—from which he escaped by virtue of a cultivated and formally shaped expertise in the writing of fiction. Slocum finds no such good fortune, and he must learn to live with what he finds within himself as he struggles and succeeds in bureaucratic politics.

*Good As Gold* is an even more grim portrait. Here the amelioration of social problems through education appears more remote, and Bruce Gold, Ph.D., Professor of English, reveals himself to be a man on whom even the highest levels of training have had alarmingly few salutary effects. This novel also contains a significant ethnic shift. In *Catch-22* the educational satire was directed at the WASPish officers who came to war trailing leaves of ivy, whereas in *Good as Gold* the satire is more bitter when directed at Jews, at Gold himself, and, especially, at Henry Kissinger. Gold's extensive education hardly speaks well for moral enlightenment and self-knowledge as a component of the educational process: he is the least sympathetically portrayed of Heller's protagonists.

In this sense, the university theme in Heller's fiction portrays a progressive intensification of satirical antipathy toward the role of education in American society. Far from being the mechanism for the eradication of injustice that it was, or was hoped to be, in Heller's early short stories, higher education is now the object of his most acrid satire as one of the institutions that perpetuate social stratification and moral insensitivity. From this perspective, the academic theme in Heller's fiction is hardly an endorsement for American universities, but it is a concern that deserves serious contemplation even by the members of the institutions most grievously portrayed.[23]

## Notes

1. Joseph Heller, "Nothing To Be Done," *Esquire* 30 (August 1948): 73, 129–30.

2. Joseph Heller, "I Don't Love You Any More," *Story*, September 1945, pp. 40–44; Heller, "World Full of Great Cities," in *Nelson Algren's Own Book of Lonesome Monsters*, ed. Nelson Algren (New York: Bernard Geis, n.d.), pp. 7–19.

3. Joseph Heller, "Bookies, Beware!" *Esquire* 27 (May 1947): 98; "Castle of Snow," *Atlantic Monthly* 181 (March 1948): 52–55.

4. Joseph Heller, *Catch-22* (New York; Simon and Schuster, 1961). Unless otherwise indicated, subsequent references to *Catch-22*, abbreviated as *C*, are given in parentheses in the text.

5. Joseph Heller's note cards, on which he planned the novel in detail, are located in the Brandeis University Library. For further information see James Nagel, "The *Catch-22* Note Cards," *Studies in the Novel* 8 (1976): 394–405.

6. The manuscript of *Catch-22* is in the Brandeis University Library. The pages of the manuscript are not numbered sequentially; Heller frequently moved sections

about and started new numbering schemes using letters or numbers in circles that do not follow in order the numbers without circles. Therefore, references to passages in the manuscript will be made to chapters. See MS, chap. 8.

7. MS, chap. 4.

8. MS, chap. 4.

9. MS, chap. 8.

10. MS, chap. 8.

11. MS, chap. 5.

12. MS, chap. 20.

13. MS, note cards.

14. MS, chap. 6.

15. MS, chap. 25. This manuscript section was subsequently published as "Love, Dad," in *Playboy* 16 (December 1969): 180–82, 348.

16. For further development of this point, see James Nagel, "Yossarian, The Old Man, and the Ending of *Catch-22*," *Critical Essays on Catch-22*, ed. James Nagel (Encino: Dickenson Publishing Co., 1974), pp. 164–74.

17. Joseph Heller, *Something Happened* (New York: Alfred A. Knopf, 1974). Unless otherwise indicated, subsequent references to *Something Happened*, abbreviated as *SH*, are given in parentheses in the text.

18. See *Something Happened*, pp. 138, 181–82, 503.

19. See *Something Happened*, pp. 485, 489–90, 519.

20. Joseph Heller, *Good as Gold* (New York: Simon and Schuster, 1979). Unless otherwise indicated, subsequent references to *Good as Gold*, abbreviated as *GG*, are given in parentheses in the text.

21. See *Good as Gold*, pp. 20, 95, 270.

22. See *Good as Gold*, pp. 332, 362.

23. I want to express my gratitude to Joseph Heller, for permission to quote from his manuscripts, and to Victor Berch, of the Special Collections Library at Brandeis University, for assistance in working with the Heller papers.

# Saul Bellow and the University as Villain

*Ben Siegel*

FEW American novelists talk and write about the university as much as does Saul Bellow. Certainly no other subject stirs in him equal rancor and resentment. He reiterates his unhappiness with the university in lecture and interview, essay and fiction. He has done so since early in his career. His views are not totally consistent, but they are clear and uncompromising. Bellow does not underestimate the university's importance. He knows this country's literary activity is not concentrated in New York or Chicago or any city, and its literary intellectuals are not molded on Grub Street or in Bohemia. They are shaped in the university, he admits, with Bohemia itself now "relocated...near to university campuses."[1] His attitude suggests a familiar paradox. Like many American novelists and poets, Bellow remains rooted in academe while making it a frequent target. He refers to himself as a "professor" and reportedly complains at campus events lacking any "special provision" for faculty members. Where faculty privileges are concerned, Bellow proves, according to Mark Harris, "rather caste-minded, petulant, peevish, especially when he...[is] inconvenienced." He thinks "that someone should always be handy to assist him."[2] Yet he attributes much of what is wrong with this nation's culture, especially its literary culture, to the university and its professors.

## Professors and the Literary Situation

In *Seize the Day* (1956) Bellow describes the type of individual who becomes a professor. Tommy Wilhelm recalls with distaste his cousin Artie, who has been "an honor student at Columbia in math and languages. That dark little gloomy Artie with his disgusting narrow face, and his moles and self-sniffing ways and his unclean table manners, the boring habit he had of conjugating verbs when you went for a walk with him. 'Roumanian is an easy language. You just add a tl to everything.'" This same pitiful Artie was

---

"Saul Bellow and the University as Villain" appeared originally, in somewhat different form, in *The Missouri Review* 6 (Winter 1983): 167–88.

now a respected professor. "Not that to be a professor was in itself so great. How could anyone bear to know so many languages? And Artie also had to remain Artie, which was a bad deal. But perhaps success had changed him. Now that he had a place in the world perhaps he was better. Did Artie love his languages, and live for them, or was he also, in his heart, cynical? So many people nowadays were."[3]

Cynical or not, professors like Artie bear prime responsibility for America's "literary situation." This Bellovian phrase covers not only recent writers and writings but also the several decades of postwar media intellectuals shaping the country's thought and expression. Since World War II, American universities have littered the cultural landscape "with small Daedaluses who teach literature, edit magazines, write critical articles and can be seen swarming far from Crete or Dublin."[4] But then Bellow is not certain this country even has a "literary situation." What it does have resembles more a sociological, political, or psychological situation, with some literary elements. "Literature itself has been swallowed up" in the last three decades. Just prior to the Second World War, America's "highbrow public" was small, but after the war, thanks to the G.I. Bill, it exploded with a "new class of intellectuals or near-intellectuals." A college degree indicates, if nothing else, Bellow notes, an "exposure to high culture" and its creators or purveyors. The poems and novels these students read were written by "highbrow geniuses—disaffected, subversive, radical." Rejecting all "average preferences" ("CC," p. 2) for their own singular ones, these modern masters infused the young with their own radical disaffection.

The new graduates formed in turn a serious "minority readership," but one different in taste and size from "that handful of connoisseurs that had read *Transition* in the twenties and discussed 'significant form.'" Now America had a large literary community, but a bad literary culture. Yet if deficient in taste, this community or audience proved insatiable in its cultural hunger, viewing literature as both "swallowable" and "enormously profitable." Its members contributed to the "university boom" and to the expansion of journalism and publishing.[5] Hence the postwar years found the universities newly prosperous and at the center of an enlarged but artificial "literary culture." Bellow claims that in the fifties and sixties the campus became "what Paris was to Fitzgerald and Hemingway in the twenties." He realizes "Ann Arbor and Iowa City are not Paris," but then "Paris isn't Paris either," its old cultural glamor gone with Gertrude Stein, Joyce, and Gide. Indeed, all of culture's great "national capitals" ("SDL," p. 17) are gone, so artists and writers have turned for "asylum" to the universities and transformed them into "the sanctuary, at times the hospital, of literature, painting, music and theatre" ("CN," p.169).

Still, if writers find shelter on campus, they are not truly comfortable there. One source of discomfort is their sensitivity to the popular conviction that "the intellectual life is somehow not virile. Artists and professors, like clergymen and librarians, are thought to be female." This popular view, observes Bellow, forces the artist to present himself as a man of the people and to downplay his true concern with thought. "Maybe that's why we don't have more novels of ideas," and why this society's truly powerful men "hold writers and poets in contempt." These leaders find in modern literature little evidence "that anybody is thinking about any significant questions."[6] The trouble, in this "vague and shifting" time, is that novelists and poets are not clear as to their obligations. Any writer able to do his society some good, Bellow reasons, should do it. But writers seldom think of themselves as society's shields against barbarism. Generally they think about stories they are or should be writing. Their "cultural assignment" results less from their thinking than from that of professors. If a few writers believe their efforts belong to society, most simply do not care.

How does Saul Bellow view his cultural obligation? "Sometimes I'm on one side of the matter and sometimes I'm on the other. Occasionally I worry about what's happening to culture in the United States, but on other days I think there is no culture in the United States, and there's no point in worrying about it."[7] His fiction and essays do not reflect this cavalier attitude. Instead, they reveal Bellow's deep concern for the nation's intellectual life, on campus and off. He emphasizes repeatedly how damaging to humanistic thought is the university's increasing commitment to technology and to the sciences, physical and behavioral. No respectable campus today lacks "computers, atom smashers, agricultural researchers, free psychotherapy, technocratic planners, revolutionary ideologists." Ideas are flattened, packaged, devalued. So are standards and life styles. Every campus has "everything, including bohemia," or, to be precise, bohemia may have the university. Either way, the campus "is being thoroughly bohemianized" ("CN," pp. 169–70).

## The University and Its Literary Magazines

The commitment of universities to technology and bohemianism was only indirectly responsible for weakening contemporary culture. But universities contributed directly to the destruction of the nation's "independent literary culture" when they bought up most literary publications during the fifties and sixties. They did so without calculation, but their innocence made little difference. Championing the avant-garde in all its forms, the universities gathered the most adventurous literary magazines and journals and sponsored the most experimental theater and dance, music and painting. "They had it all," so unaffiliated writers soon had "no extra-institutional and independent environment."[8] The danger of such academic absorption is exemplified for Bellow by certain literary periodicals and underground papers edited by "brutal profs and bad-tempered ivy league sodomites" ("CN," p. 164). These sorry academics or quasi-academics disseminate their personal (if borrowed) cultural ideas through the captive quarterlies, which now function as "attitude sources." Such publications serve graduate students and young intellectuals as *Vogue* and *Glamour* serve working girls and housewives: they teach readers the "in-things" and "out-things." They supply not art but "art-discourse" ("SDL," p. 21), as well as prepared views for fashion or discussion.

Reading these quarterlies Bellow feels "first uncomfortable, then queasy, then indignant, contemptuous and finally bleak, flattened out by the bad writing." Who reads this stuff? Do cultivated housewives and graduate students eat "these stale ideological chocolates?" Customers and responsible individuals must pay the bills. Still the universities bear major responsibility. For literary publications are now almost all "university subsidized, as what is not these days" ("CN," pp. 164, 169).

To illustrate the fallen state of literary magazines, Bellow goes after several old adversaries—the *Partisan Review* and two of its editors, William Phillips and Richard Poirier. Bellow had published his early stories in *PR* and in the forties and early fifties was an accepted member of the "*Partisan Review* crowd." His break from that coterie marked a turning point for him. In a recent interview Bellow described himself arriving in New York in the 1940s as a "young hick" determined on "going to the big town and taking it." He was drawn to *PR*'s writers and their "sense of community." His new friends, among them Delmore Schwartz, Clement Greenberg, Meyer Schapiro, and Dwight MacDonald, "were not always friendly friends, but they were always stimulating friends." Bellow appreciated "the 'open spirit of easy fraternization' that animated their discussions. Politics, generally in the form of Marxism, tended to be mostly theoretical." In the late fifties and the sixties, however, the world darkened, and the New York intellectual mood changed. During that time "a new generation turned up." Many newcomers out of Columbia University were students of Lionel Trilling. They moved "into enterprises like *Commentary*—and suddenly the whole atmosphere in New York became far more political than it had been before."[9] Groups such as "the New York poets, the *Commentary* group, *The New York Review of Books* group, the people around Stanley Kunitz and Cal [Robert] Lowell"[10] were formed.

Bellow did not want to become embroiled "in the literary life and its rackets" and avoided choosing sides. Looking back, he explains:

People have said in their memoirs that I was guarded, cautious, career-oriented, but I don't think that's so—after all, there was nothing easier in New York during those days than the life of the extremist, and that's continued to be so. I was not comfortable with the extremist life, and so I thought I might as well go back to the undiluted U.S.A., go back to

Chicago. It's vulgar but it's vital and it's more American, more representative. [11]

By the mid-1960s his *Partisan Review* phase was history. The magazine and its staff, not to mention the New York intellectual scene, had experienced many changes. A decade later Bellow launched attacks against *Partisan Review* and William Phillips, Richard Poirier, and other of its editors and contributors. His action likely was instigated by Poirier's mean-spirited *PR* review of *Herzog* in 1965. In his 1971 essay "Culture Now," Bellow argues that reading William Phillips's article on Susan Sontag "is much like trying to go scuba diving at Coney Island in urinous brine and scraps of old paper, orange rinds and soaked hot dog buns." Its sorry babblings remind him that "One of the nice things about Hamlet is that Polonius is stabbed." Phillips does rate a few merit points from Bellow. An old-timer, he helped found a magazine that published the nation's best writers and poets from the 1930s through the 1950s. But his own prose is deplorable. "What writing!" Bellow laments. "Eleanor Roosevelt wrote far better in *My Days*." Richard Poirier also gets his lumps. "The new regime of Mr. Poirier has not improved Mr. Phillips' style. Mr. Poirier has made *PR* look like a butcher's showcase, shining with pink hairless pigginess and adorned with figurines of hand-carved suet which represents the very latest in art, literature and politics. Hoarse Mr. Phillips also is up to date, and gives the *dernier cri*" ("CN," pp. 164–65).

Shifting from Phillips's prose to his critical views, Bellow scoffs at his reference to an inactive audience as an "inert voyeuristic mass." As a creative artist or "virtuoso," Bellow expects a receptive but not an "active" readership or audience. He accuses Phillips of dismissing as perverse the spectator who sits still by insisting everyone *do* something, grab "a piece of the action." Phillips contends, according to Bellow, that every person "must create," as all true art is a collaboration and the only true artist is "the public itself" ("CN," pp. 165–66). Bellow rejects this confusion of actor and spectator and by extension writer and reader. Phillips's new political stance also angers him. A lifelong Marxist ideologue, he now embraces a New Left devoid of theory or program. Phillips is convinced, quotes Bellow, "'that only an antitheoretical, antihistorical non-Marxist, unstructured movement like that of the youth today could have created a new left force in the West.'" [12] This declaration, "in its idiocy," is for Bellow "really rather touching." One must realize, he observes, that "in surrendering his Marxism," Phillips is rejecting "forty years of his life." Why? Bellow's guess is that Phillips fears he may not be making it with the young and that New York radicals will dismiss him as "a silly dry old stick who is out of it" ("CN," p. 166). Bellow expands upon this attack later while implicating the universities in the destruction of the "literary situation." Rutgers University acquired *PR* just as its founding editors were succumbing to age and fatigue. Taken over by new people, the magazine quickly grew "very corrupt and doddery."[13]

The old animosities were stirred anew by Poirier's 1975 partly revised review of *Herzog*. In his opening paragraph, Poirier describes *Herzog* and *Mr. Sammler's Planet* as "efforts to test out, to substantiate, to vitalize, and ultimately to propagate a kind of cultural conservatism which [Bellow] shares with the two aggrieved heroes of these novels, and to imagine that they are victims of the cultural debasements, as Bellow sees it, of the sixties."[14] Not given to forgetting or forgiving, Bellow used a recent interview to strike back:

> People who stick labels on you are in the gumming business.... What good are these categories? They mean very little, especially when the people who apply them haven't had a new thought since they were undergraduates and now preside over a literary establishment that lectures to dentists and accountants who want to be filled in on the thrills. I think these are the reptiles of the literary establishment who are grazing on the last Mesozoic grasses of Romanticism. Americans in this respect are quite old-fashioned: they're quite willing to embrace stale European ideas—they should be on 10th Avenue where the rest of the old importers used to be.
>
> They think they know what writers should be and what writers should write, but who are these representatives who practice what Poirier preaches? They're, for the most part, spiritless, etiolated, and the liveliest of them are third-rate vaudevillians. Is this literary life? I'd rather inspect gas mains in Chicago.[15]

Shoddy thinking and writing typify not only *PR*, says Bellow, but also most quarterlies, the "university subsidized" ones in particular. The academic publications share with popular magazines like *Playboy*, *Esquire*, and *Evergreen Review* a bohemian disdain for serious art. Despite surface differences, they all swing "against a background of high or formerly high culture" ("CN," pp. 171–72). A Leslie Fiedler article in *Playboy* offers an example. In his "Cross the Border, Close the Gap," Fiedler charges Bellow (as well as John Updike, Mary McCarthy, and James Baldwin) with writing "old novels." Without mentioning the critical jab, Bellow attacks Fiedler's desire to "close the gap, between high culture and low, belles-lettres and pop art."[16] He resents this call, as he puts it, "for more obscenity, more of the *mantic*, the *mad* and the *savage*." Why does Fiedler advocate the standards of "pop art," asks Bellow, and of "the media-managing intellectuals"? His own class interests are at risk. His pupils are among the "college-educated swinging, bearded, costumed, bohemianized intellectuals [who] are writing the ads, manufacturing the gimmicks, directing the shows, exploiting the

Woodstocks." A partisan rather than an objective observer, Fiedler is pushing "his own product" by rating "the worst sins of the masses... [above] the dead virtues of high culture" ("CN," pp. 172–74). His call for new literary standards derives from the popular conviction that literary modernism is dead. The age of Proust, Mann, and Joyce, as well as T. S. Eliot and Paul Valéry, has been replaced by a new "postmodernism," and this new era, according to Fiedler, demands a "death-of-art criticism." Those writers not fortunate enough to be under thirty-five have to be "reborn" to become relevant to the moment and the young.

Bellow finds Leslie Fiedler's theories to be as "dismal" as they are amusing. They are too close "to madness" for Bellow "to keep smiling." Even worse, this madness is old and unoriginal, offering implications of fascism instead of wit. Fiedler may intend only to scare the reader over thirty-five with talk of the death of his mind and imagination. In past years Leslie Fiedler, says Bellow, most likely would have written for Hearst's Sunday supplement. His undeniable "hatred of liberalism, love of an imaginary past (Cowboys and Indians), somnambulistic certitude, praise of tribalism and of Dionysiac excesses, the cult of youth, the chastising of high culture by the masses, the consecration of violence—all...suggest fascism." Hence history is important to Fiedler for its disposable elements. "Considerations of style, quality or degree are irrelevant." What this professor advocates is part of "an old story—an ancient religious belief, really. Destruction purifies." Jung and Lawrence, among others, have repeated this myth: "after the holocaust, the Phoenix...after Death, Resurrection" ("CN," pp. 173–74). By urging his readers to "shake off the dead past" and to rely solely on the future, Fiedler perpetuates this old motif.

So Fiedler is for Bellow merely one more intellectual opportunist. Equally opportunistic was another renowned professor—the late Marshall McLuhan. A high-pitched McLuhan review of a Mick Jagger film reveals to Bellow what the avant-garde and Ph.D. literature programs have combined to give this society: "apocalyptic clichés; a wild self-confidence; violently compact historical judgments; easy formulas about the 'cancellation of a world.'" Can anyone miss in McLuhan's views (all copyrighted by McLuhan Associates Ltd.), asks Bellow, "the presence of money"? In America time and recognition alter all, even the most perceptive. McLuhan, who long warned this country of the media's seductive powers, finally seemed himself "a medium." The avant-garde may have formed him, so that he "started out esoteric," but he ended up speaking "to a great public." Ours is "an amazing country," concludes Bellow. Even McLuhan did not "know the half of it" ("CN," pp. 163–64). As a result he was absorbed and transformed by the very forces he opposed.

### Antiquarians and Moderns

Most literature professors, Bellow realizes, are neither populists like Leslie Fiedler or Marshall McLuhan nor advocates of a New Left like Poirier and contributors to *PR*. Still, they are primarily responsible for the university's pernicious influence on literary thought and culture. He divides professors into two general types. The first is the "antiquarian," who, in his concern with the classics, serves as our "custodian of the cultural valuables." He and his colleagues insist that these heirlooms have been so "edited and catalogued, [and] sufficiently described" that there is "little more to do about them." Nurturing a "modest pride," they feel "separated from the unseemly, thrashing, boring, dangerous world." They resolve to hand over their cultural treasures only to the next generation's "qualified curators" ("SDL," p. 21). These "stony old pedants" amuse Bellow. Two generations back they "refused to discuss anyone newer than Browning." A small minority, he admits, are "quite useful; others are harmless enough, textual editors, antiquarians and fuddyduddies. Others are influential interpreters. Or misinterpreters" ("CC," p. 2). Over all, however, the antiquarians are no longer significant. Their power was broken in the 1930s, he declares, when the universities turned to modern literature and contemporary writers.

So Bellow's anger is reserved for the second academic species: the modern lit prof. He (always *he*, never *she*) and his thousands of colleagues turn out the "millions of graduates in literature" ("CC," p. 2). Not only do they deal in the recent literary masters, but these profs often also take the same figures as role models. "When I was an undergraduate," Bellow recalls, "there were teachers of literature who looked Tennysonian, Browningish, Swinburnian, pre-Raphaelite or Celtic Twilight." Later many were influenced by Hemingway, a highly popular model. Some profs who grew up in the twenties opted for "the Fitzgerald style of the sad young man who drank too much and had a nutty wife. (Many wives obliged.) Now we have Lawrentian profs, Dylan Thomas profs, Becketts, Ionescos and Mailers, wood-demons, sons of Pan Dionysians, LSD godseekers." Many Americans encourage this role playing. Conditioned to consume good things and to make them their own, such people render culture and cultural models "personally applicable" ("SDL," p. 21).

Yet these modern lit profs, like the antiquarians, also wish to keep any literary culture limited and manageable. So they proclaim the novel's imminent demise and that of literature in general. Such academics are for Bellow much like property owners. "They have their lots surveyed. Here the property begins and there it ends. A conservative instinct in them, which every lover of order will recognize and respect, resists extension, calls for limits." They are vocal and numerous. "For every poet now there are a hundred custodians and doctors of literature, and dozens of undertakers measuring away at coffins." These crepe hangers affect both students and writers, with the literature students lining up happily. "'Thank God!' they say, 'it's over. Now we have a field. We can study.'" Their attitude is understandable. Libraries and secondhand bookstores are packed full, as is "the physical universe [that] overwhelms us with its immensities." Must man's writing "flood us as well?" Still, Bellow cannot help wondering whether novels can be studied or even read with much profit if writers do not continue to write them. "Not professional study but imagination," he warns, "keeps imagination alive." The trouble is that by such negative talk the novelist is affected and made uneasy. "Trained to take words seriously," he assumes he is hearing serious words. "He believes it is the voice of high seriousness saying 'obsolete. Finished.'" What if the voice were to prove "the voice of low seriousness instead?"[17]

The role playing and dire prophecies of such people are bad, but even worse is their ineptitude. Bellow is astonished "at the ignorance of learned people." Many who teach literature or writing are so poorly prepared that they should attempt a novel simply to grasp how a book is constructed. "I suppose that the maker of a thing, however clumsy he may be, acquires a sort of knowledge for which there is no substitute."[18] If the knowledge of university scholars is defective, their prose is more so. Most of it—literary and nonliterary—lacks "poetry." During the past half-century academic jargon has grown steadily more deviant. While he can appreciate the knowledge of this country's highly intelligent economists, sociologists, lawyers, historians, and scientists, Bellow reads their prose "with the greatest difficulty, exasperated, tormented, despairing."[19]

Yet even if tin-eared, these societal specialists do not offer the major danger, "the academic danger." The humanities profs pose much the greater risk. These "humanist intellectuals" have stirred Bellow's strong dislike through the years. His next-to-latest novel, *The Dean's December*, makes clear that his feelings about academics, especially those in the humanities, have changed little. He reasserts his dissatisfaction with the intellectual rigidity and parochialism of both scientists and humanists, but he is, as always, more bitter toward his humanities colleagues. Geologist Sam Beech invites Bellow's hero, Albert Corde (a veteran journalist turned professor and college dean), to help turn his scientific findings into a prose accessible "not only to the general public...but also to the Humanist." Corde is puzzled. "Who were these Humanists, and why should Beech imagine that they were a group to whom any case could be stated? And if there was such a group, why should it be inclined to pay attention to Corde? He considered how to discuss this with a geologist like Beech. 'You want to understand humanist intellectuals? Think of the Ruling Reptiles of the Mesozoic [Age]."[20]

Corde is not suggesting humanists alone are flawed in thought and knowledge. Scientists, too, are shortsighted and insensitive to many moral and aesthetic implications of their own efforts. He reasons that "if pure scientists had really understood science, they would have realized the morality and poetry implicit in its laws. So it's all going to run down the drain, like blood in a Hitchcock movie." But the humanists, of whom more is expected culturally, "also have flunked the course. They have no strength because they have no conception of what the main effort of the human mind has been for three centuries and what it has found" (*TDD*, p. 228).

What most annoys Bellow about these tenured faculty humanists is that despite their ignorance they never suffer writer's block and are able always to supply literary articles so cheaply they have "all but wiped out...professional competitors." They want to wrench literature from writers and keep it for themselves. They remind Bellow of "the British princess who said to her husband during the honeymoon, 'Do the servants do this too? Much too good for them.'" These professors and their disciples (the next crop of literary intellectuals) are convinced literature is much "too good for contemporary novelists, those poor untutored drudges." Identifying with figures like Henry James and James Joyce, Marcel Proust and the French symbolists, they offer themselves as each master's only true heirs and agents. Their stance enables them to "enjoy a certain genteel prestige. They are the happy few" ("CC," p. 2). What are these cultural impresarios doing with their appropriated literature?

> Why, they talk about it; they treasure it; they make careers of it; they become an elite through it; they adorn themselves with it; they...take masterpieces and turn them into discourse in the modern intellectual style. I'm against that, of course. I am not for the redescription of *Moby Dick* by Marxists and existentialists and Christian symbolists, respectively. What does that do for *Moby Dick* or for me? It doesn't do anything. It only results in the making of more books—King Solomon has already warned us against that in Ecclesiastes.[21]

### Academics as Critics

Issues more serious than the mere accumulation of needless reading matter are involved here. This academic redescribing of basic texts, by relating them to myth, history, philosophy, or psychology, Bellow complains, renders them "less accessible" to readers. It means that for human emotion or response, professors "substitute acts of comprehension" ("CC," p. 2). They are obsessed with meaning, especially hidden meaning. They are convinced fiction is not to be taken literally. They resemble for Bellow those Christian fathers who expected Scripture to "yield the higher meanings." Yet such academics are not, like church fathers, nurturing "sublime conceptions of God and Man." If they were "moved by the sublimity of the poets and philosophers they teach, these humanities profs would be the university's most fervent and powerful members. Instead they rest at "the lower end of the hierarchy, at the bottom of the pile" ("SQA," pp. 55–56).

What fervor academics can muster they devote not to creating imaginative literature but to "manufacturing 'intellectual history.'" In a position to recruit writers and artists who best meet their needs, they fashion a congenial subculture for themselves and their students. They consider seriously only books whose "attitudes, positions or fantasies" please them, even if such books are "little more than the footnotes of fashionable doctrines" ("CC," p. 45). For these works are now "their material, their capital." Taking from them what they need for their journalism or social critiques, they produce "hybrid works." These efforts are "partly literary" and occasionally interesting, but mostly they reveal contemporary literature's "decadence or obsolescence." The professors want people to think they are lifting modern literature into "a higher, more valuable mental realm, a realm of dazzling intellectuality" ("CC," pp. 2, 44). They are not.

Despite this culture capitalism, Bellow does not oppose proper literary discussion. "[T]here's no reason why people shouldn't talk about books. There is a prerequisite, though, which is that they should be deeply stirred by the books. They should love them or hate them." But they should "not try to convert them into...chatter....[S]o much of literary criticism is babbling." He refers here to those critics who "translate" important books by writing them again in their own "fashionable intellectual jargon." The books that result "are no longer themselves. They have been borrowed by Culture, with a capital C." Such borrowings move Bellow to distinguish between two types of art. One type has a "direct effect on people." The other type proves "a cultural commodity [and]...a fertilizer for the cultivation of languages, vocabularies, intellectual styles, ornaments, degrees, honors, prizes, and all the rest of that. That's Culture with a Capital C." A recurrent process, its prime model has been "the Christian religion, which started with faith and ended with churches."[22] Such transmuting of the spirit into the text is seldom uplifting.

Bellow guards against becoming himself a Culture object. "I think we must all be on guard against it," he warns. "I don't want to become a support of the new clergy. Why should I? It's none of my business!"[23] What is his business? To sound the alarm. In recent years this classroom clergy has obscured the connections between the literary present and past, between contemporary writers and their predecessors. Such teachers have "miseducated the young," he declares, neither developing their tastes nor creating a public sensitive to the arts. Instead they have contributed to their students'—in Thorstein Veblen's phrase—"trained incapacity" ("CC," p. 45) by reducing novels to cultural objects and dehumanizing art. In fact,

Bellow suggests that the "dehumanization of art" that Ortega y Gasset lamented may well result from those pressures for meanings university intellectuals exert upon art. Each literary generation cherishes the novel as a cultural object of high importance. But each treats it also as a historical artifact whose "ideas...symbolic structure...position in the history of Romanticism or Realism or Modernism...[and] its higher relevance require devout study" ("SQA," p. 55).

Bellow does not deny the merit of literary study and analysis. Even redescriptions and labels can be "intriguing and useful," he admits, but Americans often overdo "this comedy of terms. We pay psychologists to penetrate our characters and redescribe them to us scientifically. ... We are delighted to hear that we are introverted, fixated, have a repression here, a cathexis there, are attached to our mothers thus and so." We pay happily for cultural or personal analyses, but they have little to do with novels and novelists. Writers and readers—unlike professors—desire from literature "the living moment." They wish to read about "men and women alive—a circumambient world." Instead of such vital responses, students and readers get from professors laborious explications. These academic critics restate and redefine "everything downward, blackening the present age and denying creative scope to their contemporaries" ("CC," p. 2). Bellow considers their criticism too "linear" or "sketchy." A novelist does not "feel he's got anything until he has it in all the density of actual experience. Then he looks at a piece of criticism, and all he sees is the single outline of thought. It's not the same thing. And you can't deal with a phenomenon that way. So he never really trusts criticism, because it lacks the essential density."[24]

Yet the "cultural bureaucrats" on campus shape things to their liking by ignoring all contradictions, aesthetic or social. They are bothered little, therefore, by gaps between their theories and practices. For instance, they "have absorbed the dislike of the modern classic writers for civilization. They are repelled by the effrontery of power and the degradation of the urban crowd. They have made the Waste Land outlook their own." At the same time, these university functionaries accumulate "money, position, privileges, power." They enroll their children in private schools and enjoy "elegant dental care...[and] jet holidays in Europe. They have stocks, bonds, houses, even yachts, and with all this, owing to their education, they enjoy a particular and intimate sympathy with the heroic artistic life. Their tastes and judgments were formed by Rimbaud and D. H. Lawrence. Could anything be neater?" ("CC," p. 44). The force of this argument is perhaps lost on the bemused college teacher reading this glittering catalog of his wealth and power, his jet holidays and his yachts; he can only wonder where Bellow encounters such privileged academics—or the "middle-class writers" against whom he levels similar charges.

But the hypocrisy of literature professors concerns Bellow less than does their intellectual rigidity. Their actions in and out of class result largely, he insists, from the tenured stability and confidence they gained from huge postwar enrollments. Lionel Trilling voiced a similar complaint, Bellow points out, in *Beyond Culture*, where he dismissed as culturally flawed the student hordes then exposed to modern classics.[25] These graduates convinced Trilling a literary education could be "a mixed blessing" ("CC," p. 44), as the critics, writers, and executives sent by English departments into society were too ill-prepared to contribute intellectually. Still they helped change, by sheer numbers and needs, both the literature curriculum and the reading public. They demanded that contemporary literature be part of the curriculum. Before them, every educated person was thought capable of reading a novel without the help of "ten manuals." But burgeoning classes enabled faculty members to assert their intellectual authority by implementing "a gloomy preparatory region, a perfect swamp," that every student has to cross before he can "open his *Moby Dick* and read 'Call me Ishmael.'" The result of this is that "He is made to feel ignorant before masterpieces, unworthy, he is frightened and repelled." At best this method "produces B.A.'s who can tell you why the *Pequod* leaves port on Christmas morning. What else can they tell you? No feeling for the book has been communicated, only a lot of pseudolearned interpretations" ("SQA," p. 55).

### Readers, Writers, and University Intellectuals

Critical of postwar education, Bellow found instruction little better in his student days. His unhappiness with professors stems in part from his own undergraduate experience, which he feels helped confuse his natural interplay of ideas and emotions. To this day, he states, "I avoid the assumption that I know the origin of my own thoughts and feelings. I've become aware of a conflict between the modern university education I received and those things that I really felt in my soul most deeply." He now trusts increasingly the impressions of his soul, despite being taught he has no soul. "The soul is out of bounds if you have the sort of education I had. I got my bachelor's degree as an anthropologist. And I read Marx and Bertrand Russell and Morris R. Cohen. I read the logical positivists. I read Freud and Adler and the Gestalt psychologists and the rest. And I know how a modern man is supposed to think.... [Charlie Citrine, the hero of *Humboldt's Gift*,] says, 'If you put a test before me I can get a high mark, but it's only head culture.' The fact is there are other deeper motives in a human being."[26]

Bellow is hardly alone in his confusion. His encounters with readers suggest their educations have proved even less adequate than his own. Always grateful to learn someone expends the time and trouble to read his books, he is "also a bit depressed" when a reader asks, "'What does it mean?' As if a novel were a puzzle, or a code, to which only the author and certain highly erudite readers had the key."[27] This question offers him further proof of the "demoralizing effect" of literature teaching in the universities. "Things are not what they seem," students are taught, and unless things "represent something large and worthy, writers will not bother with them. Any deep reader can tell you that picking up a bus transfer is the *Reisemotiv* when it happens in a novel. A travel folder signifies Death. Coal holes represent the Underworld. Soda crackers are the Host. Three bottles of beer are—it's obvious. The busy mind can hardly miss at this game and every player is a winner." How then are readers to approach a work of fiction? "Are we to attach meaning to whatever is grazed by the writer? Is modern literature Scripture? Is criticism Talmud, theology? Deep readers of the world, beware! You had better be sure that your seriousness is indeed high seriousness and not, God forbid, low seriousness."[28]

Equally troubling is the sad truth that many writers contribute to this mystification process. Like the academic critics, these novelists, by relying as much on symbols and analysis as on imagination, also help to separate literature from life and to weaken a basic literary function—the raising of moral or social issues. Claiming to feel "no such temptation" to symbolize, Bellow complains that many modern writers do. "Take somebody like Joyce, especially in *Finnegans Wake*. He is writing for a small public of intellectuals—of highly skilled readers, people who know the history of modern literature and are amused by puzzles. The same thing is true of Thomas Mann. Of Eliot. Of all the small public writers."[29] These writers want their writings to be "a little deeper than average," so they pander to the "deep readers." In fact, this century's best poets and novelists, led by James Joyce, have promoted "this deep reading." So they should not complain or expect critics to downplay their symbols, much less ignore them or view them as "accidental."

> A true symbol is substantial, not accidental. You cannot avoid it. You can't take the handkerchief from *Othello*, or the sea from *The Nigger of the Narcissus*, or the disfigured feet from *Oedipus Rex*. You can, however, read *Ulysses* without suspecting that wood shavings have to do with the Crucifixion or that the name Simon refers to the sin of simony or that the hunger of the Dubliners at noon parallels that of the Lestrigonians. These are purely peripheral matters; fringe benefits, if you like. The beauty of the book cannot escape you if you are any sort of reader, and it is better to approach it from the side of naiveté than from that of culture-idolatry, sophistication, and snobbery. ("DRWB," pp. 365–67)

This emphasis upon symbols (substantial or peripheral) has produced a readership that prefers meaning to feeling. Students learn to do what "most civilized people do when confronted with passion and death. They contrive somehow to avoid them." So do writers. They publish novels woven entirely of abstractions or meanings. Oh, meanings may be important, Bellow admits, but the "need for concreteness, for particulars, is even greater. We need to see how human beings act after they have appropriated or assimilated the meanings. Meanings themselves are a dime a dozen. In literature humankind becomes abstract when we begin to dislike it." What is to be done? Bellow is specific: "We must leave it to imagination and to inspiration to redeem the concrete and the particular and to recover the value of flesh and bone." Just as they are, flesh and bone and life's other commonplaces "are mysterious enough" ("DRWB," p. 368).

No matter how unhappy with symbolist or "abstract" writers he may be, Bellow is most angry with the academy. In *The Dean's December* he updates his disenchantment with academics and their former students, the media intellectuals. His secondary commentator here is Dewey Spangler, a noted journalist and childhood friend of protagonist Albert Corde. In his newspaper column Spangler quotes Corde's private comments and interprets his public ones on the media and on his fellow professors: "Professor Corde is very hard on journalism, on the mass media." He accuses journalists of failing "to deal with the moral, emotional, imaginative life, in short, the true life of human beings." They employ their great influence, Corde charges, to prevent "people from having access to this true life. What we call 'information' he would characterize as delusion.... [He] thinks that public discussion is threadbare...that our cultural poverty has the same root as the frantic and criminal life of our once great cities." For this the Dean blames the communications industry, seeing it as the breeder of "hysteria and misunderstanding" (*TDD*, p. 301).

But if tough on the media, the Dean is tougher, Spangler observes, on university intellectuals. Corde has expected much of them, believing their "privileges" obligated them to be different from everybody else. They have disappointed him by not accepting their differences and not making the cultural contributions society needs. Their challenge was "to produce new models," but these humanists have failed to "lead the public." They have not clarified society's "principal problems" nor depicted "democracy to itself in this time of agonized struggle." In short, the professors, as Corde sees them, have been as dominated by consensus or public opinion as their fellow Americans. So instead of "irradiating American society with humanistic culture," these academics have revealed themselves to be "failures and phonies" (*TDD*, pp. 301–2).

Spangler suggests that Corde, by revealing his disappointment in two *Harper's* articles, "must have offended his colleagues deeply." He then adds mischievously that his friend may not appreciate "the magnitude of the challenge" facing professors. Who is capable, after all, of making "high human types of the business community, the engineers, the politicians and the scientists? What system of higher education could conceivably have succeeded?" But Dean Corde, declares Spangler, "is unforgiving. Philistinism is his accusation. Philistine by origin, humanistic academics were drawn magnetically back again to the philistine core of American society. What should have been an elite of the intellect became instead an elite of influence and comforts." The Dean does not claim the professors could have stopped cities from decaying, Spangler concedes, but he does feel "they could have told us...what the human meaning of this decay was and what it augured for civilization." Corde is angry because scholars who supposedly "represent the old greatness" failed to "put up a fight for it. They gave in to the great emptiness. And 'from the emptiness [Corde has written] come whirlwinds of insanity'" (*TDD*, pp. 302–3).

Pondering Spangler's summary, Corde realizes his private statements will cost him his job. "By a process of instantaneous translation," he reads them with the eyes of his Provost and colleagues, and he decides "the trouble is all in the nuances. Oh, the nuances!" Yet he knows his old crony has caught his basic hostility to academia. Even missed nuances cannot mitigate the caustic gibes Spangler quotes. Typical is his observation that while most professors do work hard, "a professor when he gets tenure doesn't *have* to do anything. A tenured professor and a welfare mother with eight kids have much in common" (*TDD*, p. 303). But if Albert Corde is embarrassed, Saul Bellow is adamant. Such views are his own, and he has altered them little over the years. Indeed, few academics of conscience, he suggests, should deny their painful validity.

### Making a Go of It

Despite the rigidity of the university and its professors, Bellow finds self-defeating the acceptance by many American writers of the popular stereotypes of "professors, clergymen, artists and all males in 'genteel' occupations as women, not men." Nor are such writers helped emotionally by their failure to find on campus adequate cultural compensation for this psychic abuse. They expected the university to offer "a unified intellectual life" rather than "dispersed specialties." Under ideal conditions a common integrated culture could "coalesce about university-sheltered artists," Bellow concedes, but such conditions are not likely. Instead, universities and government agencies, channeling their interests and rewards into the most practical areas, intensify the differences between humanists and those in the hard sciences. The physics professor, for instance, is reassured by his "sense of being needed (by the Air Force and the Navy and Oak Ridge)"; the literature professor, however, may feel "he is foolishly watching the rats in the vegetation while he ponders the problems of Hamlet's uncle." He has no visible connection "to the gas tanks behind him and Sputnik overhead." Hence he and the

other humanists "often have a keen sense of their inferiority to the great
mass of Americans. Is the real realer where the mass is thicker? So they seem
to believe." They also may believe that it is "shameful for grown men...[to
be] sitting with a parcel of kids in a corner."[30]

This defeatist attitude helps explain why writers find in English departments "discouraged people who stand dully upon a brilliant plane." These
sad individuals may be "in charge of masterpieces," but they are "not
themselves inspired." Still, no determined, lively writer, declares Bellow,
need reject a faculty position. "If he knows his own mind and if the university thinks it can get along with him—well, why not?" He may not only
make a go of it, but he may also find in university communities good
conversation and even perhaps a Whitehead or Einstein who will prove "as
well worth writing about as [any] saloon-keepers or big game hunters."
Everything rests with the writer, with the energy he has "the boldness to
release" or the environmental restraints he can disregard. He needs to ask
himself whether he can be bold in Greenwich Village but not on campus.
Does it matter whether he is on land or sea? Can he display courage in the
mines or on an assembly line but not in "the literary life"? An occasional
writer does love "to knock around" in rough company. If so, he should feel
free to do so. Certainly he should feel as free as did Walt Whitman to "go
into the streets, ride up and down Broadway or go and dig clams." But he
should never do "these things deliberately...[or merely] for the sake of
writing" ("UV," p. 362). In short, a writer should do what he feels necessary,
but he cannot rely upon any formula or prescription.

Yet, if upbeat about the dedicated writer resolving his internal difficulties,
Bellow is less sanguine about the external pressures confronting him.
Serious writers are beset by an array of scholars, historians, and teachers
who have educated and now dominate the reading public. This highly
critical readership also includes psychologists and psychotherapists,
ideologists and various other "professional custodians of culture." Together
these "shapers of the future" pose countless questions to satisfy themselves
as to which writers merit attention. But the fiction writer and poet, Bellow
observes, can respond to such queries only "with sadness and sighs."[31]
They appear to have little else to offer so pragmatic an American reading
public in these technological times.

For campus writers such problems of relevance are compounded. Isolated
in English departments, with little access to the sciences or other hard
disciplines, they are unable or unwilling to formulate new literary ideas.
Instead they follow the lit profs and derive their cultural concepts from the
modern classics they grip so stubbornly. They merely restate then "the Eliot
view, the Joyce view, the Lawrence view." They also are satisfied merely to
prepare students for an expanding culture's new power positions. In short,
they wish to exploit only what is already there. They themselves are what is

new. "They are the brilliant event, the great result of modern creativity." They wear modern artistic and literary trappings as comfortably "as young ladies wear their plastic Mondrian raincoats" ("SDL," pp. 18, 21–22). This resistance to new ideas by writers and teachers has brought little change to American literary thought during the past half-century. They rarely challenge the "modernist orthodoxy" dominating most English departments. These departments serve the literary young as their cultural settings or "Paris substitutes," but they limit their creative potential.

Sadly enough, the universities want things this way. They do not hire these new people to think creatively but only to turn students into professional writers. The schools wish them also "to bring the art-life to the campus. Bohemia. Not the vices, just the color of Bohemia." In fact, the writer new to campus finds the lit profs and some philosophers and theologians acting like writers. Should he compete with them? No, says Bellow. He should "sit down, apart, and think things over quietly" ("SDL," p. 20). He might reflect on those societal pressures that try a man's soul, especially his own. He should not expect help: the old lit profs will not admit he exists, while the modern lit profs may make him wish he did not. The philosophers and theologians, however, will welcome him. They also will use him, as they try to include what he writes in their diagnoses of man's spiritual disorders. But while he may add to their existential evidence, the young writer is not likely to learn much from them.

So he and all the creative people on campus should keep their expectations down and guard up. They should resist becoming comfortable. Some, understandably, may become teachers and others, scholars ("SQA," p. 60), but none should deteriorate into arid pedants or posturing radicals. The trouble is that writers (older and younger) have a feeble grasp of the social changes giving universities their new "revolutionary power." University-trained intellectuals dominate industry and education, politics and city planning. Yet their innocence impedes literature teachers and writers in making humanistic use of their students. Instead, these campus humanists fall prey to a studied but empty radicalism. "But it is only the manner that is radical. Few things can be safer, more success-assuring than this non-threatening radicalism." Endangering no one, it relies, "at bottom, on the stability of institutions" ("SDL," p. 26).

In fact, recent radicalism has had no home other than the university. Why? To Bellow the reason is obvious. Having inherited a romantic tradition essentially "anti-authority," or at least "hostile to institutions," writers, unlike most academics, enjoy little tranquility in their campus sanctuary. Their psychic unrest or "bad conscience" pushes them into "exaggeratedly radical attitudes" ("SDL," pp. 25–26) and into positions of social concern. So they invent "a false radicalism," while lacking any coherent idea of what "they are opposing or upholding as radicals." They are more concerned with "style than substance." Too often they nurture feelings "of being Promethean when they're only having a tantrum."[32] The public compounds their confusion by turning them into popular figures and convincing them their political gestures should not be confined to campus. Such literary radicals, Bellow warns, should realize that a forced social involvement can be ruinous. But then so can a comfortable withdrawal. José Ortega y Gasset criticized Goethe, recalls Bellow, for settling down in Weimar. Ortega believed a poet should consent to be homeless. Bellow will not go that far. Poets are not easy "to prescribe for," he cautions, whereas critics "love to have their hearts wrung" by the disasters befalling a great artist. Still he wonders if the university is not "simply Weimar in another more disgusting and intensely more bourgeois form?" Certainly campus writers in their radicalism often reveal traces "of such Weimar fears" ("SDL," p. 25).

But most American writers, he admits, have little reason not to opt for the good life. Most are from this country's middle class, and it has shaped and justified their intellectual corruption and hypocrisy. For shielded by middle America's comforts and benefits, these writers indulge an "unearned bitterness" by decrying modern man's moral and aesthetic flaws. Educated America pampers its offspring by offering them "the radical doctrines of all the ages" without teaching them that these doctrines "in their super-abundance only cancel one another out." The middle class also trains its literary young "in passivity and resignation and in the double enjoyment of selfishness and good will." It tells them to enjoy everything life offers. "They can live dangerously while managing somehow to be safe. They can be... bureaucrats and bohemians.... [They may] raise families but enjoy bohemian sexuality...observe the laws while in their hearts and...social attitudes they may be as subversive as they please." In short, they can be "conservative and radical" and about anything else they wish to be. What these writers are not taught is "to care genuinely for any man or any cause."[33] Does Bellow speak here only of cynical journalists and life-hardened novelists? He does not. "I have known blue-eyed poets apparently fresh from heaven, who gazed at you like Little Lord Fauntleroy while thinking how you would look in your coffin."[34]

His point is that neither novelist nor poet should blame only the university for his moral confusion. For what happens on campus ultimately reflects what happens—or does not happen—off campus. The creative writer who does not find in the university community an edifying inter-change of thought and feeling will not find it in society. Universities may be this nation's cultural "warehouses," says Bellow, but they do not sever anyone's moral ties to the community. Europeans see this more clearly than Americans. In Europe, writers long have come from the better-educated, socially involved classes, and they know academic life seldom differs greatly from "real life." But American intellectuals always imagine that their education removes them from ordinary events. This attitude is for Bellow "unjustifiably romantic." He points out that universities alone harbor the poets, humanists, and scholars upon whom (with all their faults) Walt Whitman, in *Democratic Vistas,* placed the responsibility of formulating the archetypal man as American. This humanistic task is a difficult one, but then so is living a moral life, off or on campus. "Let us imagine," Bellow suggests, "a man who lives in Akron, Ohio, and teaches the history of the Italian Renaissance. It is dreadful to think what he has to reconcile. Or he teaches ethics, and takes part in department politics. He behaves shabbily and his own heart cannot bear the contrast. What I am trying to say is that certain ideas can't be held idly. Attempted containment of them is ruin" ("DFW," p. 24). So university people must adhere to their vaunted humanistic standards in community as well as faculty matters.

Conversely, American society must be more generous to its writers. The late Harvey Swados stated this pointedly. "In a society which babbles interminable platitudes about battling for the minds and hearts of men," he noted, "even while it demonstrates in a thousand ways that it values the football coach and the sales engineer above the novelist and the poet, we can expect nothing but a continuation of the circumstances which drive the novelist not only into a marginal position—bad enough in itself—but into marginal utterances." These platitudes and hypocrisies produce "the false dichotomy between 'affirmative' and 'negative' writing and the vicious spiral of neglect" that isolate the writer even more and cause him "to feed on himself and his similars instead of on the social body for his material." Then the deplorable economic situation that results "from his isolation forces him into the insulated little world of the university." There the creative writer produces works that the critics receive "not with interest, attention or even compassion, but with envy and malice." They treat his efforts not merely with "scorn" but also "as an opportunity for self-aggrandizement."[35]

Harsh charges these, but Saul Bellow and so many other novelists and poets echo them so frequently they cannot be ignored. All who care about the university and its moral health, and about the creative people it harbors and abuses, must ponder them carefully.

### Notes

1. Saul Bellow, "Cloister Culture," *New York Times Book Review,* 10 July 1966, p. 2. Subsequent references to this source, abbreviated as "CC," are given parenthetically in the text.

2. Mark Harris, *Saul Bellow, Drumlin Woodchuck* (Athens: University of Georgia Press, 1980), p. 154.

3. Saul Bellow, *Seize the Day* (New York: Viking Press, 1956; New York: Viking Compass Books, 1961), p. 16.

4. Saul Bellow, "Skepticism and the Depth of Life," in *The Arts & the Public*, ed. James E. Miller, Jr., and Paul D. Herring (Chicago: University of Chicago Press, 1967), p. 25. Subsequent references to this source, abbreviated as "SDL," are given parenthetically in the text.

5. Saul Bellow, "Culture Now: Some Animadversions, Some Laughs," *Modern Occasions* 1 (Winter 1971): 162. Subsequent references to this source, abbreviated as "CN," are given parenthetically in the text.

6. Jane Howard, "Mr. Bellow Considers His Planet," *Life*, 3 April 1970, p. 60.

7. Robert Boyers et al., "Literature and Culture: An Interview with Saul Bellow," *Salmagundi* 30 (Summer 1975): 6.

8. Boyers, "Literature and Culture," pp. 12–13.

9. Michiko Kakutani, "A Talk with Saul Bellow: On His Work and Himself," *New York Times Book Review*, 13 December 1981, p. 29.

10. William Kennedy, "If Saul Bellow Doesn't Have a True Word to Say, He Keeps His Mouth Shut," *Esquire*, February 1982, p. 54.

11. Kakutani, "A Talk with Saul Bellow," p. 29.

12. See William Phillips, "Radical Styles," *Partisan Review* 36, no. 3 (1969): 397. For Phillips's response to Bellow, see his "William Phillips Answers Saul Bellow," *Intellectual Digest*, October 1971, p. 4.

13. Boyers, "Literature and Culture," p. 13.

14. Richard Poirier, "Herzog, or, Bellow in Trouble," in *Saul Bellow: A Collection of Critical Essays*, ed. Earl Rovit (Englewood Cliffs, N.J.: Prentice Hall, 1975), p. 81. See also Poirier's earlier version, "Bellows to Herzog," *Partisan Review* 32 (Spring 1965): 264–71.

15. Kakutani, "A Talk with Saul Bellow," p. 28.

16. Leslie Fiedler, "Cross the Border, Close the Gap," *Playboy*, December 1969, pp. 252, 230.

17. Saul Bellow, "Distractions of a Fiction Writer," in *The Living Novel: A Symposium*, ed. Granville Hicks (New York: Macmillan, 1957; New York: Collier Books, 1962), p. 27. Subsequent references to this source, abbreviated as "DFW," are given parenthetically in the text.

18. John Enck, "Saul Bellow: An Interview," *Wisconsin Studies in Contemporary Literature* 6 (Summer 1965): 158.

19. Saul Bellow, "Some Questions and Answers," the *Ontario Review* 1 (Fall–Winter 1975–76): 59. Subsequent references to this source, abbreviated as "SQA," are given parenthetically in the text.

20. Saul Bellow, *The Dean's December* (New York: Harper & Row, 1982), p. 136. Subsequent references to this source, abbreviated as *TDD*, are given parenthetically in the text.

21. Jo Brans, "Common Needs, Common Preoccupations: An Interview with Saul Bellow," in *Critical Essays on Saul Bellow*, ed. Stanley Trachtenberg (Boston: G. K. Hall, 1976), p. 61.

22. Brans, "Common Needs," p. 61.

23. Ibid., pp. 61–62.

24. Ibid., p. 68.

25. See Lionel Trilling, "The Two Environments," in *Beyond Culture: Essays on Literature and Learning* (New York: Viking Press, 1965), pp. 229–33.

26. Brans, "Common Needs," pp. 58–59.

27. Joseph Epstein, "A Talk with Saul Bellow," the *New York Times Book Review*, 5 December 1976, p. 34.

28. Saul Bellow, "Deep Readers of the World, Beware," the *New York Times*

*Book Review*, 15 February 1959, p. 34. Subsequent references to this source, abbreviated as "DRWB," are given parenthetically in the text.

29. Brans. "Common Needs," p. 62.

30. Saul Bellow, "The University as Villain," *The Nation*, 16 November 1957, p. 362. Subsequent references to this source, abbreviated as "UV," are given parenthetically in the text.

31. Saul Bellow, "Machines and Storybook: Literature in the Age of Technology," *Harper's*, August 1974, p. 54. Subsequent references to this source, abbreviated as "MS," are given parenthetically in the text.

32. Nina A. Steers, "Successor to Faulkner?: An Interview with Saul Bellow," *Show* 4 (September 1964): 37.

33. Saul Bellow, "Some Notes on Recent American Fiction," *Encounter*, November 1963, p. 26.

34. Saul Bellow, "John Berryman," Foreward to John Berryman, *Recovery* (New York: Farrar Straus and Giroux, 1973), p. ix.

35. Harvey Swados, "The Image in the Mirror," in *The Living Novel: A Symposium*, ed. Granville Hicks (New York: Macmillan, 1957; New York: Collier Books, 1962), pp. 182–83.

# Making the Best of Two Worlds
# RAYMOND FEDERMAN, BECKETT,

# AND

# THE UNIVERSITY

*Melvin J. Friedman*

> I don't feel myself caught up in the New York literary life
> or, God forbid, the academic literary life, which is my idea
> of living death.
>
> —William Styron

## I

FEW individuals have combined the academy and the creative life more happily or successfully than Raymond Federman. Certainly he would be the last to agree that the academy offers the writer a "living death." He has thrived in university settings from his undergraduate days at Columbia, through his graduate studies at UCLA, to his postdoctoral teaching stints at the University of California, Santa Barbara, and the State University of New York at Buffalo—where he is currently professor of English and comparative literature. (He was originally a member of the French department at Buffalo, but as his interests shifted to writing fiction he moved over to the English department, which traditionally houses creative writers. That was in 1973, the year John Barth left Buffalo for Johns Hopkins.)

During his time at UCLA Federman developed a passion for Samuel Beckett, who became the subject of his doctoral dissertation. Since then Beckett has been the cornerstone of Federman's career, first as the "special subject" for his scholarly and critical investigations, later as the prime influence on his own fiction. He came to Beckett just when the Irish writer was finding his words more and more difficult to negotiate and his critics were finding their words with increasing ease and assurance. Federman's own writing on Beckett was part of that first wave of commentary which determined the contours of all subsequent inquiry. His *Journey to Chaos: Samuel Beckett's Early Fiction* (1965) belongs in the privileged company of those early books by Hugh Kenner (Federman's colleague at Santa Barbara), Ruby Cohn, Frederick J. Hoffman, and John Fletcher. Federman is unique in their midst, however, because he used his critical skills as an entry to a career in fiction.

He seems to have done something else quite unprecedented. I can think of no other novelist who managed, en route to his vocation, a truly imposing bibliographic work. In 1970 he joined with John Fletcher in producing *Samuel Beckett: His Works and His Critics, An Essay in Bibliography.* He did a good deal more than lend his presence and name to this enterprise: he was largely responsible for annotating the section on the criticism of Beckett's work, a herculean task handled with finesse and admirable accuracy. Many of the annotations seem literally to bear his personal signature. Even after he had established himself as a novelist, he continued his critical devotion to Beckett; he coedited two books: the *Cahier de l'Herne* volume with Tom Bishop (1976) and *Samuel Beckett: The Critical Heritage* with Lawrence Graver (1979).

Given the "dual" view I have been offering of Raymond Federman, one might expect that his first novel would include a mild flirtation with the academic scene, perhaps something akin to Malcolm Bradbury's *Eating People Is Wrong.* Professors have traditionally taken the leap from literary criticism to fiction by calling upon their campus experiences and offering them in caricatured form. Federman's *Double or Nothing* (1971) clearly disappoints these expectations.[1] How far his novel is, say, from Robie Macauley's *Disguises of Love*, Stringfellow Barr's *Purely Academic*, John W. Aldridge's *The Party at Cranton*, or William Van O'Connor's *Campus on the River*! The dust jacket alerts us: "*Double or Nothing* is a *concrete* novel— *concrete*, as in *concrete poetry*: the words are used as physical materials on the page." Indeed, it is interesting to note that Federman went the way of Beckett. He did so by turning from poetry to fiction: his bilingual collection of verse, *Among the Beasts/Parmi les Monstres* preceded his first published novel by four years. Further, one can liken Federman's critical apprenticeship as Beckett commentator to Beckett's own early critical gestures toward Joyce and Proust.

Each page of *Double or Nothing* seems to go its own visual and verbal way. All classical distinctions between image and word appear to be rendered obsolete. *Double or Nothing* is what the French might call a *roman-en-train-de-se-faire.* (Federman's readings of the great French experimenters from Mallarmé through Gide seem amply rewarded; the legacy of the symbolist imagination in both verse and prose, expressed in works like *Un Coup de dés* and *Les Faux-Monnayeurs*, has had its effect.)

We witness here the growing pains of writing a novel while we see the grudging, halting fleshing out of a story that involves the arrival in America of a nineteen-year-old immigrant. Everything is tentative, every detail of the story is subject to the caprice of the narrator. Hence names change as they do in Beckett ("in fact I'll change all the names eventually. Has to be"), situations alter on retelling, digressions wear down the narrative at every turn. It seems to take the immigrant as long to disembark from his boat as it does Tristram Shandy to get born. ("I'll never get him off the boat.")

The visual spectacle afforded by *Double or Nothing* seems more muted in Federman's second novel, the unpaginated *Take It or Leave It* (1976). This book was published by Fiction Collective, which has been responsible for a prestigious list of experimental works since 1974. Professor-writers like Federman, Ronald Sukenick, and Jonathan Baumbach have helped make the Collective a viable low-budget alternative to the large, establishment presses. *Take It or Leave It* is perhaps the most exuberant of Federman's novels. It appears part of the tradition of the French voyage-of-discovery-of-America, a tradition that includes Céline's *Voyage au bout de la nuit* and Butor's *Mobile*. (There are even references to Céline in the text, such as "here go back and reread the arrival of Bardamu in New York in le Voyage.")

The telling of *Take It or Leave It* has more than its share of exhilaration (a word used appropriately as the title for the sixth chapter of the novel). Words seem to explode on the page as Frenchy's adventures are recounted from his days with the 82nd Airborne Division in North Carolina through his trip north to Camp Drum in early 1951. (Federman himself, born in Paris, served in the 82nd Airborne during the Korean War.) The adventures, which offer something of a narrative line, are eclipsed at every turn by an elaborate series of subtexts. These comment on such unrelated matters as the differences between French and English, the theories of Derrida, and the terrible legacy of the Holocaust. Even on this crowded canvas, with its "story that cancels itself as it goes," the presence of Beckett is unmistakable. At one point Federman embellishes a line from *Murphy*: "MUST I BITE THE HAND THAT STARVES ME SO THAT IT CAN STRANGLE ME BETTER?" At another he nods fondly to his mentor: "In complete LESSNESSness my friend Sam would say where nothing is even less than nothing."

Federman coins the word "critifiction" in the title of chapter 21 of *Take It or Leave It*. His experiences as a literary critic who writes within the secure, tenured walls of the university have helped shape his novels; his narratives attempt to blur all distinctions between a sort of academic criticism and fiction. His more than two decades as a professor—with the immense amount of reading required to maintain equilibrium as classroom teacher and decoder of texts—are indelibly inscribed on his consciousness.

His four full-length novels (*Double or Nothing, Take It or Leave It, The Twofold Vibration,* and *Smiles on Washington Square*) are remarkable storehouses of acquired wisdom and literary reference. In short, the early Beckett of *Murphy, More Pricks Than Kicks,* and *Echo's Bones and Other Precipitates* has left its stamp on this critifictional phase of Federman's work.

The later Beckett, with his spare, accentless prose, clearly helped form the brief, unparagraphed, unpunctuated, bilingual *The Voice in the Closet/La Voix dans le cabinet de débarras* (1979). Welch D. Everman sees it as "a turning point in his writings, because, for the first time, the name 'federman' actually appears in the fiction." [2] A reading of *Double or Nothing* and *Take It or Leave It,* as well as a knowledge of his criticism and poetry, would seem a prerequisite for an understanding of *The Voice in the Closet.* This brief text (handsomely printed by the Coda Press in Madison, Wisconsin) looks more like an art book than a work of fiction. Federman's description of it—in a letter of 19 June 1979—is worth quoting: "A complex double book—system of mirrors, echoes, boxes within boxes to accommodate my plural voice."

Federman's "plural voice" is heard again in his *The Twofold Vibration,* brought out by the Indiana University Press in 1982. Three narrators are at work here, and they trip over one another's telling. Federman once again avoids anything resembling linearity. Digressions frustrate the progress of the narrative at every turn, recalling perhaps Sterne's *Tristram Shandy* or Byron's *Don Juan.* This time he goes directly to Beckett for his title: *The Twofold Vibration* is part of a sequence in *The Lost Ones.* (Federman quotes the passage in one of two epigraphs preceding the novel, and he slyly acknowledges the author but not the title. He apparently expects his readers to be as familiar with Beckett's work as he is.) Again the Beckett presence is evident in storytelling technique and in frequent references. These include: "he sounded like old Winnie sinking into her mound of earth, you know in *Happy Days,* casually observing her own burial"; [3] or, "imagination is far from being dead, my friends, in spite of what has been rumored lately, imagination dead imagine" (p. 5); or, "No I think of myself more as a seedy solipsist" (p. 42).

Federman commented—in an interview published in *Cream City Review* (Winter 1979)—that he was eliminating the "typographical play," which had become his trademark, from *The Twofold Vibration;* his "fundamental experiment" here is "syntactical." Thus he relies on commas as the only punctuation, and he divides his narrative into blocks of varying lengths with generous spaces in between. (Some of the pages of *The Twofold Vibration* have something of the appearance of Beckett's *How It Is.*) In fact, on the surface *The Twofold Vibration* resembles science fiction: the present time of the novel is New Year's Eve 1999, and an unnamed old man is about to be "deported to the space colonies" (p. 43). Offering a different view of his enterprise, Federman suggests that the reader "call it exploratory or better yet extemporaneous fiction" (p. 1). His concerns with the post-Holocaust consciousness are perhaps more in evidence here than anywhere else in his work.

Buffalo, where Federman has lived since 1964, makes its presence felt. "The armpit of America," as he calls it, accommodates a segment of the student movement of the 1960s. Indeed, the unnamed "old man was even thrown in jail during the student unrest, he was younger then of course, and passionate, no not in Berkeley, not at the Sorbonne in May '68, but in Buffalo, yes Buffalo" (p. 13). As leader of the Buffalo 45, the old man even managed an affair with June Fanon (read Jane Fonda).

*The Twofold Vibration*, like Federman's previous fiction, proves a kind of hybrid work, mixing as it does fiction, essay, and diary. The author parades before us his entire career as a writer and critic, never letting us forget that this career has been comfortably housed in the university. Thus Dostoevski's narrow escape from the firing squad in 1849 is given five pages, and Henry James's ritualistic shaving of his beard as the nineteenth century ended is encapsulated in a lengthy paragraph. On occasion Federman nods affectionately to university friends and colleagues who share his sympathies as critic and novelist. The names of professor-critics such as Ihab Hassan, Campbell Tatham, the late Jacques Ehrmann, Richard Martin, Mas'ud Zavarzadeh, and Larry McCaffery turn up in the text, usually in frantic Beckettian listings. (Tatham and McCaffery have written at length about Federman's work.)

Federman's most recent novel, *Smiles on Washington Square*, visually resembles *The Twofold Vibration*; however, periods seem as essential to the syntax as commas.[4] The William Styron who suggests that academic life for the writer is a "living death" makes one appearance: "Sucette seemingly engrossed in the novel she is reading. *Lie Down in Darkness*, by William Styron." Obviously Styron has managed his career admirably outside the university. Federman has placed his squarely and crucially within academic parameters. This is so even though he has never written directly about it, and despite the fact it has never been the subject of his fiction.

## II

I shall now try to account on the more personal level for Raymond Federman's unusual career in fiction. He is a novelist in every way committed to scholarship and the academic enterprise—even to the point of regularly attending Modern Language Association meetings. But he is also a novelist whose novels have virtually nothing to do with university life. To begin with, Federman never fit the classic 1950s profile of the myopic, painfully shy and repressed young man who descended on the classroom (Ph.D. and preliminary publications in hand) at the age of twenty-five. Indeed, he was already twenty-six when he first enrolled as an undergraduate at Columbia University in 1954. He was by this time, to use his own words, "the survivor and the immigrant."[5] His subject matter had already begun to take shape in his mind if not on the page: "And it is true that the material, the people, the situations in my novels so far, all that seems to come out of a pre-1954 period." In addition, Federman, despite early experiments with fiction and academic success in the form of a Phi Beta Kappa key, did not find Columbia quite the breeding ground for the future novelist that the college setting was for other writers of his generation. Nor did the move to California appear to do much to determine the future course of his creative writing. What it did do was bring him to UCLA for graduate study and later to Santa Barbara for his first teaching job. It also helped him hone his critical faculties.[6] For he came to Samuel Beckett during these years, and he finally began to discover a congenial fictional manner to accommodate the twofold vibration he felt as Holocaust survivor and immigrant.

Federman's relocation to Buffalo in 1964, however, proved crucial. He has remained there ever since, leaving only for an academic stint in Montreal and Guggenheim and Fulbright years in France and Israel. Buffalo seems to have ended his restless *Wanderjahre* and provided him with a permanent and secure sense of place. Still the profile is somewhat distorted. Restlessness for many academics of Federman's generation seems to set in late rather than early. The comforts of tenure, gained after many years of exemplary academic behavior (Phi Beta Kappa, graduate fellowships, publication in the elite journals), often turn into midcareer crises; these may involve changes of wife, locale, and life style. While colleagues on all sides were trying to refashion their lives, Federman made alterations not in his life but in his fiction: he has never ceased to be an experimental writer.

Even more surprisingly, the university has proved for Federman a place to celebrate rather than denigrate. His academic contemporaries who have set their novels on college campuses (Alison Lurie, Malcolm Bradbury, and David Lodge, among others) generally concentrate on the ungenerous, unseemly aspects of university life. The comic undermining of the academic enterprise by insiders can be traced from Mary McCarthy's *The Groves of Academe* (1952) and Kingsley Amis's *Lucky Jim* (1954) down through David Lodge's *Small World: An Academic Romance* (1984). But the satirical approach seems to go against the grain of Federman's genuine and serious appreciation of his professorial commitment. He is not ungrateful, as other writers seem to be, for what he considers to be a gilt-edged security. He dwells fondly on the time-and-money advantages afforded by his employment: "The university gives me that time. It expects of me to sit at home and write (and consequently publish what I write). It pays me for that partially."

Federman sees still another serendipitous side to his situation: he can indulge himself in the writing of noncommercial, "non-nutritious" (Sartre's expression) fiction with no expectation of financial gain. He sees this as a "freedom to write experimentally." He revels in the fact that he can obstruct "the linear movement of the narrative...eliminate plot, setting" without fear of rejection from commercially minded publishers. He can bypass the expectations of such publishers with his high-risk, low-sale Shandyean novels. (They all prove to be typesetters' nightmares because of their visual, verbal, and syntactic eccentricities.) Federman is fully aware he could have more ready access to commercial publishers if he would settle into the easy, safe, expected form of the academic novel. The splendid irony is that the university has supplied him with the financial security to avoid writing such fiction—or about his university experiences.

As mentioned above, Federman is singularly dedicated to his professorial career. He takes his classroom obligations and committee assignments quite as seriously as he does his writing. He continues to write criticism with the same enthusiasm he writes fiction. Recently he became director of SUNY Buffalo's Creative Writing Program, further evidence, surely, of his con-tinuing commitment to the needs of the university. Federman perceptively identifies two species of campus writer: "The type who acts like a writer and therefore is looked upon and dealt with as though he were some kind of strange creature, some kind of *malade*. And the other type (I fit that category, I suppose) who acts like a professor, and therefore surprises people that he can also write good fiction." The former is a familiar presence in academic novels, and his restless, itinerant ways make him a short-term writer-in-residence at innumerable colleges. His allegiances are usually not to the university, which offers him, he feels, the convenience of a regular paycheck and little more. The second type is far less usual, although it includes such talented American contemporaries as William Gass, John Hawkes, John Barth, Ronald Sukenick, and Federman himself. (It is inter-esting to note that with the possible exception of Barth, with his *The End of the Road*, none of these writers has published a conventional academic novel.) This impressive roster of committed academics, interestingly enough, contains *only* experimental writers. They appear to reaffirm Federman's assertion that "The university in a way gives me this freedom to write experimentally."

Federman describes his work habits as being chaotic and disruptive. "Disruptive" is a word of which he is particularly fond; it has been used by critics with telling effect, in quite another sense, to describe not only his work but also that of a number of contemporaries. [7] Again he sees his position in the university as offering him an edge. It provides "a certain advantage. I can be disruptive. I can corrupt the rules and regulations, the conventions, not only of writing but also of teaching." The only pattern he imposes on this seemingly "erratic" behavior is his regular confrontation with the blank page. The university offers him the luxury of afternoon classes, with mornings free for writing: "I am at the typewriter by 8:30 or even 9:30. I write every morning, six days a week, when I am writing, for about four to five hours. Sometimes less, sometimes more, depending how the writing is going."

But there is even something disruptive and "digressive" (another word he likes) about this regimen:

> Yet that does not mean that the four or five hours I spend in my study (supposedly writing) are spent writing. I can be there doing other things, like writing letters to my friends, or scribbling notes to Melvin Friedman about what it means to be a writer in a university, or simply re-arranging the books on the shelves, or rereading old things I have written. But nonetheless I am there, in my study, writing or pretending to be writing; that much can be said for me. But after those four or five hours, I need to get out.

His escape hatch is conveniently the university: "But I appreciate the fact of having a place to go—the campus—where I know I will always see some-one with whom I can sit for an hour or so and talk about books, about his or her work, about my work, yes, a colleague, but more likely a group of students." For Federman this retreat from his workshop to the more expansive contours of the university is the core of his authorial existence. He cannot imagine a life dedicated to fiction without this other life involving colleagues and, especially, students.

Indeed students have always mattered a great deal to Federman. His approach to the teaching of creative writing shares in the "disruption" discussed above. Having no specific method, he depends a good deal on improvisation. He underscores one aspect of his teaching role: "I try to have my students realize that between an experience and the written form of that same experience, there is a distance, a process, a looseness in the sense of play, a space of transformation where fiction takes place." To enhance this "sense of play," he encourages experimentation in his fiction workshops, which are conducted on both the undergraduate and graduate levels. But he is careful not to do so at the expense of quality. He urges students to "question those conventions which they tend to use by reflex." Federman measures the success of his efforts by the number of students who remain in touch with him after their graduation. Many still send manuscripts to him, seeking his advice and criticism. Three graduates of the program at Buffalo, fiction writers Charles Baxter and David Porush and poet Donald Revell, have achieved distinctive levels of recognition.

Federman views his role as director of creative writing in a very modest and self-effacing way: "To tell the truth," he observes, "a Creative Writing program runs by itself. Once the students are in it, the most important aspect of it for them is that they form a community of young writers who share the same purpose, the same goal. I think sometimes they learn more from one another than from the teachers." One achievement to which Federman points with pride is the annual festival of poetry and fiction readings he launched several years ago. This week-long event pairs distinguished visitors with campus colleagues and students. In 1984, for example, the occasion centered on the visiting South African writer J. M. Coetzee.

It becomes clear then that even if the settings of his novels have little to do with college campuses, the university scene matters a great deal to Raymond Federman. Those who know him find it impossible to imagine him operating outside the classroom, away from the lecture circuit. Indeed, he is one of those well-traveled professors who lecture and give readings across America and Europe. It could be argued that he merits honorary membership in some mythical global campus. Should Federman be interested in reading "the book of himself," he might turn to Malcolm Bradbury's *Rate of Exchange*, with its traveling professor-hero, Angus Petworth. Yet, unlike other writers-errant, Federman remains devoted to a single university to which he keeps faithfully returning: the State University of New York at Buffalo.

The final words belong to Federman: "The university, as my refuge, as the place where I was able to study, think, reflect, experiment, question, made me the kind of writer I am."

## Notes

1. Federman speaks of an earlier novel, still unfinished and unpublished, with the title *And I Followed My Shadow*; he mentions it in *Double or Nothing*.

2. Welch D. Everman, "Raymond Federman," *Dictionary of Literary Biography Yearbook, 1980* (Detroit: Gale, 1981), p.199. See also my entry on Raymond Federman in *Contemporary Novelists*, 3d ed. (New York: St. Martin's Press, 1982), pp. 209–10.

3. Raymond Federman, *The Twofold Vibration* (Bloomington: Indiana University Press, 1982), p.156. All subsequent references will be to this edition and will be cited parenthetically in the text. See my review of *The Twofold Vibration*, "'Surfictional' Exuberance," in *Newsday* (" Ideas" section), 31 October 1982, p.19.

4. Jerome Klinkowitz writes interestingly about this novel in his *The Self-Apparent Word: Fiction as Language/Language as Fiction* (Carbondale and Edwardsville: Southern Illinois University Press, 1984), pp. 3–6.

5. These words and others that I quote throughout are taken from a lengthy letter Raymond Federman wrote to me on 10 January 1984. I have Federman's generous permission "to use me, use this, as you wish."

6. It should be remembered that another Jewish writer, Bernard Malamud, left New York for the West Coast a decade earlier than Federman. After spending a

dozen years teaching at Oregon State University, in Corvallis, Malamud published the only college novel of his career, *A New Life*, in 1961, just before returning to the eastern seaboard.

7. See Jerome Klinkowitz, *Literary Disruptions: The Making of a Post-Contemporary American Fiction*, 2d ed. (Urbana, Chicago, and London: University of Illinois Press, 1980). Another useful discussion of Federman's techniques is found in Charles Caramello, "Flushing Out *The Voice in the Closet*," in his *Silverless Mirrors: Book, Self & Postmodern American Fiction* (Tallahassee: University Presses of Florida, 1983), pp. 131–42, 233–36. See also Richard Pearce, "Riding the Surf: Raymond Federman, Walter Abish, and Ronald Sukenick," in his *The Novel in Motion: An Approach to Modern Fiction* (Columbus: Ohio State University Press, 1983), pp. 118–30, 150–51. Valuable material about Federman may be found in a number of interviews. See especially two interviews with Larry McCaffery: "An Interview with Raymond Federman," *Contemporary Literature*, 24 (Fall 1983): 285–306 and "An Interview with Raymond Federman," in *Anything Can Happen: Interviews with Contemporary American Novelists*, conducted and edited by Tom LeClair and Larry McCaffery (Urbana, Chicago, and London: University of Illinois Press, 1983), pp. 126–51. Finally, one should turn to Jerzy Kutnik's *The Novel as Performance: The Fiction of Ronald Sukenick and Raymond Federman* (Carbondale and Edwardsville: Southern Illinois University Press, 1986), pp. 149–227.

# The Poet on Campus

# A Personal View
# POETRY, PEDAGOGY, PER-VERSITIES

## *Theodore Weiss*

MY forty years of college teaching have roughly coincided with the establishment and remarkable growth of creative writing in the university. So my patching out this paper with personal reminiscences seems justifiable. Some seventeen years ago, having decided to accept a post at Princeton University as a writer-in-residence and a professor of English, I informed Bard College's president. He flustered me by asking what it would take to keep me at Bard. I assured him my decision was mainly prompted by a feeling that, after twenty years at Bard, whatever my affection for it, a different teaching experience and a different world made sense. At that he said pensively, "I know, physicists and poets are the people most desired in the academy." I did my best to reassure him by stoutly denying this notion, at least for poets. Yet he was on to something: a tremendous change was indeed taking place.

Elizabeth Bowen, some years ago serving as a visiting writer in the Princeton Writing Program, well expressed the chilly, unpromising background from which that change had sprung. In a moment's confidence she said, "Just between us I think teaching writing quite absurd." Before I could respond she went on, "But then I also consider it absurd to teach English literature at the university. In earlier days it was taken quite for granted that a young man of good family, come to Oxford or Cambridge, would have read English literature, certainly modern things, at home." To my asking, "Well, why was that teaching introduced?" she replied, "Oh, for Indians, Australians, and other colonials." "And for Americans?" I injected. "Well, yes, since you say so." I had already encountered her attitude at Oxford in 1963. Victorian literature was as modern an event with which its English department could be bothered. Writers were rare birds little invited to perch in those bosky groves. Recent poetry was the exclusive concern of the large—some one hundred members—sober Poetry Society. Rather touchingly, its members seriously assumed that at least their then chairmen would become prominent poets. And those two young men flapped about importantly in the loose slippers discarded not too long before by W.H. Auden—when Stephen Spender had nearly tread on his worn-down heels.

Since American English departments copied English and German models, modern literature in this country met similar resistance. Harvard University, at least the more strongly entrenched parts of it, strongly opposed the establishment of a department of modern languages. George Ticknor, Harvard's first Smith Professor of the French and Spanish languages, made that alarmingly modern work, *The Divine Comedy*, central to his teaching. Given the conservative nature of early humanities departments, made up of those who regarded the university as a grand museum (its chief function being the preservation of the antiquities), this was not surprising. Indeed, official status for an even more upstart subject, American literature, no doubt long continued to rankle. Still more barbaric and outrageous—after all, what studious length of years, what scholarship, research, rigors, had hallowed it?—was the intrusion into the university of the creative writing workshop. With the Ivy League's inclination to regard the arts and writing as chiefly pastimes and hobbies, the writing workshop has naturally had a hard time at most old-line institutions. Elizabeth Bishop, surely an eminently acceptable poet, told me that she never met the members of the Harvard English department. They apparently did their best to pretend the writing program did not exist. Similarly, in the not too distant past, a prominent member of the Yale English faculty confessed that his department was embarrassed by the whole matter of creative writing and did not know how to handle it. Years ago, when I was an instructor at Yale, I was favored with a course of my own in writing, but I was firmly ordered not to encourage or accept any creative work.

Even more personally, therefore, in 1938, when I finished college, the idea of pursuing graduate work in English seemed, to put it mildly, quixotic; certainly it seemed far beside the point for anyone planning to concentrate on writing poetry. Like a good little embryo scholar, bent on researching the matter, I consulted many university people in high places. Unanimously discouraging, they assured me I was courting disaster; this was especially so when they learned that I, aside from being primarily concerned with poetry writing, was Jewish. I had already collided with the problem at my undergraduate college; its dean, also my Greek professor, felt obliged to tell me one day early in my senior year, most startlingly to me, since I had never contemplated or desired the possibility: "I'm very sorry, but we shan't be able to offer you a position here." A Lutheran college, it specialized in the making of ministers.

But my stubbornness, as well as my inability to think of any other course, took me to the English graduate department at Columbia University. It had a number of attractive professors; several actually encouraged me in my interests. However, the only one who came anywhere near to what I was after and helped to keep me going was Mark Van Doren. A catalyst in many ways, a poet and critic, he won me at once because he acted as though literature, whatever its age, mattered and fundamentally now. Yet even he, though he consented to look at some of my poems, rarely allowed himself anything more critical than a "very interesting" or a dry chuckle at some outlandish image. Perhaps, considering the quality of the work, he was being kind. At that I felt most grateful, even naively encouraged. With the department's expectations hardly my own, I soon realized how right my consultants had been: the life of the scholar was not for me.

Fortunately, by this time the extraordinary change that I mentioned earlier was beginning. In colleges and universities the so-called New Critics, usually men of proper background in both education and station, were making their bid for place if not for power. And gradually, through their successes, it became possible to consider criticism a legitimate substitute for scholarship. My first teaching after Columbia, a summer job at the University of Maryland, brought me into close contact with Harry Warfel, who befriended me and my writing. He saw to it that I was invited that fall to a post in the University of North Carolina's English department. He felt it was the right place for a poet. On my arrival there the new head of the department gave me a gracious audience and admitted that he had also been —I did notice the past tense—a poet; however, he went on to say, "Now that you are here of course you will get on with the serious business of your graduate work." Luckily a position at Yale came along, and he helped me to it, even as he assured the Yale English department that my religion was not its concern. For such able, generous colleagues at Yale as Maynard Mack, Richard B. Sewall, W. K. Wimsatt, Jr., Louis L. Martz, and Norman Holmes Pearson, and friends like Paul Weiss and Wallace Fowlie, I shall always be grateful. My work and I prospered, as did my and my wife's magazine, the *Quarterly Review of Literature*, started at Chapel Hill. But when several colleagues began to urge me to bring my graduate work to Yale, though I was tempted, I knew the time had come to move on. I left for Bard College, an experimental college, still part of Columbia, and one more than willing to regard poetry as an adequate substitute for scholarly work.

Meantime, however, an even more surprising change was occurring. A number of the New Critics were writing poetry as well as criticism, and T. S. Eliot, the panjandrum of criticism, was impressing the academy not only with his interpretations of past literature but also with his unusually erudite poems. These things meant poetry writing began to be a possible, if not yet a wholly respectable, undertaking for young men (if not for young women!). The heroic dedication of the critic-poets Pound and Eliot, the work and devotion of poet-critics like Ransom, Tate, Winters, and Blackmur (especially since they were academy-based), and the careers of important academic critics like Trilling and Levin—deeply occupied with literature as a living entity as well as with recent writing—were all doing much to accelerate the presence of writing in the university. Criticism of poetry (its close analysis, by way especially of the Brooks and Warren textbook, *Understanding Poetry*) swept through the country. It still awes one to think of thousands of students and teachers bent with an almost rabbinical fervor over "texts" by Yeats, say, or Eliot. One might well be surprised that their poems, after such relentless scrutiny, have survived at all.

Then, following hard on the heels of the New Criticism, at the very moment that movement was consolidating its triumph, a larger revolution shook the university. As though to break loose from all that indoor industry of analysis, poetry erupted. Dylan Thomas heralded this change. Playing the minstrel, troubadour, pied piper, he romped through America. So persuasive was his larger-than-life mellifluence, his flamboyancy, that even the academic, would-be-poet lambs, who had written tight, metaphysical, properly formal New Critical poetry, sheepish as ever, did their best to change from sheep to goats and began to bleat high-blown verses. And in the sixties, when the Beats took to the open road, widening the highway Thomas had blazed into a headlong, ragged, bemired runway, poetry, now of a most exclamatory nature, enkindled vast numbers of the young. In the revulsion many thousands felt at technology, with the sciences apparently in collusion with government, the military, and big business, the arts—for their encouragement of the individual—boomed. The young clamored for the arts' active presence in the university and, whatever their elders' reservations and dismay, the young prevailed.

Under the skillful command of Paul Engle, creative writing had already established itself as an important enterprise at the University of Iowa. A way station for most of the promising young poets of the time, Iowa's workshops served as a pilot program and great-grandparent to the generations of workshops after. Just as token Jews, having made their way first through the sciences and then the social sciences (for the humanities tended to consider these barbaric subjects), were becoming something like a fact of life for English departments, so now at least one writer sidled into many departments (to be followed in time, of course, by token women and blacks). The cultural revolution was on in full force. Princeton offers an example. In a very few years, the arts there went from one resident novelist and one poet, these usually on a one-year or two-year appointment (the university was not ready to grant tenure to writers), and one painter and one sculptor to twenty-three teachers. Fairly rapid fission followed, with one program becoming two and then three. Since writing instructors were proving popular with students, some English faculty members continued to resent the presence of such unreliable, shady characters. (How could *they* be expected to honor the regularities essential to the classroom or to deal objectively with students?) Writers, many academics believed, were best when dead and fumigated and tidied up by time and scholarship. One of my colleagues, retiring during my first Princeton year, said to me (I've never known whether he knew me, whether he was being confidential or just cleverly nasty): "I'm glad I'm leaving this place, and just in time. I won't be around to see it swamped by creative writing!"

On the whole, the arts have had to be satisfied with a gradual, backdoor entrance into the university. Music and composition, by their established rigorous study programs, first attained respectability and a secure place. The fine arts, having developed institutions of their own, took their own time about developing collegiate curricula. Then they did so in a fairly marginal way. At the small, embattled progressive colleges—like Bennington, Sarah Lawrence, and Bard—however, the arts already occupied an important, if not central, place. Bard College, for instance, had a superb English faculty comprised principally of writers, distinguished ones at that. At one time or another it included Saul Bellow, Ralph Ellison, Mary McCarthy, William Humphrey, James Merrill, Anthony Hecht, and many others. Not yet sought after by conventional academies, such writers were in fact generally *persona non grata*. Gradually, however, abetted by our churning times, the cultural experiments and educational innovations of progressive colleges found their way into the more orthodox schools. But rarely were the pioneering efforts of these progressive colleges acknowledged; these schools were too small, too poor and struggling, too bohemian to be strongly respected.

Today the arts occupy a prospering, if not prominent, place in university life. As the clergy once accommodated poets in seventeenth and eighteenth century England, so now the university provides refuge to an always increasing population of writers. Few poets escape a stint of teaching, and novelists are also becoming more visible on campus. Whatever risks residence in the so-called ivory tower of the university may entail for a writer, large benefits also accrue. Aside from being in the beneficent presence, at least ideally, of learning and of a diverse breadth of intellectual activity, resident writers enjoy a greater leisure than they would in most other work and a livelier relationship to literature itself. In addition, they often form a community among themselves, their students, and other interested faculty members. Such community is rare among American writers. Like John Berryman and others, I have at times thought of looking for different work, have somewhat wistfully thought of the lives of poets like Stevens and Williams. But, on second thought, like Berryman and others, I have always thought better of it.

Moreover, in one way or another, creative activity does affect the university. Even as workshops often attract the liveliest, if not the best students, so what goes on in them tends to overflow and color the more conventional offerings. And the resident writers usually bring other distinguished writers to their universities for readings and conferences. As a consequence, the university has become, as much as any other place, the center of literary activity. Indeed the workshop has proved of greater importance than is often perceived. For when measured against the rapid proliferation of courses in the novel and in those recent forms of criticism little interested in literature itself, the workshop has proved one of the last and most vital mainstays of poetry in the university.

At times, I must admit, I do regard my students and their workshops with some wistfulness, envy, even misgivings. For these young people tend to take for granted what I in my student days would not have dared to dream of—namely, working with professional, established writers, as with groups of like-minded contemporaries who, if one is lucky, help to spur one on; at the same time, they themselves get credit for that work! For the likes of me writing was usually a secret and lonely, if not furtive, affair. I have to admit that some of my students know rather more than at their age I and my contemporaries knew. But then I console myself by saying: "Of course they know more. They know us and what we have taught them. They have the great advantage of learning directly from us what we struggled in lonely isolation to learn." And now and then I wonder whether a good deal of what they learn does not come to them too easily, too painlessly, too much from the outside. Therefore, is their knowledge not likely to be superficial? Or, is this wondering mere puritanism on my part?

Whatever its effects on students, the workshop has done a great deal for me. Beyond putting me in the company of similarly occupied and so sympathetic workers, as well as of stimulating colleagues in English and in related fields—and, perhaps more importantly, not so related—it has provided some official status for what I do, a kind of societal approval. The workshop also has obliged me to sharpen and to justify my own attitudes toward writing, to rationalize and articulate them. Thus it has ripened my awareness of what I am—or ought to be attempting to do. Able student writers also alert their elders to new possibilities by keeping them in touch with the immediate times. Often they challenge even an established writer's basic predilections. Accordingly, I agree with Berryman that, if such teaching is consuming and may seem at times too close to what one is personally doing, it is also nourishing and invigorating. The classroom then provides a potential shield against that isolation and consequent eccentricity to which many writers are prone.

The workshop constitutes a small, unique community. It does so by its size and concentration, and by the steady, cumulative ensemble playing of students and teacher as they come to know each other's special strengths as individuals and as writers and critics. Now and again the workshop produces results that transcend the classroom and its immediate lessons. Lively, enduring friendships, for instance, are formed. For rarely in our society do people live so closely and so intimately together; rarely do they share such common, progressive aims. Their intimacy increases as they learn to quarry and to reveal deeper and deeper parts of themselves and of the personal worlds in which they live.

To encourage discovery of those deeper parts, I find certain assignments (offered as options) to be pertinent and useful. (Of course, if a student has a writing head-of-steam on, I do not interrupt it. At times, however, most writers run dry; then exercises in translation or imitation can help.) A class, whether a beginning or advanced one, usually benefits from a round of assignments graduated in ambition and complexity; these may be concerned with content as well as form. For no matter how promising the young writers, they are often helped along by assignments aimed at extending their awareness of what has been—or can be—done in poetry. Such assignments also serve to amplify their realization, not only of the diverse resources buried in themselves, but also of the riches of the world at large (and at small) waiting to be tapped. All writers, young and old alike, need to exercise their senses. Most can afford to be reminded of this. Poets generally, even much-published older ones, rely mainly on seeing. Our present world, after all, is shaped by its great distances, its passivities, its attempts at objectivity, and its principal public media (eye-and-ear-focused purveyors of spectator life and sports). These elements encourage a strong if abstracted dependence on sight.

As a writer I, too, find such assignments valuable. For they also remind me of objects and methods to which habit tends to lull us. To up-scale the assignments, I move the students from local concentrations to larger, more complicated occasions. Finally, I urge them to attempt one of the major forms of our time; it is one that has much occupied me, namely, the *sequence*: a suite of poems bound by various often subtle, if not subterranean, ligatures. Practice in such a mode intensifies the students' sense of the potentiality and resourcefulness of their materials and themselves. Meantime, for each assignment (as a model, or *after* the students have tried their hands) I introduce published poems that have satisfied the assignment. I believe it sensible to keep young writers in good, not to say the best, possible company. (Conversely, they should be tested at times on poor pieces as well.) To ensure such valid company, it is important to require a good deal of reading of accomplished poets.

At the same time, students need to *read aloud*; they should read aloud their own poems, as well as those of others, as frequently as possible. Young poets, even gifted ones, generally read indifferently; often they pay little attention to their poem's sonant, syntactic, or expressive values. A poem does not fully come alive until it takes its shape on the air. A paper poem is a Lazarus waiting to be summoned forth; its embodied life depends strongly on this natural respiration. By his breath, the reader gives the poem voice and a voiced intelligence. Once students are alerted to such potentials, it is impressive and gratifying to see how quickly they expand their critical awareness and creative capacity. It is this growth that has kept me teaching poetry writing all these years, despite my initial skepticism of the workshop.

On the side of per-versities, it is true that some students are seized by the desire to become instant poets, to be published almost as soon as they begin to write. This is a basic problem: the lack, among English faculties and students alike, of adequate respect for the arduous, lifelong discipline genuine writing must be. Since we are—unlike our relation to the materials of painting and certainly composing—born to English, many of us think writing ought to be spontaneous; it ought hardly to be studied like a foreign language, say, or a science, or composing or playing an instrument. So why should the first lines one puts down not be poetry?

But, at the same time, poetry remains for most people remote and mysterious; hence they cannot believe it is teachable. Poets, they have heard and so assume, are born, not made. When some of these individuals skeptically ask, "Can you really teach students to write poetry?" I some-times counter with Goethe's reply to a question about what he would like his children to be taught—to wit, what cannot be taught. More often I say, "No, but I can teach them to rewrite." And with little prompting I gladly go on about the relevancy and pleasures of revision—and how much more it may finally matter than vision. That is, I can try to get students to respect at least the potentiality of what they are doing; in short, I try to move them to give what they have put down the application it deserves. This I do by keeping them at the same time in the presence of critical standards and of good, not to say great, poetry. My point is that preliminary to their becoming good poets, students must become good readers.

I should say that, whatever recurrent doubts I have about such teaching, I experience a change of heart each term when I see how astonishingly much students can and do learn. Thus I have long felt that were I an English department head (fortunately I am not) I would do my best to require one term of creative writing of all English majors. My idea would be not so much to make poets of them as to introduce them to the inner workings of poetry. One does not, as someone said, have to lay an egg, especially a golden one, to appreciate a fine omelet. Still, trying to lay it might intensify one's respect for the achievement. Students' efforts, if serious enough, are bound to extend their awareness of the painstaking accomplishment genuine poetry represents. More conventional English courses, no matter how splendidly taught, rarely bring students into such intimate relation with a work of art. And, who knows, such offerings might in liveliness even affect, if only by proximity, English faculty members. So I would, as English department head, try to involve as many colleagues as possible in the teaching of workshops.

But, as with all academic developments, especially once they have become established, problems or per-versities do accumulate; this is particularly true of writing programs. Aside from the glibness such workshops may encourage, writing faculties (particularly their younger members), to prove themselves, often feel obliged to produce quickly publishing writers. Some time ago the English man-of-letters Ian Hamilton, now best known for his biography of Robert Lowell, was giving readings and talks throughout the United States. Late in his tour, during his visit to Princeton, he cited, as one of the most extraordinary phenomena that he had met, all the busy credit collecting of the young poet-teachers. Their talk, according to Hamilton, centered on the magazines in which they were publishing and no less on their students' published efforts. To some considerable extent those teachers were simply responding to their universities' expectations. But such busyness and such often untimely publishing might well be questioned.

Fortunately or not, the very limitations of publishing tend to save students from themselves. But though in any large commercial sense students may be spared the pitfalls of premature exposure, swarms of little, thoroughly ephemeral magazines do indiscriminately gobble up vast amounts of so-called poetry. Such modest publishing may do little harm. Still, gifted students deserve to be warned that, since they can normally expect to live for some time, they should avoid becoming superficially professional and blasé. In short, before they burst on the world it would make good sense for them to become somebody. First they should have a substantial body of experience on which to draw. Workshops can provide a promising beginning, but only that. Just as introductory medical courses do not make full-fledged doctors, neither do workshops produce fully developed writers; young writers need to submit to a sufficient apprenticeship to their art. Obviously their development as feeling, thinking individuals is of the first importance. And while they are on campus, since poetry is made up of rather more than just the innards of the poet, they should take advantage of the cultural riches of the university.

Another potential per-versity to which the workshop is liable is imitation. The complaint that any university's workshops produce one style, so that all their writers' poems look anonymously alike, is sometimes relevant. Yet, it is a danger primarily if the style imitated is a very limited, highly idiosyncratic one. Precisely because of its fashionable cultivation of idiosyncrasy, such a style is bound to afford scant nourishment beyond its own devices. But usually a real poet recovers from such an experience. In the great medieval and renaissance art periods, young men apprenticed themselves to masters so dutifully that at times the apprentice's style could not be told from the master's, or vice versa. In fact, the master required such aesthetic submergence from his helpers. Yet, if the apprentice was a genuine artist, not only did he benefit fundamentally from his apprenticeship, but also once he was on his own he soon developed a personal style. Clearly, the test lies partially in the worth of the teacher, but it lies even more in the gifts and the capacity for growth of the student.

Beyond all this, one might ask what these several decades of poetry workshops have accomplished. It is a little early still for the results to be clearly tabulated. However, the fact that the university has become willy-nilly a major patron of the arts—the chief sanctuary for poets already well on their way—may be considered a positive happenstance. More person-ally, I have been an editor of a literary magazine for many years, as well as an editor for several university poetry-publishing series, and I can report that the amount of poetry being written has grown prodigiously. A poetry competition is likely to receive as many as 1,600 book manuscripts, and poetry magazines may expect thousands of submissions. Apparently there are many more writers of poetry than readers. This curious development suggests we may be breeding a new kind of poet: one who can write but not read. More to the point, the quality of the present work generally far exceeds that of the home-grown, amateurish efforts of twenty to thirsty years ago. And if it is difficult to discover an Ezra Pound or a Wallace Stevens in the jostling crowd, we can certainly relish the fact that, for the first time in the United States, hundreds of able, dedicated poets are hard at work. As far as I know, except maybe for historic periods in China, there has never before been so profuse a flowering of poets and poetry.

My favorite poem on this subject seems relevant here, Pound's "Cantico Del Sol." Pound worked more fervently than anyone, in his very American passion for culture, to broadcast the right reading list—that is, his version of the indispensable classics. Still he was self-aware enough to say:

> The thought of what America would be like
> If the Classics had a wide circulation
> Troubles my sleep.

Imagine what he and his sleep would have been like could Pound have known the consequences of his efforts: the wide circulation through the United States—if not of the classics—of poetry, or at least the frenetic attempts at writing it. Not often do we do more than we dream of doing. The sorcerer might well goggle before the antics, the sudsy waters over-flowing, of his countless apprentices!

# The Playwright on Campus

# A Personal View
# THE ACADEMY AND THE
# "YOU KNOW?" GENERATION

## James Ragan

In 1981 I agreed to teach playwriting in the University of Southern California's Professional Writing Program. I did so with much anticipation. After all, I had learned that William Inge had been a former and founding member of the playwriting faculty and that Friedrich Durrenmatt and Eugene Ionesco had only recently completed residencies there. Yet, even with the promise such tradition offered, I remained hesitant. I had been witnessing in the prose and poetry of so many contemporaries a dissolution of a marriage, a "falling out of love" with language. So I expected little gratification in attempting to revive the linguistic flame in graduate writing students who were products of the "You know?" generation. Their infatuation with media imagery was rapidly replacing their love for the written word.

To accept my new position I felt I had to reevaluate my need to participate in academe, a process that has led me by invitation to further investigation here. Let me begin by posing some broad personal observations on the state of language in the arts and by adding some historical perspective relevant to the problems I have encountered when addressing them in the classroom.

## I

Language by the masses from the 1960s to the present seems to have been enjoying a romance with minimalism while moving toward a popular illiteracy caused by public apathy to accurate communication in general. Society has given up any sense of responsibility for precision in words, spoken or written. Indeed, its love affair now is with the media arts or any new forms of communication synthesized by the classical electronic media—radio and film. The "New Mediaism"—television, video tapes and discs, audio books, personal computers, and the like, with their visual and audio contexts vastly improved by technology (witness the *Star Wars* cinematic special-effects boom in the past decade)—has replaced the written word as the nation's primary communication tool. The result has been a "semantic redux," or what playwright Edward Albee, in a recent visit to my class at USC, called a "semantic collapse" of language in America today.

Unfortunately, the stageplay has not escaped the semantic redux. Lately, I have been witnessing in drama (and all the arts) a phenomenon I call the "telegenic revivication" of language. This is a reconstitution of language promulgated by the media arts, which, ironically, in their exponential forms are the very sources contributing to language's decline. This dilemma in itself does not appear to be irreversible. But it does continue to pose the most significant challenge in the classroom, where more and more I find the New Mediaism exercising its telegenic influence on both spoken and written language. No single explanation will cover this erosion of proper word usage. Much of it may be due to a post-Kennedy anti-intellectualism: the nation's new life, reflected in a devolving language during the Johnson-Nixon years, proved media-inspired, script-annotated, and sound-simplified, and suitable for television's instant broadcast and audience consumption. Sadly enough, this new life was destined also for semantic disintegration. Like television's instant flashback, "instant imaging" became the vehicle for instant truth and gratification. This telegenic impulse to "instantize" or "formulize" the visual image at the expense of language has provided also the model for much of the mimetic new drama in the eighties; it is a drama weaned on media dialogue and dependent on "hi-tech visuals" and spectacle. Marshall McLuhan was correct in predicting that the electronic media would be "subtly and constantly altering our perceptual senses."

For the most part, I have found it difficult to convey my concerns to a new generation of graduate writers who have been weaned on television and the computer sciences. For them the technology of "instant imaging" has supplanted the polysemy of the written word. They comprise the "now" generation that has popularized the acceptance of cliché, double-speak, no-speak, the noncompleted simile "like...," and the interjected "You know?" as norms of minimalist communication. They literally have fallen in love with the technical virtuosity of the visual "close-up" rather than with metaphor. Because playwrights (like poets) rely so heavily on words as metaphor, I have found it imperative in my opening lectures to confront the issue of language directly.

My course on the "Principles of Dramatic Structure" is an advanced workshop limited to eight students each semester. Hence I am able to work with a select group of promising playwrights, several of whom entered the class with stage credits. They have won Lorraine Hansberry playwriting awards, showcased off-Broadway, or had successful regional productions; in short, these are people who take their playwriting seriously. Many then earn a seat in Jerome Lawrence's master class in order to have their plays performed in his successful "Octet" stage readings. Several even get to compete in our nationally recognized USC One-Act Play Festival, where judges as various as Paul Zindel, Arthur Hiller, Mark Rydell, and Piper Laurie come to critique their work.

With such outlets for their creativity, they might be expected to experiment and take chances. They do not. In fact, as more and more student writers come to a campus where, in the past, reevaluations of classical structures were the building blocks to bold experimentation, their expectations are directed increasingly at the glamorous New Mediaism. Unfortunately, their collective "originality" also appears to feed upon the worn plots and characters culled from television or rock videos. Their plays (like so many recent novels) are being written with a film or MOW (Movie of the Week) foremost in their minds. Their writing heroes generally are Judith Krantz and Jackie Collins, and their structural models are action-spectacle dramas or musicals (*Cats*, *La Cage aux Folles*, or *42nd Street*) simply because these works make it to pay dirt—the miniseries or the great "Broad Way." Their plays are not intended to disturb so much as they are intended to pacify. The result is their greater acceptance of mediocrity.

Ironically, the response of these same students to my concerns tends to be positive. I have found "telegenic revivication" or "semantic redux" a good point from which to launch the workshop, since either addresses the immediate problems confronting potential writers in a post-bookreading culture. My students often want to achieve instant success and gratification without benefit of a *craft*. As a rule, these new writers are more ambitious, competitive, and entrepreneurial than their predecessors; they are also less patient and less experienced both in artistic sensitivity and sensibility. Unfortunately, while most can learn sensibility (craft) in the classroom, some have arrived there without the sensitivity so vital to artistic creation and vision. Many wish to substitute tricks, "high concepts," or gimmickry for craft. (Has not much current drama done the same?) They want to achieve their goals with as much expediency and as little creative pain as possible. Instant gratification is best, they believe, and for obvious media-inspired reasons. For our McLuhanesque media society has influenced would-be writers to believe that the condensed or abbreviated version of anything is best. They see less craft as better—and more in keeping with their all-purpose "You know?" minimalist response. Their slang identifies them. A popular fifties word like "cool"—which developed in the sixties to "deep," in the seventies to "heavy," in the eighties to "awesome"—has now been reduced to "unbe" (short and minimalist for "unbelievable") or "rad" (for "radical"). Indeed, these last two are appropriate abbreviations for our rock-video culture.

This, then, has been the essence of my dilemma: how to place metaphor legitimately back on the written page and by performance back on the stage. I also have had to decide whether to stay on as permanent director of the Professional Writing Program after agreeing originally to act only on an interim basis. I have John Rechy, David Scott Milton, Robert Pirosh, and the late William Goyen to thank for encouraging me to accept the permanent position. I am grateful to them, because they have placed me among the finest faculty people I have ever known.

## II

I cannot deny an inexplicable need to create an academic forum for a new kind of playwright's workshop. I envisioned one that would bring language and metaphor (rather than spectacle and special effects) once more to the forefront of the stage performance. I also thought that by teaching an imaginatively conceived course in playwriting I would be confronting the question of unchecked illiteracy. I was thinking principally of our many student playwrights who soon would graduate and move on to disturb and educate an apathetic and escapist public. Had not Jonathan Kozol, in his book *Illiterate America*, documented the sad fact that one-third of contemporary America is illiterate or semiliterate? Should this illiteracy not be a fundamental concern of the playwright-as-artist, when the very basis of his craft—his language—runs the risk of being mismanaged, misappropriated, and misunderstood? Poet William Carlos Williams had warned that corruption in language portended an inevitable corruption of morality in government.

I now realize I was not alone in my pedagogic idealism. I had returned to academe after working as a screenwriter at Paramount Pictures, where I was under contract to Albert S. Ruddy Productions (producer of *The Godfather*). Proud of being a serious writer of poetry and drama, and considering myself singularly committed to literary quality, I nurtured strong concerns about the future of "artistry" in writing. But I soon found there were other playwrights—fledgling and accomplished alike—challenging head-on the same issues of language and craft. Still, I realized that posing the challenge to the New Mediaist student was not enough. I had to become convinced the academic classroom could provide him stylistic and substantive answers.

Another factor in my remaining in the classroom has been my conviction that Los Angeles is capable of becoming the center of the nation's arts by the turn of the century. I am convinced also that by virtue of its distinguished professional faculty the University of Southern California can serve as the core of this region's cultural conscience. But more fundamental questions continue to haunt me; these relate to my own motives for wanting to believe the university can play so culturally important a role. For example, what was it that led me and others like me who believe still in the principles of artistic integrity openly to embrace a university? For it is the university itself, through its conventions of specialization and provincialism, that has been largely responsible for a kind of self-generating literary inwardness. After all, academe, with the best of intentions, trains writers to become teachers of writers, who in turn become teachers of other writers, who then turn out even more teachers of writers. This academic process produces instructors rather than artists with a knowledge of craft based on a hands-on, multidisciplinary approach to writing and life experience.

After much reflection, I now believe that there is one dominant explanation for the many insistent causes that drive the conscientious writer into the academy. I think this situation developed primarily during the sixties. For in that decade the New Mediaism inadvertently contributed to a mass movement to university campuses of nonmediaist writers. Some came to escape the rape and aberrations of language, others for economic reasons. In either event, it was they who then in the seventies contributed to the proliferation of writing programs—perhaps the last holdouts for true literary or "premise" writing across America. At first I chose to think that such migrations resulted from a selfless desire by writers to protect the purity of language and the literary crafts from the dollar-inspired pseudo-artistry hyped by television, the newest medium on the block. However, a little deliberation moved me to conclude that this migration was also a response to the recent emergence of an unlikely counterculture group called appropriately the "leisure class"; its interest in the media and in fifty-cent popular paperbacks had provided the impetus for a book explosion unparalleled in American letters. The clones of Rod McKuen and Leonard Cohen joined those of Jacqueline Susann and Harold Robbins to become the new interpreters and communicators of language and, indeed, of the entire New Mediaist culture.

By the eighties the campus version of this culture had become a matter of pure economics, as university writing programs proved the new "in" subject in Yuppie career preparation. Clearly an aesthetic dichotomy confronted the writers who took up the challenge and explored the possibilities of the media. Even as playwrights turned TV and film writers, some of them defended the integrity of their art against the creeping Mediamania. Their need for artistic integrity emanated from deep inner tensions and visions. I was quick to include myself in the latter group, and I knew that my play-writing colleagues at USC were inclined to do the same. Jerome Lawrence, William Goyen, John Rechy, David Scott Milton, James Leo Herlihy, and Donald Freed—all veterans of the Broadway and off-Broadway stages—proved unflinching allies in "my cause." More than once they responded beyond the call of their academic duties to deplore publicly the lack of subject-worthy plays on the nation's professional stages. A return to universality of subject is what film- and television-actor Raymond Burr had in mind when he asked me to write the play "Commedia" (or "Ardor Under the Arbor"). He then produced it in San Francisco as an attempt to resurrect the commedia dell'arte tradition, a lost art form whose moral purpose is suggested by the blending of contemporary and mythical materials. In researching the form, I discovered how much Samuel Beckett, Eugene Ionesco, and several of the absurdist playwrights were influenced by this tradition.

## III

This worthy-subject idea proved to be yet another major pedagogic hurdle. Students reasoned that anything they found "interesting" was worthy of dramatization. Few saw the need for the moral premise or universal insight. Scenario after scenario was flawed by a lack of originality and, by extension, a lack of artistic vision. My "solution" was to conclude the opening lecture of my Principles of Dramatic Structure class with a request that each student submit a "premise" page; this statement was to delineate the germ of an idea emotionally charged and deriving from some deep pain in the gut as much as from the mind. I considered it important for the new writer of plays to connect his or her own experience to a more general human experience—that is, to consummate aesthetically a marriage of the private to the public mythos. I wanted him to strive for those levels of human truth, those subjects of universality that have perplexed, mortified, or simply intrigued generations of playwrights and audiences. Lajos Egri, in his *The Art of Dramatic Writing*, a book I recommend (along with Aristotle's *Poetics*) in my course, refers to such universality as the basis for any true dramatic premise. For example, the premise in *MacBeth* is "Ruthless ambition leads to self-destruction." But too often the beginning playwright formulates a plot that lacks even the germ of a premise. He mistakes the "situation" of a plot for his premise, and he finds himself telling a fair enough story while failing to move the audience on any cathartic or emotionally responsive level.

When I was invited to sit in on Jerome Lawrence's first master class of the semester, I was pleased to hear him echo in his introductory remarks the exact sentiments I had been advocating. First, Jerry confirmed my own conviction that most of the plays then on the national stages were not subject-worthy. In addition, he called on each student playwright to begin his every drama by responding to his own deepest feelings. The student was to dramatize only those issues that matter not only to the individual but also to society at large. In effect, Jerry Lawrence wished his students to connect the artist's private mythos to a discerning public's more universal concerns. Thus from the co-writer (with Robert E. Lee) of such classic plays as *Inherit the Wind*, *First Monday in October*, and *The Night Thoreau Spent in Jail*, I received welcome affirmation of my own belief that responsible artists still cared about what the theater had to offer. There were still creative people who cared about moral purpose as artistic premise, and who were not swayed by the promised fame and wealth of the video and special-effects revolution. A similar concern for the efficacy of art was expressed publicly by John Rechy, whose New York–bound play, *Tigers Wild* (adapted from his novel *The Fifth Angel*), was previewed recently in Los Angeles. After several audience members had praised the tightness of his plot structure and the metaphorical levels of his language, John warned against the reductivist tendencies of today's dramatists. Too many carelessly or cynically simplify their artistic intentions and allow drama to fall into the minimalist trap. This reaffirmed my own view that current playwrights often provide mere spectacle at the expense of substance; they give the audience only what it wants (or recognizes from the small or big screen), and thereby deny their own personal vision.

Clearly the video revolution launched in the fifties helped push these two playwrights (as well as other established playwrights, poets, and novelists) into the universities for intellectual sustenance and asylum. In the eighties many more of this country's most successful playwrights are turning to the universities as a means of protecting their creative balance and artistic integrity. Like Lawrence and Rechy, such campus-based playwrights as Edward Albee, Mark Medoff, Jean Claude Van Itallie, Paul Zindel, Robert E. Lee, Murry Medwick, and Marsha Norman are striving in classrooms and on stages to nurture and champion the playwright's craft. For a return to craft is the one pedagogic mandate they all have found crucial for the future of serious theater. While certainly not all student playwrights have embraced the shlock-art plots and characters of television, rock videos, or action-spectacle films, most of them seem content to share in the popular neglect of the true dramatist's craftmanship.

I was a different young writer. When I arrived at USC, I brought with me all my cultural idealism. I planned to put a sense of craft back into every student's regimen and the word "artist" into his working vocabulary. But some still deeper, more fundamental impulse was troubling me. I felt a need to justify my presence in the university. At one time playwrights had populated New York's lofts and studios for artistic community; now I had personal reasons for turning to the academy, and not the least of these was financial security. But there was also the fact that Los Angeles, like many other urban centers, was fast replacing New York as the major setting for the most promising experimental work the theater had to offer. Most significantly, perhaps, many successful playwrights were finding the academy a satisfying hedge against the increasing New Mediaist pressures of Manhattan's commercial stages. The eastern theatrical Establishment now was attempting to resolve the largely self-inflicted new dilemma of having nearly priced itself off its own stages. But playwrights wanted to resolve the self-imposed old dilemma of the apparent conflict between their practical and artistic needs. I could relate to this latter problem, since it evoked still another old issue: How does one survive professionally without sacrificing artistic integrity? For the New Mediaist student, however, this did not appear to be a grave concern.

## IV

To further my own understanding of the role of the contemporary artist, I felt it necessary to address certain philosophic questions posed for the artist by society. I began with the aesthetic tensions governing the human psyche that Nietzsche in the *Birth of Tragedy* and later Freud in *Civilization and Its Discontents* referred to as the "antagonistic roles" of Dionysius and Apollo. For I found the same dichotomy in my separate roles as a citizen and as a teacher. Often I attempt in my lectures to illustrate the significance for the artist of this tension. I allude then to Pentheus (Euripides' *The Bacchae*); his conflict between "the chaos of the passions and the order of reason" exemplifies that existing between the writer's "lived" life outside the academy and the "relieved" life within. To the artist the *passions* attached to the chaotic "real world" have always conflicted with the idealized *reason* celebrated by the academy.

I am not reluctant to place such philosophic concerns before a play-wright's workshop. I wish to remind its students of the importance of these issues to contemporary theater. But would-be playwrights today seem not to understand the significance of this passions-versus-reason tension when they write their plays. Yet it is what Erich Heller described recently as "the wilderness of luxuriating darkness" at odds with the "designs of the mind's urbanity." More specifically, it is the chaos of the practical world versus the order of the academy. And order is the very aspect of creativity the students need most, yet are apt to deny. Craft is the best means of achieving that order, and Aristotelian structure is still its most effective form. Therefore, I devote a major portion of workshop time to working out in each student play several time-tested Aristotelian structural principles. These include *exposition*, in which the situation, protagonist, and conflict are introduced; the *rising action*, wherein tension is built up through *complications* exacerbated by the antagonist's role in the action; then the *climax*—the highest crisis point of the plot where protagonist and antagonist meet in inevitable confrontation. We deal also with the *denouement* of the action; this is the turning point that occurs when the protagonist's "epiphany" plunges the plot downward in a *falling action*; this is also the beginning of the end, as it were, of the protagonist's pursuit of his goal. Finally, we pinpoint the *resolution* or outcome of the protagonist's pursuit. ("Epiphany" signifies the protagonist's moment of self-recognition. It is the most widely neglected principle in the beginning dramatist's craft, despite the fact that its neglect often eliminates any possibility of the audience's achieving emotional catharsis.) If, through the centuries, some playwrights have deviated from these structural principles, the modern student of the *Poetics* still should recognize the importance of Aristotle's tenets to the initial outlining of his plot.

These are but a few of the ordering principles in the construction of any sound play. What students fail to grasp, I find, is that a drama or comedy is based on conflict. Hence I point out that conflict should be rendered on the *overt* and *covert* levels. (Oedipus's overt conflict is to end the plague on Thebes. His murder of his father is the covert conflict or hidden motivation precipitating his later actions.) Students even tend to forget that a play must have a beginning, middle, and end (but not necessarily in that order). This basic Aristotelian principle often goes unheeded by those who fail to see plays as having either a "linear" organization (Ibsen's *Hedda Gabler*) or "spatial" structure (Miller's *Death of a Salesman*). I emphasize also that the playwright must "hook" his audiences by making them *care* about the protagonist and his fate. This is where the premise comes in: being the philosophic or moral stance taken by the playwright, it should speak to the audience on a universal level. But it requires the playwright to have developed his personal vision (private mythos) so that through it he can portray the more public or "universal" level of truth (public mythos). These are only several of the many points I—and my students—develop and discuss in the name of craft (and with some inevitable name-dropping). We do so by a close page-by-page examination of each student play. Structuring a play, every neophyte playwright discovers, is not a simple task. The process often requires the help and involvement of actors and directors in the Playwright's Workshop or master class before the student writer achieves the fullest realization of his work. In short, the student realizes that the creative process is a slow and complex mixing of imaginative, philosophic, and practical elements.

## V

With each passing year, society appears to submit increasingly to the pressures for minimalist media awareness and response. I sympathize with any serious "struggling artist," especially the student writer, bullied by the media's mandates for escapist entertainment. I feel universities have always protected the ambitious writer from his Dionysian half. I refer to that chaotic and passionate self so emotionally prepared to swallow whole the popular view of the world. The academy, however, tugs at his Apollonian half; it urges him to exert his reason and to beware the Philistines and be saved artistically. Writers appear to be experiencing this dualism most acutely since the advent of the New Mediaism. This dichotomy may be related to the demise of metaphor. I now believe the Apollonian order imposed by academe may offer the artist his best chance of returning metaphor to the written page: the classroom engenders in teacher and student a recognition of metaphor's power through an orderly reading of dramatic works.

More specifically, I attempt to place metaphor back on the playing stage by referring my playwriting students to a 1941 essay by Delmore Schwartz on "The Isolation of Modern Poetry." In it, Schwartz, a seasoned poet and university teacher, argued that in the twentieth century "the only life available to the man of culture has been the cultivation of his own sensibility; that is the only subject available to him if we may assume that a poet can only write about subjects of which he has an absorbing experience in every sense." I agree. At a time when society—or its government—generally ignores the needs of its artists, the academy appears to offer the most appropriate forum for the cultivation of aesthetic sensibility. Schwartz is reminding his readers that true artistic development comes hard; he is underscoring the sad fact that the modern artist writes as he must and not as he might have were he living in a society that provided him access to a range of subjects beyond himself. I, too, have found that a majority of my students have had a limited access to a range of experience outside themselves. One result is that they feel compelled to write only of what they think the audience wants or dictates. Yes, there are an enlightened few who share Schwartz's vision. Indeed Schwartz, according to Richard Ellman, was "concerned with divisions within his own consciousness—between the *apprehending self* and the baffling *exterior world* with which the self must come to terms." I find this tension to be still the major cause of writer's block for the maturing artist, and it remains the stumbling block with which the beginning writer is least equipped to cope. The truth that emerges is clear: the more the writer *lives in the world*, the more mature his vision.

Still, there remains an element of the Kafkaesque in this approach to writing—and living. For the exterior world around us can be so hostile and without order that an ordering principle imposed by the apprehending self is needed to give life meaning. Wars, crimes, and personal tragedies abound. Art has always provided that ordering principle by interpreting through the imagination the extremes of human passion. But the art inspired by the New Mediaism has lost its basic integrity and interpretive powers. This loss of aesthetic integrity seems to have occurred during the seventies. Before that time (in the Kennedy sixties), our universities nurtured a limited, perhaps, but nonetheless an energetic audience open to the experimental. Recently, the award-winning playwright Edward Albee visited the Professional Writing Program at USC as the William Inge Residency Lecturer. On several occasions he discussed these very issues. He spoke bluntly: coincident with the election of Richard Nixon, our society began an intellectual and artistic retreat. There surfaced in America an understanding "that reality and total consciousness may be just a little bit more than what is safe to participate in." This attitude, said Albee, helps explain the retreat of the post-Vietnam and Watergate theater public from the realities of "lived" life to the "relieved" life of escapist entertainment. This cultural shift may explain as well the artist's retreat to the "relieved" life of the academy. Total consciousness of and participation in reality have always been at the root of the artist's struggle for truth. Traditionally, the creative artist has needed a place of privacy and order away from the irrational Dionysian world. Yet danger lurks in academe: he who elects to live totally in the "relieved" life and who elects not to engage in the "lived" life trades his fantasy for pedantry. He risks intellectualizing his life, his passions, even his art.

In flatter terms, the playwright-as-artist experiences a division of consciousness between the Apollonian apprehending self and the Dionysian exterior world. Thus he (or she) is confronted with the predicament of wanting to create a drama of ideas while living a life of passionately personal experience. Recent dramatists have sought to resolve this dilemma by moving to the academy (at least part time), because it is a place of enforced order—albeit more of the mind than the body. After all, it is reason and order that cultivate the artist's sensibilities, and, by extension, his craft. As to the body, the carnal and drinking reputations of writers on campus seem to suggest that any enforced order at times breaks down. In such instances, the artist appears to be insisting that the passions of his personal life, whether on or off campus, provide his most deeply felt subject matter. Richard Ellman points out that many recent artists have refused to choose the basic options offered by the world and the academy. Instead, they have "attempted the final transcendence"—as did Delmore Schwartz—by accepting "the famous charge that America is the land of happy tragedies." Dylan Thomas also fits this stereotype of tragic inevitability, as do F. Scott Fitzgerald, Thomas Wolfe, and Tennessee Williams. Today dramatists and poets are increasingly reluctant to accept the artist's traditional role of alienated outsider. They prefer to accept instead the image of America transmitted by the New Mediaism as the land of "tragic happiness." This image of instant escapism was created by the television world of "Dynasty" and "Dallas," and too many writers eagerly embrace it, both emotionally and intellectually.

I do not wish to be misunderstood. I am not inclined to deny the academy's intellectual and cultural shortcomings. But I am convinced that the university does help the artist to resolve the struggle with his psyche. It provides the last bastion for serious premise writing for any playwright whose work derives from his personal vision of truth. After all, the "populist" vision, hustled by media hype, is well and thriving outside the academy. Take, for example, the frequency with which Judith Krantz's books appear on the national top-ten best-seller list and the rare appearance there of a book by a Saul Bellow. Note, on the Broadway stage, the prominence of an Andrew Lloyd Webber musical as opposed to the more substantive dramas of Peter Shaffer or Samuel Beckett. More than ever before, there is a division in our collective artistic consciousness. Serious writers experience an emotional and intellectual tension when attempting to function in that performance world the media now dominate. Finding it almost impossible to deal aesthetically with the chaotic societal elements of the "baffling exterior world," the sensitive artist struggles to reduce them to order within the confines of the academy.

But the New Mediaism does not make this adjustment easy. Lately the artist's desire for personal order has been less and less realized, because all human conflicts appear "resolved" for us in current media art forms. Television's structured dilemmas and its instant news, as well as Hollywood's escapist or revisionist impulses (*Rambo*), may suggest order. But in fact they only heighten man's darker inclinations toward disorder. This may be another reason why playwrights have turned to the academy. Happily or unhappily for them, they encounter there an order imposed by a bureaucratic overlay of workshops and curricula, formal lectures and faculty committees. Still, some writers satisfy on campus their Apollonian need as "apprehending selves" to function in a formalized setting or institution. (Note the irony of this term when related to Robert Lowell, Sylvia Plath, or Delmore Schwartz.) These writers have placed themselves among students in a classroom where limitations are placed on their own Dionysian impulses. There the serious and gifted artist can strive to apprehend his world as he must rather than merely as he might have.

At a recent conference in San Diego, several colleagues (including screenwriter Robert Pirosh, playwright Donald Freed, and film director Ivan Passer) grappled with a concern I had voiced. I suggested that the playwright—and by extension the screenwriter—must write the "truth" as he sees it, for himself and not for the audience. He must dramatize *his* vision as opposed to what the audience wants to see. We focused primarily on how screenwriters now viewed this premise. It had become clear that "writing for the audience" long had been the dominant approach of screenwriting students in the academy. More recently, the New Mediaism, with its commercial orientation, had been "subtly and constantly altering" the literary inclinations of its writers. To what degree, we asked, had the writing teacher or professional-as-teacher supported this tendency? Are we in the academy teaching students to give the audience what it wants? Or are we teaching them to be creative purveyors of universal truths—no matter how nonremunerative or noncommercial that stance may prove? Can we, should we, be teaching again the distinction between a serious novel and a pulp novel? We may feel that Saul Bellow has earned his place in the classroom, but should Jackie Collins—now so broadly accepted—be allowed entry?

## VI

Several years ago, in *Esquire* or *The Atlantic*, a writer argued that there may be no major novelists today—no one writing on the literary level of a Proust or Faulkner or Joyce. In my playwriting classes I, too, feel an increasing need to advocate serious or "premise" writing as opposed to commercial or "nonpremise" writing. I say "need" with some surprise, as ten years ago I could not have imagined defending such "literary" writing. Let me repeat: premise writing, simply stated, contains at all times the writer's clearly delineated moral or philosophic stance. The absence of premise can be seen most predictably in films, especially pulp films. However, the premise also has been increasingly absent in recent drama. Edward Albee contends that were a mirror held up to our theater audiences, they would prefer it to be a distorting funhouse mirror. He is unhappy that playwrights in this country are encouraged and rewarded far better for lying to people than for telling the truth. Ironically, in Russia, where my play *Commedia* was produced recently by Anatoly Elizarov, I was surprised to find that a strong dramatic premise is considered crucial.

The artistic distortion to which Albee refers seems to have long been the special purview of escapist films, but this approach has become increasingly evident in drama as well. Film critics acknowledge readily the clear difference between, say, a *Chariots of Fire* and a *Smokey and the Bandit*. In class, we refer to this difference as between the premise "A" film and nonpremise "B" film, and we extend the distinction to drama as well. For, sadly enough, both the television situation comedy and drama have polluted the traditionally cliché-free space of the stage. Now plays like *The Crucible* or *The Glass Menagerie* are passed over for Michael Frayn–type comedies that rely on B-level nonvisionary situations and actions. Even Neil Simon manages on occasion to sustain a classical structure strongly dependent on an underlying premise. At one time I believed one should not attempt to compare the quality and artistic integrity of playwriting and screenwriting. After all, Irwin Panofsky and Susan Sontag had established the aesthetic dissimilarities between the stage's "static art" and the film's "fluid art." I contended then that each film needed to be justified as art, while a drama should never have to be justified. In those days the world—that is, the street or the park or the soapbox—provided potential stages for all forms of theater—mime, guerrilla, opera, "living," or verse. In recent years, however, the stage, like life, has been changing.

The recent popularity of writing programs has created a fierce all-out competitive search for students to populate the classrooms. Simply to survive, such programs are forced to extol the virtues and potentials of the New Mediaism. There are too many programs, too many writers (and writer-teachers), and too many bad results. One may argue that such needless proliferation stems from the nation's current escapist mentality or the hustle-hype of the New Mediaism. It hardly matters: the sad fact remains that the American audience now readily accepts less quality in its art. Indeed, it embraces an inordinate degree of mediocrity as it contentedly assents to its transformation into an escapist and an aesthetically nondemanding society.

Reasons for social or cultural changes are not always easy to determine. For example, we do not have to accept one historian's partial explanation for the downfall of Roman civilization. He claimed that once satire was banned on the stages, the people lost their ability to laugh at themselves. Now I do not expect our civilization to collapse in the near future—at least not while paradigmatic figures like John Rambo are defending our way of life. Still, it may be that our society has become too comfortable laughing *with* and not *at* itself. We Americans appear to accept the world's present ills as if they were the norm and not aberrations, and as if they all have their origins elsewhere. Box-office guardians today expect playwrights to entertain but not disturb us. Most television offerings reinforce this attitude. No one seems prepared to take individual responsibility for the withering of moral and cultural values. This attitude is clearly evident in our society's response to its drama. Not surprisingly, many social critics label us the "turned off" society. Ours is the world's only democratic society whose youth, as Edward Albee points out, are not at the political-intellectual forefront. They are not at their society's cutting edge, Albee observes, because they are not the children of metaphor. Having been seduced by escapism and distortion, by instant gratification and minimalism, they have lost any sense of responsibility for precise communication. Albee explains that historically "we are the only animal who consciously has taken the metaphor to identify ourselves to ourselves, to identify consciousness to ourselves. We have a responsibility to metaphor. It is a part of our evolutionary process."

However, there may be an interesting turn in all these events. Whereas the quality of playwriting has grown somewhat uneven in recent years, screenwriting as a craft has somehow risen in quality; at least it has done so in terms of what film at its best allows. Perhaps some of the positive cinematic impulses have come from a concern in the academy for film as art. I refer specifically to those campus workshops in screenwriting that stress the "premise" levels of writing. Such concern is evident in graduate-degree programs—like my own Professional Writing Program, where strong attention is paid to screenwriting as both an art and a craft. Admittedly, serious dramatic film is still not living up to its full potential, and neither is comedy. Indeed, comedy in many current films appears to be little more than "Saturday Night Live" television sketches transformed to the big screen. I have developed this situation into a class lecture that has proved increasingly popular with my students.

Some years back, Richard Corliss, in a *Time* magazine review, rightly lamented that in the prior two decades movie directors and writers had "snapped the straight spine of traditional drama into a series of vertebral vignettes." Lately, I have come to the same conclusion about the stage. I see the "Saturday Night Live" reductive method gradually infiltrate the subject matter of drama and work its telegenic minimalism on the typical stageplay. Classical dramatic forms are lost as more and more plays depend for audience acceptance on a parade of short scenes interspersed with punch lines and pratfalls. The standard comedy structure, Corliss points out, "gave way to anthologies of slapstick punctuated by expletives. The story became so much dead air between explosions of pain and laughter." As a result, the Bill Murray–type films and much current screenwriting— especially in comedy (*Stripes, Caddyshack,* and *Vacation*)—offer little more than expanded versions of "Saturday Night Live" sketches; they exemplify "telegenic revivication" of language and craft at its most obvious.

Michael Frayn's latest plays, *Black and Silver* and *The New Quixote,* are good recent examples of television situation comedies transferred to the stage. An actor describing his role in *The Unvarnished Truth,* a play by Royce Ryton, reveals its one-dimensional plot. He plays, he declares, "a frantic literary agent of a murder-mystery playwright. The bodies of accidentally murdered women start piling up in his house. It's a true farce— people coming in, confusion, fast-forward movement." A listener need only substitute "situation comedy" for "farce" to grasp what is happening: the "Disease of the Week" television movie has now become the "Malady of the Month" stageplay. Even widely praised Broadway plays like *Children of a Lesser God* and *As is* (a play about AIDS) were inspired by television movies of the week. Obviously, the theater must rethink its purpose and its goals. It has to refrain from competing with—much less imitating—the New Mediaism's telegenic impulses. The impetus for this reevaluation can only begin at the university level.

## VII

I am reminded of what the late Richard Hugo wrote about creative writing classes. "I believe worthwhile things can't be justified," he observed. "I would never try to justify sex, fishing, baseball or Mozart. My Grandfather used to say that some whiskey is better than others, but there is no bad whiskey. That might well apply to sex and Mozart. They seem to be in a class of their own." Hugo then added: "Creative Writing classes seem better put in a class with fishing and baseball. I've had bad fishing. I've seen and played bad baseball and I've seen and taught bad creative writing classes." Hugo's words have an authoritative ring, but then the same things have been said about drama, past and present. Some of Shakespeare's plays are better than others, but there is no truly bad Shakespeare. The same, I feel, can be said of a host of playwrights—Ibsen, Chekhov, Shaw, Miller, Williams, and Pinter, among others. They comprise a class all their own. Film and television, however, belong in a class with fishing and baseball. Lately, I have been seeing both badly played. My deeper concern is that I also have seen a lot of drama both badly played and crafted. In the arts as in life, the future lies with the coming generation of creative minds. Hence in drama the future belongs not to the children of the "You know?" generation but to the children of metaphor.

Tennessee Williams liked to quote a William Saroyan observation "that purity of heart is the one success worth having. . . . In the time of your life—live! That time is short and it doesn't return again. It is slipping away while I write this and while you read it, and the monosyllable of the clock is LOSS, loss, loss, unless you devote your heart to its opposition." This is the primary message I hope to leave to my student playwrights at the end of each workshop. Live! Live! And Write!

# The Novelist on Campus

# A Personal View
# THE "REAL LIFE" FALLACY

## *David Madden*

IN my first published novel, *The Beautiful Greed*, based on my experiences as a teen-age merchant seaman, there is a scene in which the young writer who has gone to sea to experience real life in the raw is reading E. M. Forster's *A Passage to India*. A deckhand ambles into the fo'c's'le. "That book's junk—it's a bunch of bull! *You* ever been to India? Well, I have. I know every bar and whorehouse in every port in India!" In real life and in my novel, I told him that there was more to India than bars and whorehouses. But I was on that ship bound for India because I shared with that deckhand and with the general public, and with most students, teachers, and writers, the assumption that the serious writer must gather his raw material from real life as an eyewitness in pursuit of a higher journalism. This assumption asserts that real life is the kind of life rendered in realistic detail in novels characterized by the term realism: life in the fields or in the mean streets, in hard labor in an unjust system, in crime, drugs, sex, violence, political corruption, war, aimless travel, Life on the Road, decidedly not life in a parlor in Amherst, Massachusetts.

From this real-life assumption there follows the charge that "Life in the university is not really real life." Although my own life, my writing, and my teaching seem to offer a host of contradictions, I declare both the assumption and the charge to be fallacious.

### I

It is not because I have had no other life that I make my sometimes contrary declarations about the writer in the university. I have had plenty of experiences in both the real and the unreal worlds. I was born and raised in a poor family in Knoxville, in Appalachian East Tennessee. I was a thief, I was a rebel in school, I was often suspended, I failed the ninth grade, never made above a C in English, never read a book until I was thirteen. My boyhood friends and my older and younger brothers served terms in reform schools and in state and federal prisons, with the likes of James Earl Ray. My family and my environment richly endowed me with all the raw material that novels of realism thrive on. I drew on that raw material to write my "poor family" novel *Bijou* and my con man novel *Pleasure Dome*.

Before I ventured to the Mecca of small-town writers, New York City, when I was nineteen, I held numerous dust-jacket jobs, starting at age nine: beanpicker, paperboy, curbhop, movie usher, delivery boy, busboy, elevator boy, baker's helper, file clerk. In Greenwich Village, I tried the community of artists just as Bohemia was dying—Maxwell Bodenheim in a trenchcoat selling his poems broadsheet in San Remo's. I sailed as a merchant seaman to Panama, Chile, Aruba, Hawaii. And so with my first novel, I contradict what I want to declare here—for *The Beautiful Greed* is a subject-dominated novel, a sea novel, based on my own real-life experiences. My army novel has been in outline for ten years. During the McCarthy-Korea era, I refused to sign a loyalty oath and the army exiled me to Alaska. If I want it, there it is, real-life raw material, with complex political implications.

In pursuit of my fitful academic career, I went to San Francisco State College, as it was called then, drawn to another literary community, North Beach and the Beatniks, at the time when Ginsberg's *Howl* was on trial. I had hitchhiked back and forth across the continent many times. Jack Kerouac's *On The Road* struck me as routine use of familiar raw material. I found the Beats strangely conformist and boring. I was writing a novel that would take me fifteen years to finish—*Cassandra Singing*. For me then and now, the important thing was not that it was true to my life but true to my imagination—none of the characters is drawn directly from my real-life experiences; all the events are dreamed up, made up, imagined.

Did *I* learn to write in writing workshops? Walter Van Tilburg Clark was, we all agreed, a saint, but he simply rephrased with conviction what I already knew. I got a fellowship to study playwriting at Yale Drama School with John Gassner, but in writing thirty plays on my own from age twelve, I had already learned the techniques that excellent man taught there.

After living for a year in one of the world's most fascinating cities, I turned my back on real life and began to teach—at Appalachian State Teachers College, in the mountains of North Carolina at Boone, highest town in the East. But I still had an imagination and it continued to work on *Cassandra Singing*, mostly in the summers. From there to Yale Drama School, from there to Centre College, Danville, Kentucky, for two years, on to the University of Louisville for two years, teaching writing for the first time, then to work on *The Kenyon Review* and to teach writing for two years, then to Ohio University for two years, ending up as writer-in-residence at Louisiana State University, a job casually offered me at MLA in 1968. For sixteen years, I have taught there only one course every other semester, on proportionate pay.

So I have been out of circulation in the real world for twenty-five years, half of my real life. But if I was no longer out there gathering experiences like a cosmic newspaper reporter, I still had an imagination, out of which came thirty-two books—novels, short stories, poems, stageplays, movie scripts, reviews, essays, critical books, and textbooks. If what I have written was engendered in a cloistered atmosphere, none of it has remained in the files; everything that I have merely imagined has proved relevant to the lives of readers out there in the workaday world: the sea captain who told me my sea novel was the most authentic he had ever read; the nurse who told me she uses my *Playboy* story "The Day the Flowers Came" to teach other nurses the five classic stages of grief; the motorcyclist who told me that I, who have never ridden a motorcycle, describe the experience perfectly; the ninety-year-old author of the Hardy Boys books who told me *Bijou* is about *his* childhood; the murderer on death row who told me my imagined story about a college kid moved him deeply; the Chinese, Hindus, and Poles who have heard from me over the Voice of America, though I have not heard from them. Whether my fiction is based on personal experience in the real world or created almost entirely out of imagination, the responses are the same: I am told that I "tell it like it is." Ungrateful to real life, I declare that I owe it all to my imagination.

I have gone then from the smokestack of poverty to the garret of Manhattan to the Ivy Tower, but I am happy as a Holy Roller to testify that I have never left the Ivory Tower of art. For though I was raised in the oral storytelling tradition of the southern mountains, and was influenced by images of Hollywood movies and the disembodied voices of radio drama more than by the literary tradition in which I now participate, I am an alienated Appalachian aesthete who feels as if he was conceived on the planet Mars and was born in a universal Ivory Tower.

## II

"Write about what you know" (your own personal experience) is the most misused piece of advice ever pontificated upon young writers. "What you know" *can be* a rich world created out of your imagination. The killer who sent me reams of cliché-ridden prose tells me he has finally understood what I meant when I told him he had not yet developed a rich enough imagination to write about what it's like to live on death row.

As a part-time teacher, I spend more time in the Ivory Tower than in the Ivy Tower. Into that Ivory Tower sometimes intrude people from the real world of work—plumbers, repair men, who walk out of the Acadian sunlight into the gloom of my book-congested study with its single light, like a police interrogation lamp, over my desk. With rising nausea thickening in their voices, they ask, "How can you stand to be cooped up in here all day?"—never dreaming that what they see that day they could see every day. I am invariably shocked to discover that they do not assume what I clearly know, and envy me—that before they interrupted, I was having an intensely fantastic experience in the sunlight of imagination that would overshadow any experience that they or I could have just had out there somewhere in the actual sunlight.

Attitudes and assumptions about my life in the Ivory Tower are very similar to those people apply to my life in the Ivy Tower. As if over a public address system, I hear: YOU ARE NOT LIVING A FULL LIFE. I like what James Agee, with whom I share Knoxville as a hometown, said the year he died about the full life: "I wonder whether those who go, as I do, for a Full Life, don't get their exact reward, which is that the Full Life is full of crap." To Agee, who shunned teaching because he regarded education as a conspiracy to stifle the imagination and individuality of the young, but who spent all his life in schools or in circumscribed working conditions among classmates, fell halfway into the real-life trap when he went down to Alabama during the Depression to write about impoverished, exploited sharecroppers, then swamped the facts he gathered with his imagination. In his real life, he shared the almost universal American preconception that heavy smoking and drinking and talking until the crack of dawn in bars or at parties keep the cloistered writer in touch with reality. Among writers and academics, no less than among Cajun moss gatherers, I feel a misfit at being one who no longer smokes or drinks, having decided that the imagination thrives on clarity. Nor, as an inverted snob, do I fish or talk football (as John Crowe Ransom did while living his last years with Verlaine).

The point that is being made to me that I do not miss is that I am *missing* real life, even what is available to those who live mostly within the precincts of Ivy Towers. It will surprise no one, least of all me, to learn that for the past five years, I have confined myself to my Ivory Tower to write a novel with the most blatant subject-dominance—and commercial-formula tradition—a Civil War novel. But this novel, called *Sharpshooter*, treats the subject and deviates from the commercial formula in ways that *miss* all the given opportunities. In fact, the key word in the novel's conception is the word *missing*. The narrator, who became a sharpshooter at the age of fourteen, and who writes fitfully about the Civil War experience over a period of seventy years, asks himself: "Why, if I am the sharpshooter who shot General Sanders, and I am reasonably certain that I did, have I felt for the last seventy years that I somehow missed the war?" He was a sharp-shooter with Longstreet in most of the major battles East and West, including Ft. Sanders at Knoxville, and he was a guard at Andersonville Prison. He was, to use Wright Morris's phrase, "the man who was there" and can give us a factual, honest, truthful report of the matter. But after looking at his individual experience and at the experiences of five other very different kinds of people over seventy years, he concludes that in our national preoccupation with what really happened, and in the gathering of facts to prove it, we have all missed the Civil War. The irony and paradox that I want not to be lost upon the reader is that as the sharpshooter struggled to gather and sift the facts, his emotions, his imagination, and his intellect were so stimulated as to produce a very full life indeed. There are more ways than one to be a sharpshooter and to be on target.

Like the sharpshooter, I, as a writer in the Ivory Tower who teaches part time in the Ivy Tower, am always consciously taking, without needing to expect ever to pass, F. Scott Fitzgerald's test. "The test of a first rate intelligence is the ability to hold two opposed ideas in the mind at the same time and retain the ability to function." For me, the two opposed ideas are: (1) I must live in the real world; (2) I must live in my imagination.

For me, the conflict is not between reality and imagination or facts and fantasy but the inclination to cultivate one to the diminishment or exclusion of the other. My problem is how, in the creative process, to enable reality to stimulate my imagination and my imagination to transform reality as a continuous and simultaneous process. To me the unimagined life is not worth living. The imagination is superior to real life. Thus I say, not glibly but out of a daily tested conviction, that a white writer should be able to imagine and write about the experiences of a black person, that a man should be able to imagine and write about a woman's experiences, as I did in *The Suicide's Wife*, a novel based only superficially on my own direct experience. Since I was three years old, my self-image has been that I am a storyteller. The real life of such a person goes on in his imagination and in the writer's creative process. The facts of the writer's public life, whether she is Emily Dickinson in the parlor or he is Walt Whitman on the road, have little to do with the writer's major experience. So I regard not *Bijou*, based on the facts of the year I was thirteen, but *The Suicide's Wife*, imagined and written in three weeks, as my true autobiography.

Given my aesthetic orientation to life and literature, I find that teaching in the university neither poses problems for me as a writer nor nurtures my creative life. General assumptions about what fiction ought to be and do, promoted and encouraged often by writers themselves, determine, it seems to me, assumptions about the life of the writer as a teacher in the university. As I study literature, I see that life and literature influence a writer's imagination and the creative process with almost equal power, even in realistic, important issue-oriented novels. But the prevailing assumption that great writing must first and above all be true to life, must tell the truth, must be subjectively honest, has persuaded many writers and teachers to promote several dominant literary fallacies: the subject-matter fallacy promotes the preconception that certain raw-life subjects, such as sex, war, drugs, insanity, endow a novel with importance. The exhortation that the serious writer deal with issues relevant to our contemporary problems and the emphasis on telling the truth about life in general result in what I call the fallacy of theme mongering or what Allen Tate called the communication fallacy. Closely related to the assumption of public relevance is the assumption that the writer must express his relevant personal feelings and depict his own experiences with an exemplary honesty and "courage." That assumption results in what I call the it-really-happened-to-me fallacy and a fidelity in reporting one's life that is, to me, just another form of journalism.

## III

The writer decides he will get himself off the mean streets of real life and make his living in the Ivy Tower of the university. How does teaching affect the writer and his work? Assumptions twitter like bats in the tower. The university acts on some assumptions of its own, which many writers take so seriously they expend a great deal of psychic energy combating them. The university assumes that the writer, even more than the scholar, will by the nature of his primary role write and be published, or perish along with the scholar. As a writer who has always had more  than enough published to satisfy the assumption, in both imaginative and critical genres, I have always felt that excellence in teaching ought to be the main criterion for judging a teacher and that being published is good but not necessary.

Many of the first teachers of creative writing did not produce a distinguished body of published imaginative work. But the expectation or the pressure to be published or perish does not wound a great many writers. The assumption that the writer and the scholar will clash has not affected me personally because I have also had criticism published. Had I not taught in the university, however, I probably would not have continued to write criticism. I had an inclination to do it, and the academic atmosphere fostered that inclination. I enjoy it very much and engage in it, not because anyone expects it of me (in fact, my colleagues, preferring to keep me in focus as a novelist, seem forgetful on the subject), but because I like it, even love it. Like the libraries that have all my criticism but none of my fiction, there are some teachers who know my critical work on the Tough-Guy Writers of the thirties, for instance, but don't know about my novel in that vein, *Brothers in Confidence*.

I have never had a problem as a writer or as the creator of a writing program with the administration. This is because I confess to the romantic notion that I owe allegiance only to one classroom in one university, and that is the one in which I am standing at any given hour, whether I have taught there fifteen years or am only a visitor for an hour. I have always had the attitude of an alien, that I am basically a creature of the Appalachian slums of what John Gunther called the ugliest city in America. I feel as if I am on a prolonged tour of imposture through the groves of academe, sort of like taking a rest from walking in the French Quarter by sitting haughtily in the lobby of the Royal Sonesta whose rooms I can't afford. Like Byron's attitude about his place in London society, I feel about academe, "I stood *amongst* them, but was not *of* them," an attitude carried over actually from my merchant seaman and army days. I imagine most writers feel that way, whether they teach or, like Henry Miller, work for Western Union. Most writers feel they are like God's spy, or like creatures fallen from Mars.

I often muse upon the assumption that one of the things that attract writers to the university is the life of the mind fostered there, where teachers teach humanistic values. Out of a naive disillusionment, I must say that my own experience has seldom encouraged me to support that assumption. Behind that assumption works the assumption that writers share scholars' primary interest in ideas and issues, that they thrive on theme mongering when discussing literature. Many do; I don't. Indeed, too often the writer's assumption about teaching in the university, going in, seems to be that it offers a way of promoting one's career. In that light, one university seems better than another. Thus, my own reason for choosing one school over another may be considered frivolous: I go where the look of the landscape excites my imagination—not to Michigan State but to Appalachian State Teacher's College.

The writer's energy and creativity are dissipated in teaching: this is another popular assumption that happens to be true, especially for teachers who bring to teaching the same creative energy and imagination they bring to their writing. I am aware of a flow of creative energy that is no respecter of channels or conduits. The imagination is conducted through phantom circuits. Teaching writing *is* more time-consuming than teaching literature. Twenty years ago, I couldn't understand why Hollis Summers, novelist and poet, refused to teach creative writing. I look back now on seven years of not teaching writing workshops, except for a week or two as visiting writer. One spring, I had only five students in a novel-writing workshop, and I did no writing that semester. I love teaching writing so much that I must not do it. A major benefit of my tenuous affiliation with the university is that I have the opportunity to give readings from my fiction as a visitor to other schools and to *talk* about writing.

"Lose touch with the man in the street," I can hear a great host singing, "and your writing will become anemic, you'll write mostly about academic life, you'll write in a stilted style, you'll cleave to conventional techniques." Sure enough, in addition to all that scholarly stuff, I have indeed written one novel, *The Suicide's Wife*, in an academic setting. My best-known story, one of my own favorites, "No Trace," is set in a small college, as are three other stories, and another is set in a large university. But none of those works derives from my own experiences or is based directly on people I have known.

Admittedly, some writers in the university do not write about real life, tuning their prose to the shout of history in the streets. Yet many others write about relevant national and international issues: civil rights, Vietnam, pollution of the environment, nuclear war, life in prison, oppression in South America. In an effort to make their lives and their writing relevant, they sign petitions, they protest, they sometimes act. In my personal life, I, too, in my individualistic manner, have always been engaged in the vital issues and causes of my time. But I feel no urgency to deal with any of those matters in my writing. Recognizable elements are there, but they do not motivate me to write. The sequestered life of the university has contributed in no traceable way to that aesthetic attitude which makes me respond to the stirrings of my imagination instead of the shout in the street. After a reading, students will come up to me and ask, "Did that really happen to you?" They are quite certain that they could not have been moved by a made-up person in a dreamed-up predicament. I always reply, "Yes, it really happened, in my imagination." "The Singer" is my favorite story. It delineates the ways in which storytellers and listeners interact to produce what I call the Pleasure Dome effect, a triumph of the imagination. An editor who put it in an anthology made it impossible for the story to affect the reader as I intended. She wrote:"But even though we may be defeated in our struggle to discover the *truth*, Madden illustrates that man possesses a never-ending desire for the truth." This all-purpose thematic statement did as much damage to the story as a direct lie.

I am distressed to hear many teachers of writing cater to the romantic preconceptions of the public and of students when they deny that writing (a mysterious process) can be taught, then go on to claim to achieve far more impossible goals—such as changing a student's life. In his introduction to *Writers as Teachers, Teachers as Writers*, published in 1970, Jonathan Baumbach, a fine critic and an experimental novelist, wrote:"The question comes up: 'Can writing be taught?' The questioner of course knows the answer in advance, the question implying the answer—'No, it can't.' Ah, then, what are we all doing in the classroom? The best we can, I should hope, since nothing—nothing worth knowing (nothing beyond the banality of facts)—can be taught. It is what every serious teacher finally discovers." I must confess that I have not yet discovered that which came so easily to Baumbach and his contributors to that volume.

In that same year, I wrote an essay in which I raised the questions myself. When I first began conducting creative writing workshops I was often asked the question, "Do you really think creative writing can be taught?" Emphatically implicit was the questioner's own answer: "No!" Intimidated, I used to respond with stuttering indecisiveness.

The question continues, relentlessly, to come up. If the questioner were honest, he would declare: "You can't teach *talent!*" and he would be right. I'm never asked the relevant question: "Can the techniques of imaginative writing be taught?" My confident answer, after twenty-five years of teaching, would be "Yes." In fact, I should have known from my invaluable experience teaching freshman English that writing can be taught. But I was skeptical when I first began teaching imaginative writing. Like most people, I still clung to the romantic misconception that inspiration is the wellspring of all facets of the mysterious process of creating a work of art. Consciously striving to acquire discipline, I was still not conscious of the extent to which I was already fascinated by techniques. Yet there is no better way to learn than by teaching. In the third year of teaching writing, I discovered that while the most important things—talent and imagination—can not be acquired in a classroom, certain things—technique and the psychology of reading—*can* be. No writing program can create talent, but it can introduce a talented writer to the techniques that all writers share. However, what is most individual in a writer must be cultivated in solitude and developed out of an inner discipline.

With some curious logic, it follows from the attitudes and assumptions of those teachers of writing who make disavowals similar to Baumbach's that if writing can not be taught, the writing workshops can achieve more moderate goals, such as these: offering himself as an example in the genial guise of a facilitator, the instructor can promote a gut sense of what literature is all about; in the course of his doing so, the students are enabled to get in touch with themselves (find their deeper, truer selves) and, despite the contradiction of this emphasis on individuality, create a sense of community. While the teacher may not presume to have very much to teach the students, those students involved in such a mystical process—misfits, malcontents, neurotics, outlaws, rebels, being the most promising participants—may be depended upon to teach the teacher a great deal: if not about the techniques of writing, then surely about ways of coping with real-life crises and predicaments. My apologies to Baumbach for exaggerating the example he provides; still, I have actually understated the situation that used to dominate the scene, but that is not now so pervasive.

Well, then what *can* be expected from the man who teaches part time in the Ivy Tower? I began by focusing on aesthetics or the techniques of fiction (point of view, for instance) and how they dictate style and how style implies far more than it overtly says. For given my focus on technique, I discovered that one way to introduce writers to those techniques was to examine commercial or popular fiction alongside fiction in the Great Tradition. To extend that assumption, I have argued for several years for more workshops in writing commercial fiction to meet the declared needs of some students.

In my lifelong pursuit of ways to express my imagination and to affect the imaginations of others, I have published in most genres and media. One very clear benefit of teaching writing and literature in the university has been that I have been able to explore all those possibilities in classroom settings. When I teach poetry, I tend to write more poems. When I teach drama or playwriting, I tend to write stageplays and screenplays. Teaching has also caused me to modify some of my views. For example, in 1970 I urged that we change the term "creative writing course" to "imaginative writing workshop"; this was in line with my ongoing effort to enthrone imagination over inspiration and raw material. Now I urge the term "revision workshop." I feel that the limited role of inspiration and the teachableness of techniques in the service of imagination can best be demonstrated if we focus on the process of revision. Close scrutiny of this process puts theme mongering and subjective preoccupations on hold as we focus on what the writer *does to* the reader and how. The student writer asks himself: Did I do to the reader what I wanted to do? Did I stimulate his emotions, his imagination, his intellect? If not, what possible techniques may I consider that will enable me to do what I want to do? I see now that technique can best be taught through primary focus on the inevitable revision needed.

The most difficult thing for students to learn is discipline. That is one of the things you can not really teach. But in a workshop setting in which the focus is on technique as learned in the revision process, you can instill a sense of the vital importance of striving to attain an inner-directed discipline.

At the risk of raising opinion to the level of pomposity, I think it is out of a misplaced generosity that so much classroom emphasis is placed on the notion that students have a great deal to teach their teachers. Acting on that assumption myself, I used to talk eloquently to my students about their role as teachers in the workshop. I must say, however, that I have seen very little of that over the years. That I learn somehow in the course of a writing workshop is a fact. Still, shocks of recognition come more often in my literature classes than in my writing workshops. This is especially true when I try innovative approaches, such as the study of pop fiction alongside serious fiction. But it was in the teaching of writing that I discovered the viability of focusing on revision as a method for teaching literature. The point here is that writers do bring special perspectives and skills to the teaching of literature. For the writer-as-teacher is more capable than the scholar of teaching literature from the authorial point of view; after all, he does so out of a firsthand understanding of how the creative process works. His skill is in teaching a novel not only as a finished work but also as a work produced by this creative process.

Among teachers of writing there is almost universal agreement that if we cannot claim to teach the "mysteries" of writing, we very clearly do succeed in teaching our students how to read. I go further and declare that it is in a scrutiny of the revision process—in the writings of students and of published writers—that both writing and reading (inseparable disciplines) can be most effectively taught.

# Contributors

MELVIN J. FRIEDMAN is Professor of Comparative Literature and English at the University of Wisconsin-Milwaukee. He is the author or editor (alone or in collaboration) of a dozen books, of which the most recent is *Critical Essays on Flannery O'Connor*. Formerly editor of *Wisconsin Studies in Contemporary Literature* and *Comparative Literature Studies,* he now serves on the editorial boards of *Contemporary Literature, Studies in American Fiction, Journal of Beckett Studies, Journal of Popular Culture, Journal of American Culture, Fer de Lance, Arete, Studies in the Novel, International Fiction Review,* and *Yiddish.* His awards include grants from Fulbright and ACLS, and he has served as Visiting Senior Fellow at the University of East Anglia (1972) and as Canterbury Visiting Fellow at the University of Canterbury–New Zealand (1985).

DAVID MADDEN has published nine works of fiction since 1961; of these the best known are *Cassandra Singing, Bijou, The Suicide's Wife,* and *The New Orleans of Possibilities* (his second book of stories). He has taught creative writing at Centre College, the University of Louisville, Kenyon College (where he was assistant editor of *The Kenyon Review*), Ohio University, and Louisiana State University (where, since 1968, he has been writer-in-residence). His many stories, poems, plays, essays, and his literary criticism have appeared in a wide range of publications—from literary quarterlies to mass-circulation magazines, to avant-garde journals. He also has published numerous textbooks and books of criticism.

JAMES M. MELLARD is Professor of English at Northern Illinois University, where he has taught since 1967. He has chaired the Department of English there and been Acting Dean of Liberal Arts and Sciences. He also has served as president of the Midwest Modern Language Association. His essays on contemporary fiction and modernist literature have appeared in such journals as *PMLA, JEGP, Modern Fiction Studies,* and the *Bucknell Review.* He has written or edited (alone or in collaboration) five books, including *Four Modes: A Rhetoric of Modern Fiction* (1973), *The Exploded Form: The Modernist Novel in America* (1980), and *Doing Tropology: Analysis of Narrative Discourse* (1987).

190

James Nagel is Professor of English at Northeastern University and the editor of *Studies in American Fiction*. He also edits the G. K. Hall series of volumes of "Critical Essays on American Literature." A former president of the international Ernest Hemingway Society, he has lectured on American literature in seventeen countries as well as at numerous American universities. His publications include some thirty journal articles as well as nine books; the best known of these are *Stephen Crane and Literary Impressionism*, *Ernest Hemingway: The Writer in Context*, and *Critical Essays on Joseph Heller*. Currently he is finishing a book based on the manuscripts of *Catch-22*.

James Ragan is Director of the Professional Writing Program at the University of Southern California. A poet and playwright, he has won, among other awards, the Emerson Poetry Prize, two Borestone Mountain Poetry awards, and the Pushcart Poetry Prize. He has published two books of poetry, *In the Talking Hours* (1979) and *Womb-Weary* (1987), and a third, *Lusions*, is in progress. His produced plays include *Saints* (1972), *The Gandy Dancers* (1975), and *Commedia* (1984, and in Russia, 1987). He also has written screenplays for MGM and Paramount Pictures.

Elaine B. Safer is Associate Professor of English at the University of Delaware. A specialist in the American comic novel and in the poetry and prose of John Milton, she has published essays on John Barth, Thomas Pynchon, William Gaddis, and Ken Kesey in such journals as *Studies in the Novel*, *Critique*, *Studies in American Humor*, *Studies in American Fiction*, *Renascence*, and *Critical Essays on Thomas Pynchon*. She also has published *John Milton's "L'Allegro" and "Il Penseroso"* (1970) and essays on Milton in the *Milton Quarterly*, *Milton Studies*, and *A Milton Encyclopedia*. Her book *The American Comic Epic Novel* is soon to appear.

Ben Siegel is Professor of English at California State Polytechnic University, Pomona. He has chaired the Department of English and directed the Annual Conferences in Modern American Writing held at the university's Kellogg West Center for Continuing Education. His books, alone or in collaboration, include *The Puritan Heritage: America's Roots in the Bible*, *Biography Past and Present*, *Isaac Bashevis Singer*, and *The Controversial Sholem Asch*. He also has written teacher's manuals for *A Quarto of Modern Literature* and *A College Treasury*. His critical essays deal with such writers as Saul Bellow, Bernard Malamud, Philip Roth, and Daniel Fuchs. He is now on the editorial boards of *Studies in American Fiction*, *Contemporary Literature*, *Arete*, *Journal of Popular Culture*, *Journal of American Culture*, *Saul Bellow Journal*, and *Yiddish*.

Eric Solomon is Professor of English at San Francisco State University, where he is now serving as provost. He has taught also at Ohio State, Stanford, and the University of California at Irvine. He has published numerous articles in nineteenth- and twentieth-century British and American fiction. He also has written or edited four books on American literature, the best known of which is *Stephen Crane*. He is now at work on a book titled *Jews, Baseball, and the American Novel*.

Stanley Trachtenberg is Professor of English at Texas Christian University, where he chaired the Department of English. Formerly a senior editor at Macmillan and at Crown Publishing, he now specializes in the contemporary American novel and in postmodernism. His essays and fiction have appeared in such journals as *Yale Review*, *Kenyon Review*, *Commentary*, and *The Psychoanalytic Review*. His most recent books are *Critical Essays on Saul Bellow* and *The Postmodern Moment: A Handbook of Contemporary Innovation in the Arts*.

Theodore Weiss is Paton Foundation Professor at Princeton University, where he also has been Poet-in-Residence and Professor of English and Creative Writing. At present he is on a Guggenheim Foundation grant and is a guest at the Princeton Institute for Advanced Study. A poet, editor, and publisher, he has coedited (with his wife Renee) *The Quarterly Review of Literature* for forty-five years. His books of poetry include *The Catch, Outlanders, Gunsight, The Medium: Poems, The Last Day and the First: Poems, The World before Us: Poems, 1950–70*, and *Fireweeds*. His prose works include *The Breath of Clowns and Kings: A Study of Shakespeare* and *Gerard Manley Hopkins: Realist on Parnassus*. His *Collected Poems* are scheduled for publication by Macmillan.

# Index

"The American Scholar" (Emerson), 16, 89–90

Barth, John, 16–18, 88–100
—*The End of the Road*, 16–17, 84, 88, 89, 91–94, 142; humor in, 93–94; as parody of education, 91–94
—*Giles Goat-Boy*, 16–18, 88, 89, 94–97; educational ideal in, 94, 95; humor in, 96; religious allusions, 96–97; scatological imagery, 95; and Swift, 95
—novels: personal elements, 88; setting, 88–89
—readership for, 18, 89, 97–98
—satire of university, 17–18
—*The Sot-Weed Factor*, 89, 97–98; demythologizing in, 97–98; Hudibrastics in, 98
Beckett, Samuel, 166; influence on Raymond Federman, 33–34, 136–37. *See also* individual Federman titles
Bellow, Saul, 114–35; attitude to university, 21; cultural obligation of, 116; *The Dean's December*, 22, 122–23, 128–29; *Herzog*, 118, 119; on humanities professors, 122–24; on literary criticism, 124–25; "literary situation," 115; Moses Herzog, 52; in New York, 117–18; novel as cultural object, 124–25; professor types in, 22, 121–23; readership for, 118, 126–27; *Seize the Day*, 114–15; on writers, 21–22, 115–16, 127–28, 129–32, 133
Bowen, Elizabeth, 149

*Commentary*, 117
Creative writer. *See* Writer
Creative writing: rise of, 149–53. *See also* Poetry writing
Creative writing workshops, 25, 26–29, 175–76; attitudes to, 150; effect of, 153–55, 158; problems of, 157; and screenwriting, 174

*Democratic Vistas* (Whitman), 132
*Dubliners* (Joyce), 48

Eliot, T. S., 151
Emerson, Ralph Waldo: "The American Scholar," 16, 89–90; and Barth, 16–18, 89–90, 98; and *The End of the Road*, 92, 94; and *Giles Goat-Boy*, 95
Engle, Paul, 152

Federman, Raymond, 136–45; and the academic novel, 34–35; biography, 136–37, 138, 140–41; and creative writing, 142, 144; "critifiction," 138–39; *Double or Nothing*, 34, 137–38, 139; as experimental writer, 141–42; influence of Samuel Beckett, 33–34, 136–37; "plural voice," 139; *Smiles on Washington Square*, 34, 140; and students, 143–44; *Take It or Leave It*, 34, 138–39; *The Two-Fold Vibration*, 34, 139–40; *The Voice in the Closet*, 139; work habits, 142–43
Fiedler, Leslie, 9, 119–20

Heller, Joseph, 18–20, 101–13
—biography, 101
—*Catch-22*, 19, 101, 102–6; academic themes in, 19; characters in, 102–4; education of characters, 111; education as emblem, 19–20; education, prestige of, 102; education, social implications of, 104–5; manuscript deletions, 102–4, 105; satire in, 103, 112
—*Good as Gold*, 19, 102, 108–11; education, social implications of, 110–11; minor characters in, 109–10; satire in, 109, 110, 112; social issues, 112
—*Hungry Hearts*: treatment of academics, 10
—preoccupations of, 102
—satire in, 20, 111

—short stories, 101–2, 111, 112; and Hemingway, 102
—*Something Happened*, 19, 102, 106–7, 111–12; education in, 106; identity in, 107

Iowa Writer's Workshop, 69, 152
Ivory tower, 31, 81, 153, 181–83; effect of, 10

Joyce, James: *Dubliners*, 48

Language: collapse of, 161–62; and playwriting, 164
Lawrence, Jerome, 166–67

McLuhan, Marshall, 120–21, 162
Madden, David: autobiography, 179–80; *The Beautiful Greed*, 31, 179, 180; *Bijou*, 31, 180, 181, 183; *Pleasure Dome*, 31; "revision workshop," 188–89; *Sharpshooter*, 182; *The Suicide's Wife*, 32, 183, 185
*Magnalia Christi Americana* (Mather), 90–91, 96
Malamud, Bernard, 10, 54–67; *A New Life*: academics in, 58; as academic novel, 54–55; Seymour Levin, 52, 55–66; and pastoralism, 11–13, 54–56; perception of academia, 12; as wasteland, 56–58, 61, 66; women in, 62–64
Marxism, 117
Mather, Cotton: and Barth, 90–91; and *The End of the Road*, 92; *Magnalia Christi Americana*, 90–91, 96
Minimalism, 161, 162, 163
Modern literature: resistance to, 150

New Criticism, 25–26, 86, 151–52
New Mediaism, 161–63, 165, 170–72; and writing programs, 174; and young writers, 27–29, 30
*New York Review of Books*, 117

Oates, Joyce Carol, 39–53
—academics in, 11, 40–41, 52–53
—ambition in, 51
—on the artist, 39–40
—and consciousness, 39–41, 50–51
—*Crossing the Border*: "The Liberation of Jake Hanley," 45, 46; "The Transformation of Vincent Scoville," 45–46; faculty wives in, 48
—*Hungry Ghosts*: "Angst," 45; "The Birth of Tragedy," 44; "Democracy in America," 41–42; "A Descriptive Catalog," 43–44; "Pilgrim's Progress," 42; "Rewards of Fame," 44–45; "Up from Slavery," 42–43
—narrative voice in, 51
—professional writers in, 44
—on Shakespeare's *Troilus and Cressida*, 51
—*Upon the Sweeping Flood*: "Accomplished Desires," 48; "Archways," 46–47; "The Dead," 48–49; "In the Autumn of the Year," 50; "In the Region of Ice," 47; "Magna Mater," 49–50; "Normal Love," 48; "A Theory of Knowledge," 50; "Through the Looking Glass," 47–48

*Partisan Review*, 117–19
Phillips, William, 117, 118
Playwrights: and artistic integrity, 165–66, 168; and audience, 172; Dionysian/Apollonian dichotomy of, 169–70, 171; and language, 164; need for craft, 163, 167; need for premise, 166, 173; student development of craft, 168–69; student playwrights, 162–63; in the university, 167
Poetry writing, 151–52; and publishing, 157; rise of, 149–53; by students, 154–56; teaching of, 156
Poirier, Richard, 117, 118, 119, 121
Princeton Writing Program, 149

*Quarterly Review of Literature*, 25, 151

Rechy, John, 167
Roth, Philip, 10, 13, 68–87
—as academic, 68–69, 86
—as academic novelist, 14–15, 86
—biography, 69
—*The Breast*, 70–74; satire in, 71–72
—and Flaubert, 82
—form and content in, 86
—and the ivory tower, 81
—and Kafka, 85–86
—*My Life as a Man*, 15, 75–82; as

academic novel, 79; "Courting Disaster," 76–78; "My True Story," 78–80; parody in, 77, 81; "Salad Days," 75–76
—*Portnoy's Complaint*, 15, 70, 74, 79
—*The Professor of Desire*, 14, 69, 82–87; as academic novel, 84–85; two worlds in, 84
—two worlds of, 68, 70, 74, 81, 85, 87
—as writer, 69, 80; and writer's values, 72–73

Thomas, Dylan, 152
Trilling, Lionel, 117; *Beyond Culture*, 126

*Understanding Poetry* (Brooks and Warren), 152
University: literary magazines of, 116–20; modern literature in, 22, 24–26; as sanctuary, 21, 35, 115. *See also* individual authors
University of Southern California Professional Writing Program, 161

Van Doren, Mark, 151

Whitman, Walt, *Democratic Vistas*, 132
Workshops. *See* Creative writing workshops
Writer: attraction to university, 164–65; benefits of university, 153; and imagination, 181, 182, 183; and literary fallacies, 183–84; problems facing, 9–10, 21–22, 23, 29, 32, 130–31; and publishing, 184; and radicalism, 131–32; and "real life," 30–31, 32, 179, 182; and society, 23–24; subjects addressed, 186; as teacher, 32, 33, 183, 184–89; as writer-in-residence, 9, 21–22, 35
Writing: creative, rise of, 149–53

# The American Writer and the University

## Edited by BEN SIEGEL

No other institution rivals the American university in harboring so many who criticize and even revile it while refusing to leave it. No other nurtures so much internal factionalism and strife. And certainly in no other area of the university are the internecine hostilities as frequent and vocal as those between its professional teachers or professors of literature and its invited poets or novelists. The latter are, of course, the "creative writers" appointed to teach literature, composition, or creative writing. Here resentments and bruised sensitivities on both sides appear most bitter and open. What are the causes of this anger? The essays gathered in this volume speak to this point.

Both "factions" are represented here: critics and scholars as well as novelists and poets. All the contributors are teachers, and several fit validly into both categories. Three deal only with their own experiences in the classroom, but they also relate these personal experiences to the general cultural and academic scenes. The others discuss seven major American novelists who have made the university an important setting or reference point—or target—in their fiction.

Hence this volume's purpose is not to suggest a debate between the university's professional teachers and its invited or appointed writers; instead, it offers differing responses of creative writers to their respective institutions or to the idea of the university and to academe's varying effects on the sensitive individual. The cumulative result of these ten essays provides fresh insights to the reader interested in the contemporary American university. He or she will derive a much